PRACTICING WHAT WE TEACH

SUNY Series, Social Context of Education
Christine E. Sleeter, editor

PRACTICING WHAT WE TEACH

*Confronting Diversity in
Teacher Education*

Edited by
Renée J. Martin

STATE UNIVERSITY OF NEW YORK PRESS

Published by
State University of New York Press, Albany

LB
1715
.P67
1995

© 1995 State University of New York

For information, address the State University of New York Press,
State University Plaza, Albany, NY 12246

Production by Christine Lynch
Marketing by Fran Keneston

Library of Congress Cataloging-in-Publication Data

Practicing what we teach : confronting diversity in teacher education
  / edited by Renée J. Martin.
      p.   cm. — (SUNY series, social context of education)
    Includes bibliographical references and index.
    ISBN 0-7914-2549-5 (alk. paper). — ISBN 0-7914-2550-9 (pbk. :
  alk. paper)
    1. Teachers—Training of—United States. 2. Multicultural
  education—Study and teaching—United States. 3. Critical pedagogy-
  -United States. I. Martin, Renée J. II. Series.
  LB1715.P67 1995
  370'.71'0973—dc20
                                                              94-32933
                                                                 CIP

10 9 8 7 6 5 4 3 2 1

Grateful acknowledgment is made to the following authors, publishers and publications
for permission to use portions of previously published material.

Class, Race, and Gender in American Education, edited by Lois Weis. © 1988.
Reprinted with the permission of State University of New York Press.

Critical Practice, by C. Belsey. © 1980. Reprinted with the permission of Methuen &
Co.

CONTENTS

ACKNOWLEDGMENTS

Practicing What We Teach: Confronting Diversity in Teacher Education has grown out of the lived experiences of multicultural teacher educators and others who share concerns about the ways in which issues of diversity have and are being represented in institutions of higher education. The authors and I have attempted to translate theoretical frameworks into daily practice in an effort to create new paradigms and possibilities for all educators. It is our hope that this work will contribute to the existing discourse and will serve as a catalyst for others to transform their pedagogical strategies in meaningful ways.

We are indebted to the students with whom we have worked who have contributed to the actualization of our personal pedagogies and to the colleagues who have supported us in our endeavors. In particular I am grateful to Christine Sleeter for her faith in and support of my scholarly work. In addition I wish to thank Kent Koppelman for his early instruction regarding issues of diversity and Julie Andrzejewski for her numerous valuable insights. I also want to express my gratitude to Suk Hoon Han for his early proofreading efforts and Dawn VanGunten for her help in the final phases of editing.

INTRODUCTION

As we approach the year 2000, it appears that many of the issues that have haunted American colleges of teacher education during the current century are destined to accompany us into the next. Numerous authors have asserted that in order to create conditions necessary for all students to be successful in schools, teacher educators must "rethink the nature of their programs and practices" (Giroux and McLaren 1987, 4). However, most proposed reform efforts have overlooked the complex relationships among culture, power, knowledge, and ideology that permeate American schools, and in particular teacher education, Instead, they have continued to focus on dominant ideological constructs that reproduce existing social structures and that reinforce boundaries between the powerful and the powerless and the haves and have-nots.

Addressing issues of diversity is a concern for all in the educational community, however the problem is particularly significant for teacher educators. The composition and fabric of American public schools and of those who will educate are rapidly changing. Demographic data indicate that by the year 2000 the population of students will be comprised primarily of children of color (Murray and Fallon 1989), while the teachers who will educate those students will be white, female, and from middle-class backgrounds (Schumann 1990). Teachers will be challenged increasingly to incorporate the diverse biographies, the multiplicity of experiences, and the cultural styles of students. But there is little evidence to suggest that teacher education institutions have initiated comprehensive programs to reform the canon or to aid educators in the quest to engage in alternative pedagogical structures that might better serve the needs of a diverse student population.

In fact, most efforts to reform teacher education have merely attempted to breathe life into archaic systems tainted with ideological constructs that have pretended to be politically neutral. Issues of race, class, and gender have been virtually absent from the design and structure of teacher education reform. In the overview to Weis's book on race, class, and gender, McCarthy and Apple inform us that "Practice in mainstream discourses has often meant the stipulations of 'workable' programs, policies designed for operation within the rules and terms of references of existing institutional structures. Practice in this mainstream sense at best merely allows for incremental modifications necessary for the maintenance of existing institutional frameworks and power relations" (Weis 1988, 30).

At the forefront of the reform debate is the battle currently being waged over multicultural education. It is a debate laden with ideological tensions out of which have emerged a number of conflicts and concerns. Specifically, there are two levels on which the debate must be addressed. The first concerns the imposition of institutional constructs that reify traditional knowledge regarding teaching and learning relative to issues of diversity. This issue is reflected in the presence or lack of state mandates, teacher certification requirements, institutional guidelines, course design, and policies and practices either formal or informal that explicate the role of issues of diversity and specifically multicultural education in teacher education. On another level are the struggles that ensue as teacher educators attempt to work within existing frameworks to create alternative pedagogies and paradigms, many of which are reliant upon altering attitudes and behaviors of individuals within their own classrooms.

Teacher educators writing for this volume have chosen to interpret this two-front battle by grounding their work in an approach known as multicultural social reconstructionist education (MCSR) (Sleeter and Grant 1994), which is an outgrowth of critical theory. Critical theory rests upon the assumptions that educational institutions "need to analyze how cultural production is organized within asymmetrical relations of power in schools" and "construct political strategies for participating in social struggles designed to fight for schools as democratic spheres" (Giroux 1989, 169). Multicultural social reconstructionism is an extension of social reconstructionist principles of earlier decades. Social reconstructionism emerged during the American depression of the 1920s and was viewed as a way to alter inequitable societal conditions predicated upon the dominant culture's interests that, it was asserted, were being served and reproduced in schools. Social reconstructionists purported that reconstructing the school culture employing democratic values would enhance principles of social justice and create a more participatory and equitable democratic society (Stanley 1985).

Multicultural social reconstructionism exists in sharp contrast to the functionalist approaches that predominate in colleges of teacher education in so much as it extends the boundaries of reform to empower students and teachers to become agents of change. By incorporating interpretive theory and its micro-level analysis of how individuals construct meaning via their social relationships, and by including a macro level of cultural analysis, critical theorists emphasize class structure and the ways in which schools magnify class differences that promote inequality of educational access and perpetuate social class distinctions (Bennett and LeCompte 1990). In addition, critical theorists speculate about the ways in which teachers and students might engage in pedagogy that offers cultural alternatives for the pursuit and preservation of social justice. Unlike dominant ideologies steeped in social transmission theories, which promote the role of the teacher as objective and indisputable while the role of the student is one of passivity, critical theory sees teachers as "transformative intellectuals [who] take seriously the need to give students an active voice in their learning experiences" (Giroux 1989, 127). This approach challenges each person to engage in a deeper understanding of pedagogy by fostering a dialectical relationship between theory and practice. Further, it encourages teacher educators to go beyond the authoritarian and traditionally didactic limitations of teacher and student relationships in favor of mutually affirming relationships within a context that values diversity and promotes social justice.

McLaren has written that "Critical theorists challenge the often uncontested relationship between school and society, unmasking mainstream pedagogy's claim that it purveys equal opportunity and provides access to egalitarian democracy and critical thinking. Critical scholars reject the claim that schooling constitutes an apolitical and value neutral process" (1993, 171). Of critical theorists, he says, "They aim at providing teachers with critical categories, or concepts, that will enable them to analyze schools as places that produce and transmit those social practices that reflect the ideological and material imperatives of the dominant culture" (171). Inherent in critical theory is the idea that human agency can mitigate obstacles to social injustice and that schools can become sites for transformation.

BARRIERS TO THE DEVELOPMENT OF
MCSR PEDAGOGY IN TEACHER EDUCATION

Many of the concepts and much of the ideology advocated by critical theorists and by extension social reconstructionists are problematic in the teacher education arena. Adoption of a critical theoretical perspective infers the disruption of the prevailing discourse regarding what constitutes excellence and equity, and it asserts the reconfiguration of a pedagogy that comprehends the relational nature of power, culture, knowledge, and ideology. In order for issues of diversity to be addressed in any comprehensive manner, colleges of teacher education must assess basic theoretical underpinnings and ideological constructs.

For example, despite the imposition of recommendations and guidelines by accrediting agencies as early as the 1970s such as those set forth by the National Council for the Accreditation of Teacher Education (NCATE), many universities still have only isolated courses that have not been integrated throughout their institutions or even within coursework in colleges of education. The NCATE standards seek a commitment to issues of diversity and multicultural education by asserting that: "Multicultural education presumes an acceptance of and commitment to cultural pluralism for all teachers and administrators . . . it is not a body of subject matter to be easily packaged in separate courses and learning experiences that are added to the teacher education program in a laissez faire manner" (NCATE Preamble).

However, even when institutions are monitored by accreditation standards suggested by agencies such as NCATE, compliance with multicultural standards is subject to interpretations of individual evaluators and administrators. Thus, great variation from institution to institution and from state to state occurs, and it is important to note that the variation is not due to cultural differences within the various institutions but rather to the subjective interpretations of teams of examiners, many of whom remain unacquainted with issues of diversity in any meaningful way.

In addition, substantive teacher education mandates for multicultural education exist in only a handful of states. While approximately twenty-seven states have advocated some form of multicultural education applicable to teacher education, only Minnesota, Wisconsin, and Iowa have legislation that is fully inclusive of the integration of issues of race, class, gender, ethnicity, lifestyle preference, and disability (Martin 1986).

Uncertainty exists regarding where in the educational arena issues of diversity should be addressed and by whom. While those advocating an MCSR approach support the integration of issues of diversity throughout all areas of the teacher education curriculum, most institutions have met multicultural standards by instituting a single course often taught by untenured faculty or people of color. Professors relegated to teaching such courses are often seen as singular proponents for a particular racial, ethnic, or other group, and they in turn end up preaching to the converted, students who are interested in learning more about the racial, ethnic, gender, or lifestyle groups to which they belong. Other institutions have addressed the dilemma through ethnic or women's studies courses. The consequence of this type of fragmentation is that proponents in women's studies and/or ethnic studies sometimes find themselves fighting for resources with those who advocate a more wholistic multicultural approach. At issue is not whether ethnic and women's studies courses should exist but how such courses should be taught in concert with a fully integrated multicultural curriculum throughout the university.

And an accompanying concern is that all faculty, not just women or faculty of color, need to be a part of the effort to redress problems and issues associated with diversity. Not to do so is to perpetuate the notion that diversity and in essence racism, sexism, homophobia, and poverty are problems to be dealt with by members of microcultural groups (people of color, women, gays and lesbians, and poor people) but not by members of the dominant culture.

Further complications have arisen because scholarly approaches to diversity have been eclipsed by neoconservative ideologues. Many have no background in multicultural education or issues of diversity, but do have access to popular media and are capable of influencing virtually thousands of uninformed listeners. These critics have argued against transformative pedagogy in favor of a more simplistic discourse centered around individual agency and the promotion of traditional meritocratic approaches to education. Their coercion of terms such as multicultural education, political correctness and historical revisionism causes confusion and diverts attention from substantive issues of poverty, elitism, homophobia, and institutionalized racist and sexist policies and procedures.

AN ALIENATED TEACHING FORCE

The entry level teaching force is composed primarily of white middle-class students who, for the most part, enter teacher education unaware of the dynamics of racism, sexism, classism, and heterosexism upon their lives and the society at large (Bennett and LeCompte 1990; Martin and Koppelman 1991). Most have attended public schools dominated by middle-class white teachers, and this pattern prevails at the university level where faculties in teacher education tend also to be 93% white and 70% male (Grant and Koskela 1986). Whiteness, heterosexuality, being middle class, and the accompanying norms and standards of the dominant culture are viewed as a legitimate foundation for conceptualizing the world and ultimately for constructing pedagogy. Hooks (1989) has recounted the frustration of her encounters with prospective teachers whose backgrounds are isolated and alienated from issues of diversity.

> Struggling to educate in the corporate university is a process I have found enormously stressful. Implementing new teaching strategies that aim to subvert the norm, to engage students fully is a really difficult task. Unlike the oppressed or colonized, who may begin to feel as they engage in education for critical consciousness a new found sense of power and identity that frees them from colonization of the mind, that liberates, privileged students are often downright unwilling to admit that their minds have been colonized, that they have been learning to be oppressors, how to dominate or at least how to passively accept the domination of others. (102)

Others have addressed the complexities of altering the dominant discourse. Lather (1991) has noted students' resistance to liberatory curriculum and their willingness to do what she has called "stay dumb." She has written of the inherent dangers and pitfalls in formulating a discourse in which we must remain constantly aware of the multiplicity of experiences and voices that we and our students bring to the classroom. She challenges us to question the extent to which the "pedagogy we construct in the name of liberation [is] intrusive, invasive pressured? (143). And hooks (1989) has further contemplated the difficulties of introducing radical pedagogy to students who have privileged interpretations of life. She comments, "Education for critical consciousness that encourages all students—privileged or non-privileged—who are seeking an entry into class privilege rather than providing a sense of freedom and release invites critique of conventional expectations and desires. They may find such an experience terribly threatening. And even though they may approach the situation with great openness, it may still be terribly painful" (102). Further,

Foucault has noted the "violence of a position that sides against those who are happy in their ignorance, against effective illusions by which humanity protects itself" (1977, 162).

VISIONS AND RE-VISIONS OF PEDAGOGICAL PRACTICE

While there has been a proliferation of literature about multicultural education and issues of diversity during the recent decade, little has been written or shared that actually illustrates the struggles and successes of teacher educators in classrooms where transformative, liberatory pedagogy in the form of multicultural social reconstructionism is being employed or practiced. This is a volume full of alternatives and possibilities for transformative pedagogy. It is part of a teacher education saga that explicates some of the grim realities and occasional epiphanies that those of us who advocate an MCSR approach to issues of diversity encounter when we attempt to practice what we teach. These authors hold up for pedagogical scrutiny the dominant discourse embodied in functionalist philosophy and by doing so we problematize privilege, radicalize race, and disrupt and analyze the politics of gender. We have adopted as our collective responsibility the challenge to present alternatives to how we construct and conduct school and specifically to the ways that we educate prospective teachers about issues of diversity.

In this work, we challenge teacher educators to go beyond the mundane and the prescriptive, to deconstruct and reconstruct what already exists and to carve out new territory for teaching and learning. The authors cut deeply into the complex and unexplored relationships among issues of diversity and hierarchical, systemic oppression and the ways in which these issues are inextricably linked to pedagogy. This work probes the confines of traditional approaches to teaching about diversity, and it explores the possibilities for redefining links between theory and practice. It thereby presents an alternative repertoire for teacher education that emphasizes the relationship between ideology and pedagogy.

Our work is "a deliberate attempt to construct specific conditions through which educators and students can think critically about how knowledge is produced and transformed in relation to the construction of social experiences informed by a particular relationship between the self, others and the large world" (Giroux 1992, 99). It expands the realm of radical discourse and advocates an ideological stance that employs multicultural social reconstructionism as a way to empower teachers to become "transformative intellectuals" (Giroux 1989). Therefore, the chapters in this volume attempt to accomplish one of the goals first cited by Sleeter and Grant when they defined multicultural social reconstructionist education and linked it with critical theory which is to create a "language of critique" that moves [teachers] toward a "language of possibility" (Giroux 1992, 167).

As authors, we believe that the emergence of a critical pedagogy of possibilities is embedded in a rigorous analysis of the experiences that arise out of our own classroom experiences. Weis (1988) has advised that "The question of critical practice is essential. . . . We have few descriptions of exemplary practices in which models of educational action—informed by the critiques of the relationship between education and differential power—actually make a difference" (31). These authors have attempted to answer her call for programs that work, day-to-day examples of how to address effectively "problems of curricular and pedagogical policy and practice *and* also lead beyond themselves to further possibilities of organized cultural, political, and economic action (Weis 1988, 31).

The authors pose counter-hegemonic questions and dilemmas that challenge the positivistic, functionalist positions of our predecessors and that attempt to dismantle fundamental metaphors for what constitutes teaching and learning. In doing so, they disrupt the false sense of security that is engendered in teacher education programs that purport to train students to become effective teachers. Instead, we offer sometimes subtle, often complex suggestions for framing and expanding educational boundaries.

It is not happenstance that these authors represent variations on the MCSR theme. Their shared concerns and similar pedagogical strategies act as further testimony to the validity of their experiences and to the necessity for transformative pedagogy. Their work is shaped by efforts to give voice to questions about emancipatory praxis within the bureaucracies and intricacies of the teacher education arena. Influenced by critical, liberatory pedagogues, the various authors in each of the book's three sections grapple with questions such as the following. What are the political, systemic struggles in which multicultural educators engage? What role do our histories and personal biographies play in the production of pedagogy? How do our personal belief systems intersect with theory and practice? How might we demystify pedagogical practice that is multicultural and social reconstructionist? What are the relationships among power, culture, knowledge, and ideology? How do they inform pedagogy?

ALTERNATIVE TEMPLATES: BUILDING NEW FOUNDATIONS

The creation of meaningful pedagogy derived from critical theoretical constructs remains a challenge for even the most astute teacher educator. In the first section of the book, the authors set the stage for an investigation of the nature of teaching about issues of diversity by reflecting upon, dismantling, and reconstructing prevailing pedagogical structures. In chapter one, "Teaching Controversial Issues in Higher Education: Pedagogical Techniques and Analytical Framework," Julie Andrzejewski provides us with insights to address institutional conflict as well as individual resistance from predominantly white, middle-class students in multicultural education courses. The author discusses pedagogy that attempts to reduce defensiveness and establish openness toward developing and creating a framework for understanding issues of oppression. The chapter chronicles her struggles and those of the institution, the college, and the department in a state that mandates a multicultural/human relations teacher education program.

In "Thinking about Diversity: Paradigms, Meanings, and Representations," Robert Muffoletto discusses the social construction of knowledge. He uses two major paradigms, functional and interpretive, to explore our understandings of the world, and he guides the reader through an explication of semiotics and post-semiotics relative to those paradigms. Muffoletto then notes that "when considering diversity and multicultural education, the overt and covert messages delivered through various forms of media and technology must be considered and unpacked." Finally, he assesses the implications of the models for multicultural representations and classroom practice.

Next, Kathleen Farber, in "Teaching About Diversity through Reflectivity: Sites of Uncertainty, Risk, and Possibility," explicates a model for reflective pedagogy that actively engages students in the reconstruction of their own experience through problem posing. Using reflectivity grounded in Dewey's notion of democratic education, she discusses ways that students' and teachers' personal knowledge can be valued and validated via critical reflection. In addition, she examines the risks involved in the use of a reflective model to address issues of diversity, and she underscores that prospective educators must be able to reflect upon the ways in which the transmission of culture affects the production of knowledge and the relationships of power between teachers and students.

Chapter four, "Deconstructing Myth, Reconstructing Reality: Transcending the Crisis in Teacher Education," suggests that teacher education must be reconfigured at both the institutional and the individual levels in order to create an understanding of the dynamics of the complex intersection of notions of power, ideology, culture, and knowledge. In this chapter, I provide examples of how students can become engaged in an analysis of the structural dynamics of the classroom and of the ways in which prospective educators can examine, integrate, and critically analyze their own experiences and construct opportunities for the realization of democratic ideals and liberatory pedagogy. Examples of classroom activities arising out of student inquiry and cognitive struggles exemplify strategies that teacher educators might incorporate into their own repertoire.

"What's All This White Male Bashing?" is a chapter by Carl Allsup that examines teaching about issues of diversity within the framework of institutions that embrace hegemonic leadership and endorse dominant cultural values thereby marginalizing opposition to those values. Allsup quotes bell hooks noting his own efforts to reconceptualize sites of resistance which have operated to define and maintain a dominant center. The author notes the obstacles and limitations of disengagement from the centered, dominant discourse, and its accompanying ideological constructs, and the distortions that one encounters when educators attempt to reconceptualize issues of diversity for a more inclusive vision.

IMPACT AND IMPLICATION OF BIOGRAPHY

As noted earlier, at the heart of many problems associated with teaching about issues of race, class, and gender is the inability of a predominantly white, female, and middle-class teacher-education population to identify with issues of oppression. This inability often leads to misunderstandings and misconceptions about how to translate effectively what they learn about issues of diversity into alternative pedagogical strategies. The section of the book entitled "Impact and Implications of Biography" is characterized by accounts of ways in which educators can integrate their own biographies and those of their students in order to gain insights into the creation of more equitable and meaningful pedagogy.

In "Multicultural Teacher Education for a Culturally Diverse Teaching Force," Carmen Montecinos expresses the concern that "teacher education research has thus far failed to advance a discourse that is committed to the education of a culturally diverse teaching force. She examines and summarizes the ways in which a core of empirical studies on multicultural education describe the ethnic backgrounds of participants. Montecinos then explores some of the implications inherent in the development of multicultural teacher education programs that fail to understand the significance of such identity. She challenges us to develop alternative paradigms and notes areas of research that need to be addressed in order to accomplish her vision of a culturally diverse teaching force.

In her chapter entitled "Teaching Whites about Racism," Christine Sleeter describes a process that she has used with white preservice students to help them recognize the limits of what they know about social stratification so that they can begin to reconstruct their perceptions. After analyzing the social construction of identity, she discloses a variety of class activities designed to expose students to alternative paradigms for understanding issues of diversity. In so doing, she combats the notion that ownership of issues of diversity is vested within marginalized groups.

"Creating Classroom Environments for Change" is a chapter in which Keith Osajima discusses how his students are taught to think reflectively and analytically about the nature and impact of racism in the United States. Osajima centers his discussion around a course he teaches that is governed by three primary questions: 1) How have educational institutions served as vehicles both to oppress and to liberate people of color in this country? 2) How have white and minority students been miseducated about the nature and history of racism in the United States? and 3) What strategies and actions can students adopt to address how racism affects their lives?

"What's in It for Me: Persuading Nonminority Teacher Education Students to Become Advocates for Multicultural Education" is an account of how Kent Koppelman and Robert Richardson address value structures and moral dilemmas that students experience in a mandated teacher education course on diversity. The chapter transports the reader through a series of concrete examples of the authors' struggles in their own lives and teaching. In the context of these examples, they discuss the imposition of popular culture, the impact of language, and other cultural artifacts to investigate notions of power and oppression in society.

Multiple Realities: Multiple Enactments

The final segment of the book discloses some of the complexities of transferring liberatory, multicultural social reconstructionist theory into practice. In chapter ten, "Reflecting on Cultural Diversity through Early Field Experiences: Pitfalls, Hesitations, and Promise," William Armaline reflects on cultural diversity in early field experiences that involve a critical sociological analysis of schooling as portrayed in an entry level course with an accompanying field experience. He discusses an evolving pedagogy designed to interrogate students' perceptions, expectations, constructions, and ideological positions with respect to how they learn, what is important to know, and how we teach. Armaline discusses a research study in which preservice teachers employed reflective thinking and journal writing to inform this practice.

Elizabeth Quintero and Ana Huerta-Macias in "To Participate . . . To Speak Out: A Story from San Elizario, Texas" highlight pedagogical practices that interrupt and work against patriarchal systems. Their case studies of parents participating in a three-year family literacy project extend the concept of social reconstructionist education to familial and community education. The personal experiences of the women in a family literacy project for limited English-speaking families are used as a "point of departure to explore some of the more difficult questions regarding critical transformation" (180). Through the eyes of the participants, the reader is exposed to the complexities of transformative pedagogy, the social context of literacy classes, the family situations, and the community context in a small border town in Texas. What emerges are numerous implications for restructuring schools, redefining curricular issues, and rethinking development programs for teachers.

Lourdes Diaz-Soto and Tina Richardson relate two interactive and reflective methodological approaches, and the accompanying learning experiences of the facilitators and participants, in their chapter "Theoretical Perspectives and Multicultural Applications." The first set of experiences they recount occur in a required multicultural education course for graduate students whose voices depict their experiences in the course. The second set of experiences occur in a multicultural education course in counseling and psychology. The authors explain how they enable these students to identify key concepts and address new awareness regarding issues of diversity and the potential impact of those issues on the cultural contexts created in the counseling and mental health professions.

In chapter thirteen, we are exposed to the ways in which physical education acts as a site for socially, politically, and culturally constructed spheres of oppression. In "Beyond Bats and Balls: Teaching about Knowledge, Culture, Power and Ideology in Physical Education," Robyn Lock uses her own experiences as an athlete and teacher-educator to address the ideological boundaries of traditional pedagogy for physical education and to examine the possibilities for teaching transformatively. Her work is informed by a research project in which she demonstrates the application of critical theory to a physical education component in teacher education. Lock's discussion encourages us to create alternative lenses for viewing the traditional and the taken-for-granted courses that all children encounter in public education.

Evelyn McCain-Reid's pilot study in the chapter "Seeds of Change: A Pilot Study of Senior Preservice Teachers' Responses to Issues of Human Diversity in One University Course" sheds light on the impact of two models of instruction on students' learning in a multicultural education course—the Societal/Curriculum School Curriculum Model and the Multicultural Education Infusion Method. McCain-Reid frames her discussion within the context of a ten-week senior level social cultural foundations course, and she employs student voices in her discussion and investigation. This chapter causes us to reflect upon the dynamics inherent in classrooms where educators of color are faced with the limited perspectives of students from white middle-class backgrounds who are steeped in dominant ideological constructs.

The final chapter, "The Coalition for Education That Is Multicultural: A Network of Advocates for Educational Equity," describes and analyzes a coalition between educators in a teacher education program and teachers in a public school district. The long-range goals of the project were to increase knowledge of preservice and in-service teachers and administrators relative to multicultural education; to promote the development and implementation of multicultural curricula; and to provide placement sites for student teachers with teachers who are conversant with multicultural strategies. Marilynne Boyle-Baise offers the reader insights about the commitment and participation of members of the coalition that can serve to deepen and broaden our understanding of the complexities of the network of relationships to be considered as we create culturally congruent classrooms for the future.

REFERENCES

Bennett, K. P. and M. D. LeCompte. 1990. *How schools work: A sociological analysis of education*. New York: Longman.

Bonacich, E. 1989. Inequality in America: The failure of the American system for people of color. In *Race, class, and gender: An anthology*. Edited by M. L. Anderson and P. H. Collins, 96-110. California: Wadsworth Publishing Co.

Foucault, M. 1977. The political function of the intellectual. *Radical Philosophy* 17:12-14.

Giroux, H. A. 1989. *Teachers as intellectuals*. Massachusetts: Bergin & Garvey.

————. 1992. *Border crossings: Cultural workers and the politics of education*. New York: Routledge.

Giroux, H. A. and P. McLaren. 1987. Teacher education and the politics of engagement: The case for democratic schooling. In *Teachers, teaching and teacher education*. Edited by M. Okazawa-Rey, J. Anderson, R. Traver, 157-82. Harvard Educational Review Series, no. 19, Mount Pelier, Vt., Capital City Press.

Grant, C. and R. Koskela. 1986. Education that is multicultural and the relationship between pre-service campus learning and field experiences. *Journal of Educational Research* 70(4):89-102.

hooks, b. 1989. *Talking back: Thinking feminist, talking Black*. Boston: South End Press.

Hutcheon, L. 1989. *The politics of postmodernism*. New York: Routledge.

Lather, P. 1991. *Getting smart: Feminist research and pedagogy within the postmodern*. New York: Routledge.

Martin, R. J. 1986. A comparative analysis of the implementation of the human relations mandates in three selected teacher education institutions in the states of Iowa, Minnesota, and Wisconsin. Ph.D. diss., Iowa State University, Ames, IA.

Martin, R. J. and K. Koppelman. 1991. The impact of a human relations/multicultural education course on the attitudes of prospective teachers. *The Journal of Intergroup Relations* 23(1) (Spring):16-27.

McCarthy, C. and M. P. Apple. 1989. Race, class and gender in American educational research: Toward a non-synchronous parralelist position. In *Class, race, and gender in American education*. Edited by L. Weis. Albany, N.Y.: SUNY Press.

McLaren, P. 1993. *Life in schools*, 2d ed. New York: Longman.

Murray, F. and D. Fallon. *The reform of teacher education in the 21st century: Project 30 year one report*. Newark, DE.: Project 30, University of Delaware.

National Council for the Accreditation of Teacher Education (NCATE). 1977. Standards for Accreditation of Teacher Education, Washington, DC: NCATE.

Schumann, A. 1990. Improving the quality of teachers for minority students. In *Making schools work for underachieving minority students*. Edited by J. Bain and J. Herman. Westport, CT.: Greenwood Press.

Sleeter, C. E. and C. A. Grant. 1994. *Making choices for multicultural education: Five approaches to race, class, and gender in American education*, 2d ed. Columbus: Merrill.

Stanley, W. B. 1985. Social reconstructionism for today's social education. *Social Education* 45(5):384-89.

Weis, L., ed. 1988. *Class, race, and gender in American education*. New York: State University of New York Press.

ALTERNATIVE TEMPLATES:
BUILDING NEW FOUNDATIONS

1

JULIE ANDRZEJEWSKI

Teaching Controversial Issues in Higher Education: Pedagogical Techniques and Analytical Framework

Twenty years ago, the Minnesota State Department of Education mandated that all licensed teachers be certified in Human Relations and our university, among others, was faced with the task of educating teachers about the issues of prejudice and discrimination. Faculty from around the campus and community leaders of color were invited to participate in concentrated professional development workshops and plan a program for teacher education students and in-service teachers. Located in a fairly large midwestern university within a small homogenous, predominantly white city, the university in which I teach draws many students from rural communities. Initially, in-service teachers in our service area were not pleased about having a new sixty-hour requirement to meet that cost them time and money but did not lead to pay increases. Therefore, faculty often found themselves challenging unresponsive, if not hostile, participants to examine their attitudes and pedagogy in regard to race, and to a lesser extent, socioeconomic class. While the state mandate at that time did not include gender, disability, sexual orientation, or other types of oppression, the course content was considered very controversial. In this context, the Human Relations program at St. Cloud State University was created. Over the next twenty years the program developed into a Department of Human Relations and Multicultural Education serving the entire university on issues of racism, sexism, heterosexism, classism, imperialism, militarism, ageism, ableism, anti-Semitism, xenophobia, oppression based on physical appearance, and the interrelationship of environmental and animal rights issues.

This chapter will attempt to describe some of the pedagogical approaches and content of our program, including: (1) Methods that reduce defensiveness and establish openness to new perspectives; (2) Methods that introduce a framework for understanding oppression; (3) Methods that develop the framework; and (4) Methods that motivate students and address conflict. Because the content and methodology are integrally intertwined with one another, I will develop these points more or less chronologically as they are introduced to a class while moving back and forth between them to emphasize the key issues. Since most readers will be primarily interested in these rice and beans issues (a vegetarian equivalent for meat and potatoes) that may be of some value to their

3

own work, an abbreviated history of the program may assist the reader in understanding and utilizing this work.

It is important to qualify that the methods and perspectives represented in this chapter are, of course, informed by my own individual teaching and leadership experiences with the program. While the other faculty in the department share the fundamental perspectives and basic teaching methodologies described herein, each of us differs in emphasis, style, and the particular use of time and materials in the classroom. In this context, I will use the term *I* throughout most of the chapter. This is not an effort to take credit for all of the programmatic ideas and activities because some are a result of collegial interaction, but it is an effort to suggest that only I am responsible for this particular version of events.

History of the Program

As instructors, we were subjected to trial by fire. The sensitive subject matter of the class exacerbated the hostility of in-service teachers about having to meet the requirement at all. In response, some faculty neutralized their material to the point where no one objected. Others developed methods to diffuse the antagonism of the in-service teachers and to challenge them to struggle with the issues the new course presented. As the instructors educated themselves about the issues, a new framework began to emerge. It became clear that the mandate did not address oppression in as much depth or breadth as needed. After a few years, when the pressure to certify the vast majority of Minnesota's in-service teachers subsided, a dedicated core faculty continued to pursue ideas of expanding and improving the program. The mission, in the minds of the faculty, was broader than the state mandate and included working toward the reality of values ascribed to by the United States: "liberty and justice for all." Several faculty were actively involved within the community or the university with issues involving labor, feminism, antiracism, or challenging class oppression or heterosexism. For instance, my own work on the National Free Sharon Kowalski Campaign, coauthoring the book *Why Can't Sharon Kowalski Come Home?* (Thompson and Andrzejewski 1988), organizing a local women's center, and serving as a grievance officer for faculty experiencing racism, sexism, xenophobia, and heterosexism provided a wealth of practical experiences in institutional change. Our activism informed our teaching, and our program development informed our analysis and conceptual framework.

Program development was not without problems. At different times, we experienced opposition from other departments in the university as well as efforts to eliminate or curtail the program by the administration. We became experts at defending ourselves. Internal conflicts were also a source of frustration as well as growth. Partially as a result of internal debate about the inclusion of other types of oppression, we moved ahead of the mandate and incorporated issues of sexism, sexual orientation and others while beginning to examine the political and economic foundations of oppression. In 1976, our program became a core model for the Foundations of Oppression manual adopted by the State Department of Education in Minnesota (1977). Later, the state mandate was changed to include more issues. By this time, the program had developed a reputation for being challenging and exciting. A demand developed from noneducation majors for general education courses, and eventually a minor and graduate program emerged. The program grew into a center and the center eventually became a department.

PART 1: METHODS THAT REDUCE DEFENSIVENESS
AND ESTABLISH OPENNESS

Respectful Approach to Students

In my teaching experience with controversial issues, I have found it most effective to address the issues candidly and directly, and to tell students exactly what is planned and what the expectations are for the course. I am careful, however, about the manner with which I approach them. I try to explain things in a respectful and challenging way, making sure they feel they have control over what they choose to believe and that there are opportunities for challenging the information I present. I tell them that while the information presented may challenge many of the beliefs they have been taught, they are the ultimate judges of what they choose to accept. I make it clear that I don't expect them to adopt these perspectives but I do expect them to give the information consideration, to check on the materials, perspectives, and data for veracity, and to be able to articulate knowledge of them.

The First Day of Class: Establishing Ground Rules and Decreasing Defensiveness

The first few days of class are extremely important to establish ground rules, share the underlying values of the course, reduce defensiveness, and challenge some of the pervasive myths and ideologies in our culture. In this chapter, I will describe some of the activities I have developed that facilitate this process.

Because students are involved in a wide variety of in-class activities such as sharing written assignments, analyzing and critiquing media, or reacting to films or readings, a fifty-minute period was found to be inadequate. Therefore, most of our classes are arranged in two-hour blocks. Given this time, a number of key activities occur on the very first day. I try to identify and reduce apprehensions, establish ground rules for communication and class expectations, identify some personal and professional benefits of the course, and then move directly to the heart of some prevailing myths of our times to challenge and motivate them. I regularly have students write brief class reactions to monitor their understanding and feelings about the issues and materials. After the first class session, students usually express a combination of excitement, nervousness and amazement.

I begin class by asking students to share in small groups the rumors they have heard about Human Relations. (When the Human Relations courses were first offered, these lists contained many negative things, but as the program has developed these lists became more and more positive.) This gives the students the opportunity to present their apprehensions about the class without necessarily identifying them as their own. For instance, they may be fearful of being attacked or personally exposed as a racist or prejudiced person. This activity gives me a chance to address their fears or other rumors in a straightforward way. In addition, getting these issues out in the open for discussion early provides an opportunity to establish a precedent for relaxed (even humorous at times) communication about difficult subjects.

The second activity is to establish some ground rules for the class. Basically, they are:

1. Required attendance: Since we essentially are trying to challenge a lifetime of exposure to myths and ideologies, misinformation (or disinformation), institutionalized oppression, and bigotry, et cetera, each day's materials provide the background and foundation for the next and so on. Students who miss class raise questions often that were addressed previously or they never quite grasp concepts or skills addressed during their absence. Students who miss one or two classes are given assignments that are designed to replicate the class experiences as much as possible. If more classes are missed, students are asked to retake the class.

2. Honest and respectful dialogue: Disagreement and challenging of ideas (of other students or the instructor) in a supportive and sensitive manner is encouraged. However, hostility, derision, or other disrespectful behavior will be addressed promptly by the instructor.

3. Expectations of outcomes: Students are expected to be able to understand and articulate various perspectives and information presented and developed in the class. There is no requirement that they personally adopt or agree with these perspectives. It is my experience that if students allow themselves to understand the perspectives of oppressed groups without the obfuscation of ideological justifications, they tend to discover that these perspectives have validity. At a minimum, they are challenged to reevaluate their own values, ideas, and behaviors.

The third activity is to address communication, my pedagogical philosophy, and the development of some personal skills that will be useful in the class. I acknowledge that the dominant culture in the United States (and certainly the local community) does not encourage or reinforce open, honest, and respectful disagreement. Disagreement is not viewed as "polite," and those who challenge mainstream views or authority are often called "troublemakers," "communists," or other pejorative labels. In addition, there appears to be a negative judgment about people who change their minds. However, I suggest to the class that education is the process of changing our ideas and behaviors based on new information. Therefore, I propose that learning is enhanced by the juxtaposition of contradictory ideas/theories, conflicting pieces of information or evidence, and the process of searching for their veracity. I briefly share a couple of my own experiences of changing my mind when confronted with new or more persuasive information. So, I encourage the students to experiment with challenging (in a positive manner) information or arguments that I or others present. In addition, I encourage them to try to get more comfortable with disagreement and with the possibility of changing their own minds based on new information. I explain that my own teaching style is to combine challenge and support (Perry 1970). One of the most significant moments in the class is the first time a student takes a risk to challenge an idea. It is important that this effort is reinforced by the instructor or the overt message (encouragement to challenge) is contradicted by the actual response.

The Role of Self-Interest and Integrity

The faculty in our program have discovered that it is most beneficial to identify why it is in the students' self-interest to examine the issues we will present to them. Since our students are not at an elite university nor from the upper class, we are able to present information quickly about the distribution of wealth in the United States, the types of jobs and salaries available to graduates from a comprehensive versus an elite university, and the comparative resources available to them as students. Even at the tuition cost of a state university (rising rapidly in the last few years as the state deficits increase), most of our students work long hours just to stay in college. As they consider the materials presented, they quickly realize that they are victims of class oppression. I point out that students of color, women, disabled students, lesbians or gay men, et cetera experience additional types of oppression as well.

In addition to inequitable resource distribution, another component of self-interest is the maintenance or enhancement of integrity and self-esteem. I begin with the assumption that the students have developed a sense of ethical responsibility, that they have been taught and share certain values about freedom and justice. I explain that in this course they will be asked to examine their own ideas, beliefs, and behaviors as victims of oppression and as oppressors. However, I suggest that much oppression is hidden and not easily detected. If they have not studied oppression and how it is institutionalized (permeates policies and practices), then it is very likely they are unaware of most oppression against themselves or others, including whether they are inadvertently perpetuating it. As an example, I might ask how many women in class believe they have been victims of sex discrimination. When less than half raise their hands (which is often the case), I suggest that they may be surprised to discover the limitations that have affected their lives and to discover the opportunities they have been denied based on their gender. I explain the importance of examining the information in the class in light of their own personal life experiences.

Next, I indicate they will study instances of oppression they encounter throughout their normal daily activities. They will become more aware of oppression as it occurs around them and will have new tools upon which to base their responses. Finally, the class will examine how each of us perpetuates oppression. I assure them that the purpose of this component is not to make them feel bad and guilty but to give them the opportunity to change any attitudes and behaviors where they are not satisfied with the consequences. They will also be taught to identify institutionalized oppression, the use of power and resources to establish and maintain it, and the methods of social control that serve to render it invisible. To place this in a context, I explain that the class will examine how oppression operates from the global level to the interpersonal level.

I suggest that when they understand how oppression operates, they will be in a better position to make informed decisions in their personal and professional lives. I repeat that the purpose of the class is not to establish blame and guilt but to examine the circumstances, theories, and motivations for oppression and/or injustice. The students will need to be reassured at several points during the class since the materials and ideas presented result in a variety of intense emotions.

The Myth of Objectivity

The first myth I introduce is the myth of objectivity. I ask the students if they can identify societal institutions that claim to be objective, neutral or value free. If the students don't identify education, science, or the media, I add them to the list. Usually there is some discussion about whether they believe these institutions are objective or not. Beginning with education, I lay out the argument that none of these institutions are objective and give examples (e.g., perspectives of Columbus as discoverer or invader). Then, as a class, we discuss what is the purpose of fostering the impression that an institution is objective when it isn't. I ask them to consider who benefits most from the educational institutions. Who benefits the least? As they think of their own education, which group or groups are made to look like "heroes" and which appear to be "problems"? How are women made to appear? People of color? Lesbians and gay men? Working-class people? Disabled people? Countries that are "at war" with the United States? Through this discussion, the students are introduced to the idea of social control and how biases and discrimination can be hidden behind a facade of "objectivity" or "neutrality." I indicate that one of the skills they will learn in the class is how to identify hidden biases in education, the media, science, and other fields. I go on to introduce how the myth of objectivity applies to science and media.

I always end this first brief presentation with the conclusion that Human Relations classes are not purported to be objective. I contend that through the media, advertising, education, and exposure to many other social institutions they have been taught certain assumptions, myths, and misinformation about oppression and justice. As much as possible throughout the course, I will try to identify the values base of the materials so they are able to make their own judgments about the information and perspectives I am presenting. I make clear that my contention is that they have already been exposed to "the other side," and therefore I will use my limited amount of time with them to present perspectives from the vantage points of oppressed peoples.

Examination of Democracy and Citizenship Skills

Since the government has a major responsibility for the country's policies and practices that impact individuals and groups differentially within the United States as well as in other countries, it is important to introduce students early to issues that lay the foundation for examining institutional oppression at the governmental level. As I developed the next activity for at least eight years, it became clear to me that students have almost no concept of what democracy is or what types of skills might be needed for "citizenship." There are two components to this exercise. The first is to get them to begin to question some myths about the U.S. government and to explore who benefits from its policies and practices. The second is to question their own education (and therefore, the educational system) in regard to democracy and citizenship skills.

I ask the students to tell me what "democracy" is. The only consistent answers I receive are "government of the people, by the people and for the people," and some explanation of "representative democracy." I almost never get any response relating to "participatory democracy." Utilizing their definition of representative democracy for the time being, I ask them if they are satisfied that Congress is really "representing" the "people." Here I usually raise some questions and give them some pieces of information to consider, such as: How much money do members of Congress make? How much wealth do they own? How many are millionaires? What are PACs and how might they influence legislation? What kind of perquisites do members of Congress receive? How many of the congressional and presidential candidates are millionaires? What is the income and wealth of the "poorest" members of Congress? How many women, people of color, lesbians or gay men, disabled people, et cetera are in Congress? How many members of Congress are rich, white, male, heterosexual (or closeted), able-bodied, Christian, et cetera? How is legislation affected by these characteristics? Can any patterns of voting records be identified? The discussion of these questions has been enhanced dramatically in the last few years by all of the disclosures about members of Congress, their pay raises, perquisites, voting records, et cetera. Indeed, I now have a list of questions that I give to students to investigate in both the mainstream and alternative press so they can inform themselves further on these matters.

After raising questions in their minds about representative democracy, I inform them that almost every school has, as one of its objectives, to teach citizenship skills. Therefore, I ask them to make a list of all the citizenship skills they now possess. Usually there is a long silence. Then, slowly and torturously the class tries to make a list. After ten years of doing this exercise, I consistently get the same five answers and often no more than these five.

1. vote
2. salute the flag
3. say the pledge of allegiance
4. pay taxes
5. obey the laws

Occasionally, some will indicate that they were taught how government works and the system of checks and balances. I ask, "Were you taught how to influence government?" Almost without exception, the students say, "no." Occasionally, someone will say that you can write to your legislator. When I ask how many in the class have done that, it is rare that more than one or two people indicate they have. I ask them, "Do you believe you have adequate citizenship skills?" I ask them to consider why the schools are not teaching them skills geared toward a "participatory democracy."

PART 2: METHODS THAT INTRODUCE A
FRAMEWORK FOR UNDERSTANDING OPPRESSION

Moving to a Macro Conflict Model

It is not easy to encapsulate the theoretical framework of an entire course in the space of a few pages. In addition, each faculty member in the program teaches the issues in a slightly different sequence, and each chooses from a variety of films, exercises, and readings even though the overall framework is basically shared. Based on my own curriculum, I will attempt to convey here a brief sketch of the framework utilized for understanding oppression (theories, concepts and definitions) and how the framework lends itself to examining the interrelationship of issues.

The framework is based on a number of theories. These contend that discrimination is not a result of individual (irrational or ignorant) prejudice but rather a matter of vested interests and of establishing and maintaining resources and privileges. The program moved to this model in the early 1970s by shifting the examination of social problems and issues away from the victims of oppression to individuals, groups and institutions with power and resources.

By making this shift, the program essentially moved from a micro social-psychological perspective (individual prejudice model) to a macro conflict orientation (social power and resource model). Early in the development of the program, faculty primarily utilized components of various theoretical perspectives from authors of color (e.g., Deloria 1969; Carmichael and Hamilton 1967; Knowles and Prewitt 1969) and, after sexism was incorporated into the program, materials from feminist authors (e.g., Frasier and Sadker 1973; Tavris and Wade 1984; Stacey, Bereaud and Daniels 1974) as well as progressive white males (e.g., Cahn and Hearne 1970; Harrington 1962; Ryan 1976; Terry 1975). As our framework began changing, materials from alternative press publications, social change organizations, and movements, as well as from more traditional scholarly sources, were sought to inform our teaching and scholarship.

Over the last decade, scholarship emanating from many disciplines converged in similar theoretical and analytical conclusions. While it is important to qualify that substantial differences and debate are still very alive among these perspectives and that their foci may differ, they underscore the significance of structural systemic oppression. In the field of education alone the terminology that speaks to this framework differs widely. Sleeter and Grant (1988) call it multicultural/social reconstructionist and speak to the different terminology used to describe similar frameworks: "This approach, more than the others, is called different things by different advocates. For example, one may encounter terms such as *emancipatory pedagogy* (Gordon 1985), *critical teaching* (Shor 1980), *transformational education* (Giroux 1981), *multicultural education* (Suzucki 1984), *antiracist teaching* (Carby 1982; Mullard 1980), and *socialist feminism* (Jagger and Struhl 1978)" (177).

Our program has drawn from a number of these authors as well as from the works of individuals in other fields, such as Gloria Anzaldua, Benjamin Bagdikian, James Baldwin, James Banks, Franz Fanon, Paulo Friere, Eduardo Galeano, bell hooks, Winona LaDuke, Audre Lorde, Manning Marable, Peggy McIntosh, June Jordan, Michael Parenti, Paula Rothenberg, Holly Sklar, Barbara Smith, Merlin Stone, Ronald Takaki, Howard Zinn, to mention only a few.

The Use of Alternative and Activist (as well as Scholarly) Sources

To demonstrate the significance of alternative and movement sources, some examples are in order. I have purposely chosen examples that may be less familiar to those who have primarily focussed on race, gender, and class. For instance, in order to keep up with the cutting edge of disability rights, I regularly draw from *The Disability Rag*. One article, "Between Two Worlds," describes the experiences of black deaf people who encounter racism in the deaf community and ableism in the black community (Younkin 1990). Articles like this provide strong testimony for examining the interrelationships of oppressions and why educators and activists must address all types of oppression, not just those closest to their hearts. Furthermore, I am aware of no scholarly publication that addresses disability rights from the perspective of the disability activists as does the *Rag*.

The Green Party USA and the Rainbow Coalition both provide examples of movements trying to demonstrate that oppressed peoples of all types must join together to try to effect comprehensive changes that affect the majority of the population in one way or another. For instance, the Green Party platform includes education, health and healing, indigenous people, peace, nonviolence, and social justice as well as issues of ecology (Green Party 1992). At the same time that environmental groups are beginning to recognize the necessity of addressing social justice issues, Ben Chavis (one of the Wilmington 10) coined the term *environmental racism* to describe the phenomenon of toxic waste dumps primarily being located near communities of color. Small organizations such as Panos Institute have published stories of resistance to this phenomenon by various communities of color (Alston 1990). Groups whose primary concern is racism and others whose primary concern is ecology are recognizing that the issues are interrelated and that both must be addressed simultaneously because safety *and* justice are inseparable.

Lesbian, gay, and bisexual organizations and publications are also in the forefront of examining the interrelationships of issues since lesbians, gay men, and bisexual people are commonly members of other oppressed groups as well. Although a few are upper-class, white, young, able-bodied, Protestant males, the majority have other characteristics that accompany oppression (female, persons of color, disabled, poor, etc.). As a black, lesbian, feminist, Audre Lorde in her article (1983) "There is No Hierarchy of Oppressions," speaks eloquently to those who would try to dismiss or discount the oppression of others.

Finally, the animal rights movement has much to offer in the analysis of oppression. Peter Singer's *Animal Liberation* (1975) challenges some of our deepest myths, ones often used to justify the oppression of various human groups as well. People for the Ethical Treatment of Animals (PETA 1989) offers very persuasive argumentation and data showing the interrelationship between eating meat, the global maldistribution of food (and concomitant social justice issues), and the destruction of the environment.

Almost every student will find it easy to understand or identify with some issues and will struggle with or want to reject consideration of other issues. I try to find diverse ways to demonstrate that the issues are more interrelated than is immediately apparent. I suggest that students carefully examine the evidence and arguments for each issue, especially those that challenge them the most. They are asked to reflect upon where they may have developed their current opinions on a particular subject and what evidence or reasoning constitutes the basis for these opinions. Discussion groups are asked to compare and contrast the arguments used to justify the oppression of various groups, the policies and practices through which the oppression operates, and the consequences of the oppression to the perpetrators as well as the victims. Students are encouraged to apply the questions, "Who benefits?" and "Who loses?" as part of their analysis of the position or policy they are examining. There is no expectation that students will accept any or all of the arguments made about a particular issue. But the exposure to information and analysis from a wide range of issues helps them to understand that significant connections exist between seemingly unrelated topics.

Many times alternative sources such as these are at the cutting edge of analysis, challenging and juxtaposing interrelationships of oppression that have yet to be addressed by the scholarly community. Scholars operating within traditional educational institutions are subjected to many more constraints than activists within alternative organizations. While pockets of critical theorists, feminists, and activists of color have been able to survive and work here and there in academia, radical scholarship generally has not produced the rewards of tenure and promotion. Only recently has the entire traditional canon been challenged by scholars from many disciplines who insist that these new perspectives are "legitimate" scholarly activities. Rothenberg (1992), Anderson and Collins (1992), hooks (1990), Marable (1991), Minnich (1990) and others now provide important sources of information and conceptualization for teaching about oppression. In some instances, individuals from activist organizations and academia collaborate. For instance, *Looking Forward: Participatory Economics for the Twenty-first Century* (1992), written by Michael Albert (coeditor and cofounder of *Z Magazine*) and Robin Hahnel (professor of economics at American University) provides a vision and blueprint for an equitable economic system. Most of these sources validate the importance of the struggle and resistance to oppression as well as contribute to the understanding of oppression itself.

Because of the breadth of resources used, the students are exposed to a number of theoretical frameworks early in the class, many of which overlap or are useful for certain types of analysis. Feagin and Feagin (1978) outline succinctly a few theories as the interest theory, internal colonialism, and institutional discrimination. When definitions of oppression deriving from these theories are compared, common themes emerge. These themes then reinforce the basis of a framework for understanding oppression. Although the particular manifestations of racism may differ from the expressions of sexism, students can begin to identify some patterns and to formulate some of their own impressions of how and why oppression occurs.

Working Definitions of Oppression

Working definitions emerge from the theories. The Council on Interracial Books for Children (1976) identifies the components of institutional oppression as (1) systematic discrimination and exploitation of a particular group; (2) discriminatory institutionalized policies and practices that are pervasive; and (3) the possession of power by the oppressive group in order to enforce discriminatory actions and maintain exploitation. The interest theory indicates that "the motivating force behind discrimination can be the desire to protect one's own privilege and power" (Feagin and Feagin 1978). Stone's definitions (1992) of the two stages of economic racism are useful in examining a colonial model of oppression: "The first aspect and nearly always the underlying purpose of racism, is economic racism, the theft of the land, property, resources and/or labour from people of a racial or ethnic group other than one's own. . . . The second stage of economic racism is the long term control by the aggressors/conquerors of what they have taken by force and then claim is rightfully theirs. The land, property and resources of the victims are legally in the conquerors' name; no matter that they wrote the new laws themselves" (232-233). Terry (Minnesota Department of Education, 1977) outlines four interdependent components of oppression in his definition: "Oppression exists when any entity (society, organization, group, or individual) intentionally or unintentionally inequitably distributes resources, refuses to share power, imposes ethnocentric culture, and/or maintains unresponsive and inflexible institutions toward another entity for its supposed benefit and rationalizes its action by blaming or ignoring the victim" (Andrzejewski 1993, 6).

Examining Political and Economic Systems in a Global and Historical Context

The theories and definitions clearly establish the necessity for a direct examination of political and economic systems. Despite academic freedom and the first amendment, the tolerance for critical examination of capitalism and the role of U.S.-based multinational corporations or other political-economic phenomena is almost always controversial. Many scholars who have attempted to address these issues directly (like Michael Parenti) have been purged from academia. Other scholars have approached the issues cautiously and have developed language or models that try to address the same issues in a less threatening manner. However, recent political events and carefully documented exposés of the relationship of government and corporate interests by highly acclaimed investigative reporters have made such a critical analyses more difficult to attack (Barlett and Steele 1992; Grieder 1992; Moyers 1987, 1992). In any event, *it is my contention that the study of oppression within the United States is not complete without studying the United States in a global and historical context.*

PART 3: METHODS THAT DEVELOP THE FRAMEWORK

A Critical Analytical Approach

Because students come to the course imbued with all of the patriotic myths about the United States that permeate almost every aspect of our culture, I have found it effective to approach the study of these issues within the context of critical analysis. Initially, a very simple model of analysis can be introduced for comparison of stated values versus actions. Because stated values can be a form of disinformation, this model can also be useful later in studying methods of propaganda, ideologies and social control. I ask students to compare what the United States *says* it stands for and its *actual* policies and actions. This model can be used to analyze any nation, particular social institutions (schools, churches, businesses, etc.) or even individuals: what do I *say* I stand for, in comparison with what I actually do. Together, the students and I make a list of what they have been taught are the values of the United States. Many of these values (freedom, equality, justice, human rights, etc.) are identified as the basic values of the course. Then I ask the students to list any policies or practices of the United States that appear to contradict the stated values. The students easily identify numerous contradictions.

Next, I explain that I will be presenting materials that may seem shocking or uncomfortable and may challenge much of what they have been taught about the United States. I also indicate that one of the skills they will be developing in the course is the critical analysis of media in all of its forms, including an understanding of ideologies and methods of social control. I will expect them to analyze the materials I give them as critically as any others. My goal is to introduce students to materials that challenge common assumptions and ask them to check the veracity of the data, identify the underlying values in the materials, and come to their own conclusions.

The Use of Readings and Media

In the second week of class, students already are engaged in a critical analysis of the Constitution, its framers, and the Bill of Rights. They are introduced to a brief review of the role of colonialism in the world, the concepts of neo-colonialism and imperialism, and an examination of U.S. foreign and military policy. Without listing and annotating all of the readings and audiovisual materials that provide the basis for this study, a few examples may suffice. Historical selections about the framers of the Constitution and in whose interests they were operating (Fresia 1988) can be used to examine the lives of the "founding fathers" and how their wealth was accumulated from slavery, land acquisition, etc. The Constitution can be explored further in regard to protection of wealthy white males. An article about the Bill of Rights can raise questions about why food, housing, health care, and other basic necessities are not considered "rights" (Savoy 1991). In an excerpt from *Democracy for the Few* (Parenti 1988) can challenge students to examine how the "bulk of public policy is concerned with economic matters" and how the private sector influences and benefits from these policies. In *The Global Factory*, students can read about the nature of international capitalism and examine a cost-benefit analysis for the majority of people in the United States and in other countries (Kamel 1990). A pbs *Frontline* by William Grieder (Who Will Tell the People, 1992) detailing the control of government by corporate and banking interests, or Bill Moyer's famous documentary on "The Secret Government"

(1987) outlining the policies and practices of the National Security Council and Central Intelligence Agency, can challenge common perceptions about democracy.

Viewing Racism, Sexism and Class Oppression in the Global Context

At this point, some readers may think I have completely gotten off the track of studying oppression based on race, gender, class, and other issues of oppression. On the contrary, I would contend that all of the issues involved in the study of U.S. government, U.S. foreign and military policies, and international capitalism are fundamental to examining the process of, as Stone (1992) puts it, "the theft of the land, property, resources and/or labour from people of a racial or ethnic group other than one's own . . . and the long term control by the aggressors/conquerors of what they have taken by force and then claim is rightfully theirs." Furthermore, corporations prefer to exploit women of color in their countries since they can pay them even lower wages, they are less likely to rebel against oppressive conditions, and they can be subjected to sexual exploitation (Kamel 1990). The understanding of how racism and sexism function on a global level and who benefits establishes a basis for looking at how it functions within the United States or within any given institution. Individual behaviors are studied and analyzed with these larger contexts.

Critical Analysis of the Media

A second component of critical analysis taught in the class is based on the myth of objectivity. First, students are assigned readings about the mainstream media industry itself. Benjamin Bagdikian (1987) documents the concentration of ownership and control of information production and dissemination in the United States and how this affects the content, selection, analysis and reporting practices. Excerpts from *Unreliable Sources* (Lee and Solomon 1990) describe how racism, sexism, and homophobia serve these same corporate and elite interests. Information is shared on Project Censored which conducts national media research and identifies "the top ten issues overlooked or underreported by the national news media" each year (Most Censored Stories 1990, 1991, 1). Students are introduced to alternative press publications (Alternative Press Center 1991) and shown how to identify factors that influence the content, selection, analysis, and reporting in these publications.

Given this context, students are encouraged to examine the values in all media and materials. A media assignment asks students to read an article or two on a human rights issue in the alternative press, find an article or two on the same or a similar topic from the mainstream media, and examine the content and values in both. It is emphasized that both publications have values and biases. Students are given questions and clues to help them identify these, such as: To whom is the information directed? Is the publication profit or nonprofit?

Which side seems to be presented as being right? How can you tell? What evidence or documentation is presented? The veracity of any data or event can be cross-checked with other sources, and the interpretation of the data or event can be evaluated in the context of the values. Again, students are encouraged to compare what the media publications *say* they stand for and what they *actually publish*. Students are encouraged to critique and analyze the materials presented in class using these same skills. This skill is further developed later in the course when students are asked to identify racism, sexism, ableism, heterosexism, and other types of oppression in textbooks and educational materials.

At the same time, students are introduced to ideology and social control. Beginning with *Blaming the Victim* (Ryan 1976), students are taught how certain myths justify oppression and maintain the power, resources, and privileges in the hands of a few. The relationship of homophobia (the irrational fear and hatred of lesbians, gay men, and bisexuals) to the oppression of women is explored (Pharr 1988). The use of anticommunism to justify imperialism and military intervention or to prevent an examination of the ills of capitalism is studied (Cook 1989). Students examine how "The Myth of Reverse Discrimination" (Andrzejewski 1992) maintains racism and sexism. The use of the terms *political correctness* and *cultural diversity* in academia are compared and analyzed. Students study how such terms disguise political positions. Overall, the study of social control is a crucial component of critical analysis. Students are taught to ask questions such as: Who benefits and who loses if I accept this analysis? Who paid for this research? Who has been able to influence this interpretation/analysis and how? Whose interests does this "information" serve? Can these data be corroborated by other sources? How reliable are these sources? What determines the *perception* of reliability versus *true* reliability?

The Study of the Issues: Race, Gender, Class, Disability, Sexual Orientation, etc.

After these foundations, the course begins to focus on particular types of oppression. For instance, students' understanding of racism is expanded and delineated. Contemporary racism is addressed in a global and historical context. Connections with xenophobia and imperialism are made. At this point, however, the focus is on racism within the United States. Because the scope of the issues is so large, each instructor is a generalist with more in-depth expertise on a couple of the issues. However, we believe it is important for students to be exposed to specialists in each area. Therefore, our program has a small budget to provide the students with ten speakers each quarter. Since ten can never cover all of the issues, we vary the speakers from quarter to quarter but generally have speakers on the following topics: American Indian Issues, Asian American Issues, African American Issues, Latino Issues, Sexism in Education, Violence Against Women, Heterosexism and Homophobia, Disability Issues, and Xenophobia. It is not uncommon to have speakers on anti-Semitism, class, social change, ageism, children's rights, discrimination based on mental retardation, or other topics when speakers are available. The speakers we use regularly have been exposed to the curriculum and materials of the course. Therefore, they can build upon and enhance the meaning of the conceptual framework we are trying to build. Nationally known speakers brought to campus by the student body are included whenever the topic seems appropriate. We challenge students to listen with a critical ear to all the speakers.

We choose speakers who have expertise on particular types of oppression and who have personal stories and professional experiences to share. However, it is also necessary that they understand and make connections with the larger framework utilized in the program. One of the difficulties we encountered in earlier years was locating speakers who were sensitive to all of the issues. For instance, we occasionally would have a speaker on racism who made sexist or ableist statements or a speaker on sexism who utilized racist or heterosexist materials. When this happened, we explained to our students that understanding one type of oppression does not guarantee understanding others. Such an example would become an illustration of the necessity for understanding all types of oppression and their interrelationships.

PART 4: METHODS THAT MOTIVATE STUDENTS AND ADDRESS CONFLICT

Connecting the Global and National with the Personal and Interpersonal

It is not always easy for students to understand why and how global, national or even institution-wide events and policies affect their own personal and professional lives. If this connection is not specifically addressed by the course methodology, students tend to view the material with a distant or abstract manner. It doesn't seem to have relevance to their own lives and is not as salient as the experiences of school, employment, or personal relationships occurring in the present or immediate future. Therefore, faculty continuously provide ways for students to envision or experience in some small way the impact or influence of various issues, policies, or events on their personal lives and careers. Students examine the materials and issues as citizens and taxpayers; as members of a particular class, ethnic background, gender, sexual orientation, spiritual orientation, etc.; as future teachers or employees; as human beings needing air, water, food, clothing, shelter, health care, etc.; as ethical individuals operating within their own value system; as members of their family and community; as individuals with their own desires, aspirations, and hopes for their futures.

As students begin to consider how issues of oppression, power, and resources have affected and are affecting their own lives, the significance of the issues is enhanced and made more meaningful. How have the policies on the distribution of income and wealth in the United States affected their families and shaped their futures? What are the social and personal costs of imperialism, environmental destruction, runaway factories, concentration of media ownership, etc. and who will bear the brunt of paying for them? What types of privileges and/or oppression have they personally experienced in regard to racism, sexism, ageism, heterosexism, ableism, et cetera? In every class period, students are given a way to explore these types of questions in some way. By addressing issues of the course in personal terms we can arouse feelings of all kinds and create an atmosphere of intense interest.

Relating the Issues to the Lives of the Students

In addition to reading and writing assignments, the course draws upon the real experiences of the students. One assignment, the Sex Role Project, asks students to step outside of the stereotyped gender roles in some aspect of their lives to experience the pressure that is placed upon them to maintain these roles. While possible activities are listed to give them a sense of the project, the choice of activity is left entirely open to the student. The requirements of the project are: that it not be something you already do; that the project be taken seriously; that the activity occur over a span of time. Examples from the long list of activities women may consider (*if* the activity applies to their own lives) are:

1. Stop cleaning your boyfriend's apartment, doing his laundry, et cetera or renegotiate responsibility for sharing the housework in a household.
2. Stop wearing makeup.
3. Drive the car instead of the male driving.
4. Nurture yourself instead of others.
5. Reverse gender roles with a spouse or friend.
6. Make your own decisions rather than letting others make them for you.
7. Challenge sexism (behaviors, jokes, comments, sexual harassment, etc.)
8. Begin to learn a stereotypically male gender-based skill (servicing or repairing cars, carpentry, plumbing, electrical work, etc.)

Examples from the list of activities for men (again, only if they apply) are:

1. Do your own cleaning and laundry.
2. Use nonsexist language.
3. Take responsibility for child care.
4. Nurture others.
5. Reverse gender roles with a spouse or friend.
6. Consult your spouse or partner on decisions or ask her to make them.
7. Challenge sexism (jokes, comments, sexual harassment, pornography).
8. Begin to learn a stereotypically female gender-based skill: sewing, cooking, etc.

The students are given four to six weeks to work on this project as the class proceeds. Oral reports of their experiences and analysis occur in class. Students are asked to consider sharing their own feelings and/or struggles about the activity; reactions of other people to the activity; and their analysis of how these behaviors are affected by sex roles, gender stereotypes, media images, institutional policies, and educational experiences. The Sex Role Project is often identified by students as one of the best learning experiences in the class.

Another assignment that directly involves the students' everyday lives is called Identifying Oppression. Students are asked to identify and record examples of oppression they observe or experience. The examples may include: comments, jokes, actions, policies or rules, unwritten institutional practices, or written materials or audiovisual media. They may draw from any forum: home, work, school or community. Sometimes the students may be asked to look for examples of a particular type of oppression, such as racism or sexism. Students can bring their lists to class and examine them in light of the definitions and reading material. This exercise helps to increase awareness and clarify how oppression manifests itself on a daily basis. Students are often surprised to discover how many incidents of oppression they encountered in a week. These types of activities make the issues in the class very salient and give students the opportunity to examine how they wish to deal with them on a personal as well as professional level.

Addressing Questions and Conflict

Intense interest also increases class participation and debate. These are encouraged as long as the dialogue is respectful. It is important that students who question the material be able to bring these questions out into the open. Otherwise, students may discount and reject the materials internally, based upon some untested, unscrutinized rationale. Students are encouraged to challenge each other as well as the instructor in a supportive way. When students are clearly challenging the framework, the materials, or the data upon which the class is based, or if they make comments that could be characterized as prejudicial or oppressive in themselves, several different responses are appropriate within the context of our pedagogical style. Some examples follow.

1. If a student indicates belief in a stereotype or myth early in the class, the comment might be gently addressed as follows: "Well, that is a common perception. We will look at some materials that address that issue and we will examine its origin, veracity and underlying values." This response does not punish the student for bringing up a taboo subject, for being "prejudiced," or for any other negative attribute. It suggests, instead, that information exists that pertains to the subject and she/he will have an opportunity to explore the issue further.

2. If a student directly questions a particular fact, contention, article or media, the class is encouraged or assigned to check the references or origin of the data, or to check other sources (both mainstream and alternative). The student may be asked to supply material that supports her/his point of view for class examination, or the instructor may have additional corroborating materials available for class inspection. The approach is not argumentative but investigative. The point is not to win an argument with a student but simply to juxtapose the pieces of information and get the class involved in critical analysis.

3. Occasionally, a student will persist in discounting well-documented data, in rejecting any and all perceptions by oppressed groups, and in making prejudicial comments, et cetera. In our pedagogical approach, the student has the right to make such observations as long as they do not intimidate others, dominate the class, or contribute to the oppression of others in the class. Sometimes, such a student is especially threatened by the material for some personal reason, and I try to have a supportive open discussion with the student outside of class to see if there is something I can do to ease the difficulty she/he is having with the materials. Other times, a student's questions or comments may motivate other students to challenge or debate a particular issue. Sometimes, such comments serve as examples to others of the pervasiveness and depth of oppression that exists. Students are evaluated and graded in the class based on their ability to articulate an understanding of the materials, not on the state of their personal attitudes at the end of the class.

4. If honestly expressed questions or comments are oppressive to other members of the class, it is necessary for the instructor to advocate for those members if they do not feel empowered or capable of responding on their own behalf. For example, if derogatory comments are made about lesbian, gay, or bisexual people who may not wish to come out to the class, I remind the class that such individuals are certainly present in the class even though others may not know who they are. I explain the consequences of such stereotypes or myths on their lives and possibly ask class members to discuss how they might feel if such comments were made about them. Empathy is encouraged, but the person who made the comment is not made to feel guilty or bad. It should be reiterated, however, that if comments or questions are purposefully made to hurt, degrade, intimidate, or interfere with open communication, the instructor has an obligation to challenge this directly and firmly.

5. Students who are going to be teachers must be certified in Human Relations as part of the teacher licensure. This places an additional obligation on instructors to assess and challenge any attitudes or behaviors that appear to endanger future students of these preservice teachers. This type of evaluation is fraught with academic pitfalls. If you insist

that students exhibit certain attitudes, then students' sense of personal freedom and thus their willingness to be open to new information is impeded. In addition, the program or instructor can be accused of violating freedom of speech, academic freedom, and the like. On the other hand, to allow hostility, stubborn insensitivity, or other signs of intractable oppressive attitudes to go completely unchallenged appears to place us at odds with our ethical and professional responsibility to the state to "certify" teachers who will be able to provide unbiased, supportive education to all their students.

Under these circumstances, I have adopted a personal challenge approach to address these issues. I keep this process separate from the grading, which is based on the evaluation of the assignments. The process I use is less formal but carefully followed throughout the class. I write responses to comments made in ungraded class reaction papers, challenging students to examine the consequences of certain attitudes for the students they will be teaching. As a regular component of the course, I have developed some questions for small groups that ask the students to discuss the consequences of the personal biases of teachers. I ask, for instance: Based on the information available, will personal biases affect a person's teaching? What, if any, will be the impact on students? Occasionally, regardless of all educational efforts, a student persists in expressing hostility and an unwillingness to examine her or his personal prejudices toward a particular oppressed group. Under these unusual circumstances, I discuss with the student privately the possible negative consequences that may occur to her or his students and directly suggest that another profession be considered. The student is still graded only on the class materials.

Overall Student Response to the Course and Program

This program brings students face to face with the unexamined assumptions and values they had adopted. Students may experience distress and frustration at different points in the class, depending upon which issues touch their lives most directly. The faculty are very supportive during this entire process and allow students to express their distress, anger, despair, excitement, amazement, or other feelings in or outside of class. Faculty especially stress that our goal is not to evoke guilt. Indeed, guilt is usually counterproductive, so we try to demonstrate how socialization has imbued us with many of these attitudes and behaviors. We try to emphasize that this course will give them an opportunity to examine these attitudes and behaviors and to make new decisions of their own based on new skills and information. Faculty are also prepared to direct students to counseling when that is appropriate since students who may have experienced sexual assault, abuse, or hate crimes, or who are lesbian or gay students in the process of coming out may need more prolonged and intensive support than the instructor or class is prepared to give.

It has been our experience that the combination of our pedagogical methodology and framework for understanding oppression are very effective in giving the students some tools to utilize in their personal and professional lives. An External Review of the Human Relations program (Frye and Lather 1990) reported that in a survey of student teachers from 1988 to 1990 conducted independently by the Department of Teacher Development at the university, "a substantial number of students considered their HURL (Human Relations) course work to be the single greatest influence on their understanding of what it means to be a teacher. No student reported it as being the least important" (2). While Human Relations began as a single course for preservice and in-service teachers, so many other students began taking the courses that general education courses and eventually a minor was developed. It is now one of the largest minors on campus and includes students from every major. In our own student evaluations, students often identify the course as the most important or best course in their college career, a course that is relevant to real life, a course that should be required of all students, etc. They identify it as a hard course, one that took much time, energy and even agony but from which they emerged a stronger person.

Summary

The Department of Human Relations and Multicultural Education at a large Minnesota state university has developed an effective model for addressing controversial issues of race, gender, class, sexual orientation, disability, and other social justice issues. Students are treated with a great deal of respect and caring. Defensiveness and fear are reduced, and a supportive, inquisitive, investigative climate is established in the class. In this way, students learn a way of addressing differences in the classroom from both the content and methodology. Multiple theories and definitions based on the examination of social power and resources are utilized to develop a comprehensive framework for understanding oppression, one that especially lends itself to seeing the interrelationships between social justice issues. The framework examines oppression from the global level to the personal level and makes the connections between them.

The framework is developed by the use of readings and media, small and large group discussions, writing assignments, and experiential and analytical activities. Critical analysis skills are emphasized. Racism, sexism, and other forms of oppression are viewed within the context of this framework. A special focus is the examination of methods of ideological and social control that maintain and disguise oppression. Students are motivated by the open, supportive atmosphere and by the study of direct and indirect effects of all types of oppression on their own lives. Student evaluations have consistently stated that the course was among the most significant of their college careers by helping them to examine their own values and by teaching them skills they use on a daily basis in their personal and professional activities.

REFERENCES

Albert, M. and R. Hahnel. 1992. *Looking forward: Participatory economics for the twenty-first century.* Boston: South End Press.

Alston, D., ed. December 1990. *We speak for ourselves: Social justice, race and environment,* 9. Washington DC: Panos Institute.

Alternative Press Center. 1991. *Directory of alternative and radical publications.* Baltimore, MD: Author.

Anderson, M. L. and P. H. Collins. 1992. *Race, class, and gender.* Belmont, CA: Wadsworth.

Andrzejewski, J. R. 1992. The myth of reverse discrimination. In *Human relations: The study of oppression and human rights.* Edited by J. R. Andrzejewski, 81. 3d ed. Needham Heights, MA: Ginn Press.

Andrzejewski, J. R., ed. 1993. *Oppression and social justice: Critical frameworks.* 4th ed. Needham Heights, MA: Ginn Press.

Bagdikian, B. 1987. *The media monopoly.* Boston: Beacon Press.

Barlett, D. L. and J. B. Steele. 1992. *America: What went wrong?* Kansas City: Andrews and McMeel.

Cahn, E. S. and D. W. Hearne, eds. 1970. *Our brother's keeper: The Indian in white America.* New York: New American Library.

Carmichael, S. and C. V. Hamilton. 1967. *Black power.* New York: Vintage Books.

Cook, B. W. (1989, March/April). Anti-communism taints American life. *New Directions for Women,* 11-12, v. 36.

Council on Interracial Books for Children. 1976. *Human and anti-human values in children's books.* New York: Author.

Deloria, V. 1969. *Custer died for your sins.* New York: Avon Books.

Feagin, J. R. and C. B. Feagin. 1978. *Discrimination American style,* 1-18. Englewood Cliffs, NJ: Prentice-Hall.

Frazier, N. and M. Sadker. 1973. *Sexism in school and society.* New York: Harper and Row.

Fresia, J. 1988. *Toward an American Revolution: Exposing the Constitution and other illusions.* Boston: South End Press.

Frye, H. and P. Lather. 1990, August. *External review report.* Unpublished manuscript, St. Cloud State University, Department of Human Relations and Multicultural Education, St. Cloud.

Green Party USA. 1992. *The Green program.* Camden, NJ: Prompt Press.

Greider, W. 1992. *Who will tell the people: The betrayal of American democracy.* New York: Simon and Schuster.

Harrington, M. 1962. *The other America.* Baltimore: Penguin Books.

hooks, b. 1990. *Yearning: Race, gender and cultural politics.* Boston: South End Press.

Jones, S. and E. Sams, producers; F. Wiley, director; and W. Greider, correspondent. 1992, April 15. The betrayal of democracy. *Frontline.* New York: Corporation for Public Broadcasting.

Kamel, R. 1990. *The global factory: Analysis and action for a new economic era,* 1-20. Philadelphia: American Friends Service Committee.

Knowles, L. L. and K. Prewitt, eds. 1969. *Institutional racism in America.* Englewood Cliffs, NJ: Prentice-Hall.

Lee, M. A. and N. Soloman. 1990. *Unreliable sources,* 228-53. Secaucus, NJ: Carol Publishing Group.

Lorde, A. 1983. There is no hierarchy of oppressions. *Interracial Books for Children Bulletin* 14(3 & 4):9.

Marable, M. 1991. *The crisis of color and democracy.* Monroe, ME: Common Courage Press.

Minnesota State Department of Education. 1977. *Foundations of oppression curriculum.* St. Paul: Author.

Minnick, E. K. 1990. *Transforming knowledge.* Philadelphia: Temple University Press.

Most censored stories: 1990. 1991, Spring. *Northern Sun News.*

Moyers, B. 1987, November 4. The secret government. *A special report by Bill Moyers.* New York: Corporation for Public Broadcasting.

———. 1992. Who owns the government? *Listening to America.* New York: Corporation for Public Broadcasting.

Parenti, M. 1988. *Democracy for the few.* New York: St. Martin's Press.

People for the Ethical Treatment of Animals. 1989. Meat kills . . . the earth, the hungry, wildlife, the animals, you. *PETA guide to compassionate living.* Washington, D.C.: Author.

Perry, W. G., Jr. 1970. *Forms of intellectual and ethical development in the college years.* New York: Holt, Rinehart and Winston.

Pharr, S. 1988. *Homophobia: A weapon of sexism.* Little Rock, AR: Chardon Press.

Rothenberg, P. S. 1992. *Race, class, and gender in the United States.* 2d ed. New York: St. Martin's Press.

Ryan, W. 1976. *Blaming the victim.* New York: Vintage Books.

Savoy, P. 1991, June 17. Time for a second bill of rights. *The Nation*, 813-16.

Singer, P. 1975. *Animal liberation*. New York: Avon Books.

Sleeter, C. E. and C. A. Grant. 1988. *Making choices for multicultural education*. Columbus, OH: Merrill Publishing Company.

Stacey, J., S. Bereaud, and J. Daniels, eds. 1974. *And Jill came tumbling after: Sexism in American education*. New York: Dell Publishing.

Stone, M. 1992. Three thousand years of racism. In *Human relations: The study of oppression and human rights*. Edited by J. R. Andrzejewski, 231-34. 3d ed. Needham Heights, MA: GINN Press.

Tavris, C. and C. Wade. 1984. *The longest war*. New York: Harcourt Brace Janovich.

Thompson, K. and J. Andrzejewski. 1988. *Why can't Sharon Kowalski come home?* San Francisco: Spinsters/Aunt Lute.

Terry, R. W. 1975. *For whites only*, 50-60. Grand Rapids, MI: William Eerdmans Publishing Company.

Younkin, L. 1990, January/February. Between two worlds. *The Disability Rag* 11(1):30-33.

2

ROBERT MUFFOLETTO ⎯⎯⎯⎯⎯⎯⎯⎯⎯⎯⎯⎯⎯⎯⎯⎯⎯⎯⎯⎯⎯

Thinking about Diversity:
Paradigms, Meanings, and Representations

> [T]he objective reality of the social world is not a central issue. It is
> the way in which it is interpreted by human actors that is important.
> (Burrell & Morgan, 1979, p. 232)

An assumption that must be taken seriously in education is that knowledge is itself a social construction that presents the social world from a particular world view representing different interests (Habermas 1968). What is presented to students in higher education and K-12 education is a social construct with social, political, and ideological codings (Apple 1979; Berger 1963; Ellsworth and Whatley 1990). If educational knowledge presents stories about the world from a particular point of view, we need to ask: What are those stories? Who is telling them to whom? and Whose voices and meanings are being heard? For as many educational researchers have pointed out, the interest represented historically in educational discourse benefits the dominant ideology while marginalizing the views, values, and culture of others (Apple 1982a; Apple 1982b; Atkinson 1985; Freire 1971; Giroux 1989; Kliebard 1987). Naturalistic representations as a form of story found in textbooks, educational media, computer software, and instructional kits and programs (all are constructed texts) deliver the overt and covert curriculum to students and teachers alike (Apple 1979). They present stories about race, gender, class, and normalcy.

The constructed, legitimate and official school curriculum received by all involved in education results from particular world views that generate social, political, and economic benefits to some. The official school curriculum not only functions to control what comprises school knowledge by asserting authority and naturalism but also affects school practice: what teachers, administrators, and students do on a routine bases (Apple and Christian-Smith 1991). As Ellsworth and Whatley (1990) suggest, the ideologically based curriculums serve "the interest for and from which they have been constructed by offering individuals a perspective on the world, a position from which to make sense of the world and act in it in ways that serve the interest of a particular social position. The perspectives and interest embedded within a particular ideology are presented in texts as if they were natural, given, and those of the individuals being addressed" (4).

When educators consider diversity and multicultural education, they must also consider and unpack the overt and covert messages delivered through various forms of media and technology. Under the facade of naturalism and realism, the educational text presents the world as natural and accessible. The delivery of these messages becomes transparent. Neither the student nor the teacher questions the text found in the class. The world and its people appear to be natural and correct. How those messages are depicted becomes only one of the socially constructed messages that teachers and students experience on a daily bases. The legitimate knowledge of schools, the messages delivered through mass media, and what is talked about over the dinner table at home become the real world, and for many, the only world.

The bell rings; it is 8:15 A.M. The teacher, after greeting her students, walks over to a newly created bulletin board covered with photographs and large text. The board displays photographs of Angela Davis, Martin Luther King, Malcom X, Jessie Jackson, juxtapositioned with black and white, and color reproductions of conflict and confrontation. The students sit back in their seats while the teacher brings their attention to her display. The students appear to be attentive, switching their gaze between the teacher and the images on the wall. After a few moments and a pause for questions, the teacher makes a transition to a social studies lesson. The students are studying nineteenth-century, western expansion in the United States. The textbook terms the unit of study as "Pioneers and Settlers in the New West." While moving through this unit, the students and teachers alike will read and look at the textbook, view a number of videotapes and films, watch a filmstrip located in a learning center, and create a map and a number of drawings about frontier life. For extra credit, the students may select to work in their groups and create a story, using a word processor, after they have viewed and interacted with a computer software program entitled Oregon Trail.

The rest of the day, the teacher and the students will move through various curriculum materials and activities covering science, language arts, mathematics, and art. On this day the members of this classroom will read, listen, view videotapes and films, and look at numerous still pictures, illustrations, maps, and graphs. The students will also have the opportunity to express their ideas by speaking, writing, and drawing. After what may at times seem like an eternity, the school day will end. At their homes, our teacher and her students will watch television, read newspapers and look at books, do their homework and lesson plans, and before heading to bed, select their clothes for the next day. As they sleep, most will dream.[1]

Throughout their day both the teacher and her students encounter countless representations in the form of sound, images, written and spoken worlds—language and discourse. The position I take in this chapter is that everything they encounter throughout the day is representational in one way or the other (Goodman 1978). The representations refer either to phenomena believed to reside in the real world or to concepts about the world. The representations, in order to refer, have to be encoded with social and culturally accepted meanings. Representations encountered on their day's journey can only be encoded with messages about the social world, about gender, class, race, and normalcy. These messages have intended and interpretive meanings. As I will discuss later, these meanings position the reader in a social space where a continuous flow of messages works to establish and maintain the subjectivity and location of the individual in what may appear to be natural and normal. When realistic messages about race, gender, economic class, and normalcy appear to be natural and thereby correct, while corresponding to experiences and meanings from other texts, individuals (an insufficient term) will perceive their knowing about the world as correct and real. Framing everything in education as representations, representations which always refer, has critical implications for multicultural education and diversity. Representations are not natural or real. Representations are social constructs that refer to concepts and ideas about the world. Grounded in realism, they become transparent, a window to the world.

How students and teachers make sense and meaning as readers from their experiences of these realist representations, make sense and meaning from their experiences of them, how they see themselves and others as a result of that experience, and how they practice what they have learned from their experiences with representations may be best understood in terms of history, power, and discourse. It is through our historical experiences of representations and institutions as ideological discourses that we as human objects become human subjects. How we think about who *we* are and who *they* are goes beyond a concern for multicultural education and issues of diversity to questions concerning language and discourse, ideology and consciousness, and practice.

While viewing a photograph of my self, I experience a representation, an image, from which I make meaning—that is me, I see my self, and I know who I am. When I see photographs of others, I construct a meaning, giving a form to who I think they are and what my relationship to them may be. Do I see them as different or the same? Do I value or reject what I think they are? Do I see my self as being better or as lacking what I believe they have? How those interpretations and meanings (which appear to be correct) are formed, and why I see them and myself the way I do—as being natural and normal—is embedded in the ideology and discourse I have experienced in and outside the walls of the classroom, the pages of the textbook, the pictures on the wall, the frames of the film, and the examples used by my teachers.

Because representations are social constructs and mediums for expression, because they embody messages about the social world, representations have producers and readers. Who controls and directs the meanings of representations encountered in daily experiences controls the consciousness, the subjectivity, of those who experience them over and over again. Returning to our classroom, the meanings experienced by both students and teachers through the curriculum not only create the culture of education but also situate all participants within that space ideologically.

Ideology, as Bill Nichols (1981) suggests, "is how the existing ensemble of social relationships represents itself to individuals; it is the image a society gives of itself in order to perpetuate itself. These representations serve to constrain us; they establish fixed places for us to occupy that work to guarantee social actions over time. Ideology uses the fabrication of images and the processes of representations to persuade us that how things are is how they ought to be and that the place provided for us is the place we ought to have" (1). If images (representations) are "fabricated," then we must see them as intended social constructions Representations, as such, like photographs, words on a page, film and videos, and languages in general, have meanings historically and geographically. To express a concern over the meanings of representations, especially for those involved in multicultural education, is to inquire into the control, intent, and effect of those representations as texts meant to be experienced.

As educators, we use various forms of representations to communicate or engage our students with information, ideas, concepts, and procedures. This multimedia approach includes speech (lecture and discussion), written materials (books, essays, etc.), realistic images or media (films, videotapes, laser discs, photographs, and slides), and currently the computer screen (which may draw together a number of different formats mentioned above). Rarely do teachers or students ever consider the effect of the form over the content that is being delivered to them (Postman 1992). A realistic image, as well as abstract language however much it may "look like" or "sound like" the world, it is not what it depicts.[2] For at the very least, any representation is an abstraction of reality. By its very nature, a representation is a social construction. The intent of realist representations is to construct a virtual reality experience (Rheingold 1991), a reality that is and is not what it re-presents. Our recognition of this enjoins us to consider what interests work to inform the practice of representation and its effect on the lives of real people (Goodman 1978).

Diversity and multicultural curricula are not neutral representations. They refer to broader social, political, and historical relationships, meanings, and interest. In order to address concerns over such representations and meanings, we need to consider the relationship between representation, the phenomena referred to, and the reader of the representation; the experienced text. We need to consider if a direct correspondence exists between the representation and the perceived world, or if that world results from the individual's experience with "stuff." To explore these concerns and their relationship to diversity, I will discuss two major paradigms, functional and interpretive, that frame our understanding of representations and the world they seemingly refer to. I will then discuss two models of communications, semiotics and post-semiotics, as they relate to those paradigms. And finally, I will conclude with a discussion of the pedagogical implications of the paradigmatic and communication models for multicultural representations and classroom practice.

One warning to the reader of this chapter: the issues concerning representation, meaning, the formation of the subject, discourse, diversity, and multicultural education do not fit neatly into a nice box. These are complex and messy matters. They draw from different areas of interest and at times overlap. The danger for any writer in dealing with readers' understanding and interest is making the dynamic appear to be simple and easily accessible.

PARADIGMS

There are different understandings and uses of the term paradigm. Thomas Kuhn (1962) refers to a paradigm as an "accepted model or pattern" (23) that guides beliefs and assumptions, directing action and meaning. Paradigms refer to a worldview that provides a platform for guiding practice and understanding. This adherence to ways of thinking about the world form the perspective of horizon that beings to define and limit a paradigm. In an important manner, a paradigm not only fixes a worldview, but also defines that world and the relationships of objects within it. Within a paradigm, the assumptions, understandings, and beliefs are viewed as natural and correct. Truth is or can be known. In this manner, reality becomes *common place*, a place where we make decisions based upon *common sense*.

In discussing school discourse and practice, Popkewitz (1987) refers to a paradigm as a "worldview or framework of knowledge and belief through which we see and investigate the world" (193). He suggests that school discourse, practice, and institutional legitimacy are paradigmatic, framing our understanding and relationship to the institution of schooling. Burrell and Morgan (1979) suggest that in the study of social organizations, paradigms provide "a frame of reference which reflects a whole series of assumptions about the nature of the social world and the way it might be investigated" (X). Feenberg (1991) leads us to consider that "paradigms include not only concepts and theories, but also standard procedures which define objects in measuring and controlling them" (71). Paradigms as frameworks for thought and practice, as a system of values and beliefs, are not neutral. They are born and maintained in social and historical realities. They reflect human interest (Habermas 1968).

In his discussion of the nature of scientific inquiry, Kuhn (1962) comments on the recruitment of new members to a particular community or paradigm. His comments may help further understand the nature of paradigms and their social maintenance and reproduction. He suggests that those "who learned the bases of their field from the same concrete models . . . will seldom evoke overt disagreement over fundamentals. Men whose research is based on shared paradigms are committed to the same rules and standards for scientific practice" (11). Popkewitz (1984) adds to this discussion when he refers to the notion of scientific fields as "constellations of questions, methods, and procedures" (3). For Popkewitz, these constellations "provide shared ways of seeing the world, of working" in the world. He continues with the notion of social reproduction by suggesting that individuals are trained to exist within a community: "Learning the exemplars of a field of inquiry is also to learn how to see, think about and act towards the world" (3). For our interest here, we need to consider the ways in which paradigms "define objects" as subjects and control them, both physically and psychologically, and how actors and social realities are reproduced and maintained. In short, we need to realize that how we make sense of phenomena is determined by the paradigm we swim in.

Here the concept of reification may be of some use in understanding the notion of paradigm. Berger and Luckmann (1966) provide us with a rich discussion of the historical and social base that underlies concepts of social reality. Reality they argue is a social construction. Reification objectifies that reality and transforms it to one that lacks human intervention or interest. Reification is the "apprehension of the products of human activity as if they were something else than human products. . . . Reification implies that man [sic] is capable of forgetting his own authorship of the human world, and further, that the dialectic between man, the producer, and his products, is lost to consciousness. The reified world is, by definition, a dehumanized world" (89).[3] Combining the notions of paradigm and reification produces a commonsense view of the world. The world is this way because that is the way things are (Apple 1979). The power as well as the danger of a paradigm is that you may not know that you have one.

FUNCTIONAL AND INTERPRETATIVE PARADIGMS

The functionalist and interpretive paradigms are at odds with each other. They both see different worlds, different realities. Each paradigm holds different relationships to representations and significations, particularly to photographs that exist within the classic realist tradition (Belsey 1980). The functionalist and interpretive paradigms construct different unions between viewers or readers and the experienced text. They are ideologically and epistemologically different.

FUNCTIONAL, OBJECTIVE, AND REAL

Functionalism or objectivity can be traced back to the roots of natural science. Burrell and Morgan (1979) refer to Comte (1798-1857) for the roots of a social science that were based upon reasoning and objectivity to produce useful knowledge. Here the notion of "useful knowledge" is based in positivism and structuralism. Together positivism and structuralism are an analytical tool for knowing about the social world that "claims to be ideologically neutral. . . . The goal is to tell it like it is" (Cherryholmes 1988, 22). Positivism refers to "epistemologies which seek to explain and predict what happens in the social world by searching for regularities and causal relationships between its constituent elements" (Burrell and Morgan 1979, 5). A positivist approach does not value individualistic points of view. Because what are traditionally thought of as are scientific methods employed (empiricism), positivism appears to be a neutral report or observation of the world. Empiricism, suggests D. W. Hamlyn (1967), is a theory about reality that reports that "experience rather than reason is the source of knowledge, and in this sense it is opposed to rationalism. . . . To say that we have learned something from experience is to say that we have come to know of it by the use of our senses" (499).

Realism declares that "the social world external to the individual cognition is a real world made up of hard, tangible and relatively immutable structures. . . . For the realist, the world exists independently of an individual's appreciation of it. The individual is seen as being born into and living within a social world which has a reality of its own. It is not something which the individual creates. . . . For the realist, the social world has an existence which is as hard and concrete as the natural world" (Burrell and Morgan 1979, 4).

Understanding this paradigm is important when the nature of representation and meaning is considered in light of the re-presentation of racial, gender, and social-economic communities. Realistic images, like photographs and films, are believed to show the world the way it is. The photograph understood as document and as evidence removes the camera and its operator from any responsibility such as interpretation or intervention. As the events and truths of the world unfold before the observer, the medium implies, the camera operator just clicks the shutter.

Through the realist photographic image, our experiences of the world have been replaced with a representation. The photograph, seen as a neutral and scientific representation, presents its viewer with mechanically and objectively produced evidence of what was. Through the photograph our experiences and expectations of the world are satisfied. For the photograph of Uncle Joe to exist, Uncle Joe must also have existed. As a document, the photograph mirrors reality, it is truth.

The functional/objective paradigm then positions the individual not as a participant in the construction of reality, but as an observer, a reporter of sorts, telling truthful stories about what is. This paradigm also assumes that reality can be known, that what we experience through our senses is real. Authorship of the social world, or for that matter reality, does not lie within the individual or a community. It just *is*. In considering the representation of others and self, this paradigm holds that the realist photographic image presents the world as is. Meanings and interpretations of what is experienced is set from outside the image, from experiences of other types of so-called realist texts that also mirror reality and truth. From the functional/objective paradigm, representations and meanings are not ideological. From this perspective, there is no ideology.

INTERPRETATIVE, REFLECTIVE, AND CONSTRUCTED

The interpretative paradigm is grounded in phenomenology and hermeneutics. Phenomenology and hermeneutics share the notion that commonsense ideas about existence are actually products of consciousness and human interest. Phenomenology "questions the common sense taken for granted attitudes which characterize everyday life and the realms of natural science" (Burrell and Morgan 1979, 233) whereas "hermeneutics is concerned with interpreting and understanding the products of the human mind which characterize the social and cultural world" (235-36). The products of the human mind that both phenomenology and hermeneutics consider would include such human constructions as language, institutions, works of art, religions, education, dance, and various forms of social communities.

The interpretive paradigm recognizes the voice of the author. It suggests that the world as we know it, natural or manufactured, is a product of human activity. As the reified world of the functional paradigm is authorless, the interpretive paradigm proclaims all of us to be authors. As authors "we" have a voice. This voice, the language in use, is representational of a consciousness that has been formed within various frames of reference or horizons (Goffman 1974). History and geography play a critical role here. In history we find the authors of consciousness. How we think about phenomena is grounded in our historical interplay with ideas and experiences through language and institutions (Attridge, Bennington and Young 1987; Berger and Luckmann 1966; Eagleton 1984).

As a form of representation and re-presentation, "languages divide or articulate the world in different ways" (Belsey 1980, 39). This articulation is symbolic and removed. As a symbol, it is both historically and physically distant from the actual phenomenon. It is possible to speak, write, and visually talk about events, places, and objects with never experiencing them (Berger and Luckmann 1966). This articulation, this gesture, this re-enactment and re-presentation, provides both a means to interpret and communicate messages about the world and its events.

As a re-enactment, language embodies the historical and social horizons of individuals, communities, and cultures. The interpretative paradigm positions the individual within a historical framework where language reconstructs the world within its own boundaries, constructing not only the world and its meanings but the individual as well. The individual has a voice that emerged out of a history of meanings and representations that are ideologically based. Even though this paradigm localizes the external world as a product of consciousness, the formation of this consciousness is a social construction. Seeing the world from this perspective places this paradigm at odds with functionalism and objectivity. As an interpretation and as an expression that resides in the social world, the interpretive paradigm questions and rejects the commonsense notion of that world as existing outside of and removed from the individual. In this sense, the world is as we think about it and not as we are told about it.

In order to question the objective commonsense view offered by positivism, this paradigm calls for reflective action that leads to reflective knowledge. "Reflective knowledge . . . contains not only messages, but information as to how it came into being, the process by which it was obtained. It [also] demonstrates the human capacity to generate second-order symbols or meta-levels—significations about significations" (Myerhoff and Ruby 1982, 2). To be reflective is first to see the world as socially constructed, not as given but as storied by an author. Second, to be reflective is to unpack the meanings, assumptions, implications, and intentions of artifacts found within a symbolic universe. And third, a reflective act includes reflecting on one's own reflection.

Understanding the external world as an artifact and "willed into existence through intentional acts . . . man [sic] is shown to live in a world created through consciousness" (Burrell and Morgan 1979, 233). To see the world as a construction is to deconstruct it, unpack it as representative of individual intent, of an interpretive community, of an ideology. To reflect on the way things appear through various forms of representations is to reject the classic realist text. For the "strategies of the classic realist text divert the reader from what is contradictory within it to the renewed recognition [misrecognition] of what he or she already 'knows', knows because the myths and signifying systems of the classic realist text re-present experience in the ways in which it is conventionally articulated in our society" (Belsey 1980, 128).

The interpretive subjective paradigm positions the individual as the creator of significance. Meaning from this worldview is constructed through the reflective, unpacking process juxtaposed against and with other meanings generated in society. The individual, within this paradigm, not only is a reflective participant in social discourse, but also is a creator of intended meanings in concert with other members and other discourses. Whereas the functional objective paradigm points to "one" reality, the interpretive subjective paradigm refers to many realities grounded in social and historical discourses. Where the former's role is to point to the truth, the latter is to unpack it, reconstruct it, only to unpack it again.

As discussed above, the two paradigms offer two different views of reality. Seeing something called reality from either of these two positions sets the individual in different relationships to what is perceived as "truth" and to other individuals. As we read educational representations that depict different cultures, races, economic groups, genders, and the handicapped, the position the individual takes in relationship to them and their truthfulness will be different. How teachers, students, and parents understand the social curriculum of the school, as real or as symbolic, will determine how they give meaning to the representations they encounter. From one position, those representations are real and reflect reality. From another, they are constructions with intents and implications. In either case, the only tools teachers have to communicate meaning are representational in nature. This includes spoken and written language, images of all forms, body language, classroom and school environments, and the power relationships maintained between teachers, students, parents, educational texts, and knowledge. Whose notions of reality and truth are valued in schools? Do all participants see the teacher, the student, the textbook, or the test as the true holder of knowledge. Does the history text convey unchangeable information, or does it tell one of many stories told?

SEMIOTIC AND POST-SEMIOTICS

We may agree that a certain representation depicts various objects and establishes their relationships to each other within or across frames of reference. How those representations become meaningful, what stories are told, and what meanings are understood is a social and historical act. Questions concerning significance from semiotic and post-semiotic models include the following. Does meaning lie within the representation or text? Or does meaning lie within the reader's experience of the text? Either answer positions the individual in relationship to knowing and not knowing.

Semiotics and post-semiotics offer two models for understanding representations as a form of communication and as the locus of meaning within and outside of the act of representing. My intent here is not to provide an elaborate or even in-depth discussion of semiotic and post-semiotic theory (Saussure 1959). Instead I want to take from both models what is useful to our discussion of representations as situated within the functional and the interpretative paradigms discussed earlier. Semiotics and post-semiotics are rich and complex areas of study. For further readings in this area, I suggest Barthes 1964; Belsey 1980; Cassirer 1955; Coward and Ellis 1977; Freund 1987; Hawkes 1977; Holub 1984; Norris 1982; Weedon 1987; Wollen 1969.

Semiotics emerged at the turn of the century from the work of Ferdinand de Saussure, a French linguist. It is a theory based upon differences, a theory of the sign. We understand referents (signs) because we know what they are not. Central to this theory is the notion of the sign. The sign is understood to *stand in place of* what it refers to. A sign is representational, it refers. Signs function at different levels of significance: iconic, index, and symbolic.

Iconic significance refers to representations holding a strong perceptual relationship between the representation and what it refers to. A photograph of Uncle Joe and Aunt Linda looks like them. An index is a type of sign that refers to something else but is highly conventionalized and variously abstract. This would include road signs, written and spoken language, body language, and certain forms of music and sound. The major difference between the icon and the index is that the index does not necessarily convey a likeness of what it refers to, as an iconic sign does. The index gains its power and meaning through an association that has been determined by social agreement within a historical context. Sound-effect recordings are iconic. Morse code is indexical because the letters and numbers to which it refers, themselves indexical, bear no resemblance to elements of the code. Road signs function in similar ways. Symbols work in a different way from icons and indexes, even though they may look like or refer abstractly to something. As Susan Langer (1942) suggests, they are "instruments of thought" (63). Symbols refer to mythical conceptual levels of meaning, whereas an icon and index are tied to a referent.

Semiotics, a science of signs, places language, thus literature, as a signifying system. Visual representations such as photographs, films, and drawings are part of that signifying system. Communications is the signifying system in practice. Thus, when we view an educational film or look at a textbook illustration, we are engaged in a signification process. Saussure's theory of semiotics held "that language is not a nomenclature, a way of naming things which already exist, but a system of differences with no positive terms. He argued that far from providing a set of labels for entities which exist independently in the world, language precedes the existence of independent entities, making the world intelligible by differentiating between concepts" (Belsey 1980, 38).

The semiotic model further separates the sign into two components, signifier and signified. The signified is a concept or idea, the signifier a sound, image, or written figures (the material we can hear, see, or feel). The power of language is to make itself transparent and not problematic. Names, realistic images, and sounds become the idea of what they refer to and not sounds or markings on paper or light sensitive material. The name/image association of semiotics is not problemitized until the association between them is noticed. In this manner, the signifier and signified are not separated, they are seen as one. "Language can . . . be compared with a sheet of paper: thought is on the front and the sound is on the back; one cannot cut the front without cutting the back at the same time; likewise in language, one can neither divide sounds from thought nor thought from sound" (Saussure, in Belsey 1980, 38). In other words, the object named is known through language. In this manner, we know of the world through language, through representations. The world is as we speak of it—as we speak of it the world is. Language becomes transparent, a conduit to reality.

Knowing the world through representation engages a transparent relationship between the world and the language used to refer to it. From a realist text's perspective, the world is as it is shown, spoken, or written about. Language as a system of significations defines the world before we enter into it. In this manner, the world *is* as we know it, as we speak about it, and as we show it. To question this is to question the commonsense view of the world. Photograph, realism works in similar ways. Photographs work like language in that they become transparent. They present the world in what appears to be a natural way. "A photograph in effect can provide us with an objective, veridical version—an 'actual picture of' socially important aspects of what is in fact out there" (Goffman 1976, 12). Realistic photographs work because they "reproduce what we already seem to know" (Belsey 1980, 47) about the world. Representations, like realistic photographs and language, appear to be natural, objective, and free of human intervention and interest.

Realistic forms of language (written, spoken, pictured) work comfortably with the functional/objective paradigm. The camera, as a neutral tool, as an extension of our senses, only records what is in front of it. This paradigm assumes that we can objectively know the world through the realistic representation, the photograph. Both the nature of language and the realistic photograph become hidden as systems of codes behind the naturalism of discourse and depiction. The functional/objective paradigm assumes there is no difference between the reality of the world and how we talk about it or picture it. Reality is as it is.

The correspondence between the understood world and realistic representations of it have interesting implications for multicultural education. If the world is as it is depicted, then what I experience is the 'truth.' The representations of men and women, people of different races, and different economic communities are presented in relationship to each other and to others and either confirms or contradicts the experiences of other representations or stories experienced about them. In this manner, the form of representation and re-presentation become transparent. Even though we know we are looking at a realist photograph, we take for granted the correspondence between what is seen and what we 'believe' was. The question from a post-semiotic perspective is not whether we are looking at a photograph, but what meaning we are to assign to the photograph as a constructed text.

This brings us to the heart of the matter. There is no argument over the existence of the text. What is debated is the nature of signification. What does the text mean? Semiotics, functionalism, and objectivity all present a way of seeing and understanding the world as given through re-presentations. The functional/objective paradigm does not question the storyteller or the veracity of the story. The storyteller is real, belongs to the physical world, and concerns the physical sciences. The story itself concerns us here, the representation and presentation of the social world through constructed experiences or texts. Form in the semiotic paradigm does not affect the content. The world is as shown, the truth is as told.

POST-SEMIOTICS: MEANINGS AND COMMUNITIES

Post-semiotics departs from the notion of a single truth. This model supports the position that experiences of the constructed text (the representation) vary by the nature of the text's reader. Truth exists, not as an absolute or as a given, but as a social construction representing human interest and ideological positions (Habermas 1968; Nichols 1981). There is no signified, there is no meaning, until the reader says there is. Post-semiotics exists within the interpretative/subjective paradigm where reality, truth, and meaning are understood to be historical constructions created by social actors (reader theory). Meaning, from this perspective, does not reside within a fixed system of meanings corresponding to a set reality, but resides within the experiences of the readers as members of interpretative communities. This model positions the individual as a socially and historically constructed reader and not as a nonhistorical autonomous neutral receiver.

Post-semiotics positions nothing within the social world as being natural. Language, discourse, institutions, pictorial representations, and auditory reconstructions are social products embedded with social purposes and human interest (4). This interpretive model attempts to deconstruct the nature and implications of significance and naturalism, and in doing so, rejects any meanings put forth by the dominate or any other ideology found in the social world. A post-semiotic analysis of representations resists the functional objective naturalist point of view. It does so by recontextualizing signification. Such analysis makes possible alternative and oppositional readings (Cherryholmes 1988; Hall 1980). In return post-structuralism characterizes meaning to be an interpretation, informed by historical, political, and social relationships and conditions as experienced by the socially constructed individual.

As stated above, the post-semiotic perspective does not question the nature and existence of the physical world (and true to a postmodern perspective, some will disagree with me). A rock falls, liquid turns to gas under certain conditions, the photograph exists. At issue are the meanings of the photograph, the gesture, the space as a social construction. A post-semiotic analysis of a space typically questions sources of meanings and influences upon them: Who benefits from space being this way? What are the effects of this space on those who use it? Why is this space here? It is the meaning of the photograph imposed onto it from outside its frame that is of concern. Whose meaning is it? What effect does it have on those who consume that meaning? Who is that meaning given to? These are some of the questions brought to the meaning of any and all social texts from a post-semiotic analysis.

It is necessary at this point to return briefly to the notion of the individual as subject. To suggest that "we" are socially constructed may suffice for now. How we think about ourselves and others results from our experiences with various ideological texts (Belsey 1980; Berger 1963; Berger and Luckmann 1966; Berger, Berger and Kelner 1973; Muffoletto 1993). Social institutions, like families, religions, and education, inform the individual about who they are through the repetition of stories. Mass media and educational media, phenomena that individuals experience, present numerous narratives that inform us and position us in relationships to others and to social institutions. In light of experiences and discourses that are controlled by others, we come to think of ourselves as autonomous individuals when actually the *I* results from social, political, economic, and historical factors. Ideology works to form and inform us (Ellsworth and Whatley 1990; Popkewitz 1991). This is no simple matter. The social construction of individuals as subjects is mediated through various forms of representations that consume the individual. This hegemonic process, as Feenberg (1991) suggests, is not imposed by struggle between self-actualized individuals, but it "is reproduced unreflectively by the standard beliefs and practices of the society" (78) where individuals find themselves. "The self-as-subject is a social construct whose place will vary according to the construction process. It is not a fixed-for-eternity entity but a term in a relationship; and how we are termed as selves can therefore be defined as an ideological question, a matter of the position we occupy or believe we occupy within a social and cultural order" (Nichols 1981, 30). How that self is formed, maintained, or changed results from repeated social experiences. These social experiences are representations and re-presentations of various encounters in the social world. For example, continuous experiences of women in submissive and powerless positions, such as acting out trivial roles (advertisements), may with other observed phenomena affect the consciousness, a sense of self, of women and men and their perceived relationship to each other and the social order. If the vehicle for this example is codified in realism, the delivery of these continuous messages may become transparent and the message eventually reified.

Reification, realism, and naturalism go hand in hand to mask the authorship of the messages experienced. It is the use of the existing codes of realism that make the illusion plausible. The power of the realist text is to make itself appear to be real and natural. Through various modes of experiences, the realist text seems more like day-to-day life and not like the appearance it really is. "Yes . . . it is only a film . . . but it is about real life." Like the storyteller, the representation and re-presentation of the social order constructs the spaces we occupy and our sense of self. Why else would self-esteem be of interest to educators.

The struggle for control over the minds and hearts of individuals is an ideological battle. Post-semiotics as a form of discourse analysis attempts to unpack the ideological framework of naturalism and realism to reveal its subjective and political nature. From the interpretative/subjective paradigm, the representation or text is an experience created by the interaction between the intended text and the consciousness of the reader or viewer. The experienced text is the only text ever experienced. This experience is never fixed or natural, but is the result of social dynamics, agreements, and conflicts.

Two Paradigms in Conflict

As demonstrated above, the functional and the interpretative paradigms oppose each other. Each constructs its own boundaries for 'knowing' and the 'known.' The paradigms reveal the world constructed as is or as I make it. The implications for understanding 'self' in context with gender, race, economic class, and sexual preference offered by each paradigm are basic to any pedagogy concerned with diversity, justice, and democracy.

The functional paradigm positions the individual in relationship to an already existing and meaningful social world where the codes for meaning are set. You are born into an ideological position of self and others. From this paradigmatic view, the world created by the reader is not recognized or valued. Reality is as you are told, truth can be known. Through the process of reification, reality and truth are recognized and encoded in the realist text. The mirror shows us ourselves, and we never ask the storyteller why.

The interpretative paradigm recognizes the individual as a socially and historically constructed subject. It rejects realism and embraces constructivism. This paradigm understands the world to be a product of consciousness and understands consciousness as a social construction. The interpretative paradigm calls for the unpacking of the mask of realism by looking at issues of power, control, and benefit. In doing so, it proclaims not one reality, one truth but many realities, many truths.

DIVERSITY, MEANINGS, TEACHER EDUCATION

Preservice teachers are presented with a curriculum in their teacher education program. This curriculum's purpose is to educate (some programs employ the term *train*) future teachers and administrators about theories and practices related to learning, instruction, and school management. Knowledge gained by these experiences is usually presented and accepted as being nonproblematic. Few instructors have the time, flexibility, or inclination to encourage critical reflection and inquiry into the nature of the knowledge presented and tested in their classes. To do this would unmask the constructed nature of any knowledge base and experience. It would also unmask the ideological and political nature of the institution (Muffoletto, in press). To adopt a critical stance toward the curriculum being presented (I should also add selected and organized by the instructor) repositions the instructor from the center to the margins of epistemological authority. If the knowledge and experiences presented in teacher education classrooms are presented not as truthful and real, but as only one truth, one reality, then the ideological and constructed nature of knowledge and experience is exposed (Cherryholmes 1988; Fish 1980; Goodman 1978).

For reasons of either power, naiveté, or belief (and possibly all three), courses in teacher education do not unpack their appearance of naturalness of practice, knowledge, research, and theory. How teachers think about the curriculum they receive will fall into the functional or the interpretive paradigm. If future teachers are not taught to reflect on the curriculum they receive and will disseminate to their students, teachers and the knowledge they hold will become standardized and normalized. Precisely such standardized thought—naturalized knowing and common sense—raises the most resistance to seriously thinking about diversity and what a multicultural environment could be. Freire (1985) refers to this naturalness as a prescription for the standardization of thought. If we think of education as a form of mass media, his thoughts on standardization deserve our consideration: "In mass society, ways of thinking become as standardized as ways of dressing and tastes of food. Men [sic] begin thinking and acting according to the prescriptions they receive daily from the communications media rather than in response to their dialectal relationships with the world" (89). Prescriptions for knowing not only frame how we understand the world (Goffman 1974; Muffoletto 1991) but how we act in it. Prescriptions are both ideological and hegemonic. Frames, actions, and knowing relate to a social world that is either perceived as given (naturalness) or constructed (acted upon and interpreted).

Questions in teacher education programs concerning diversity and the representation of racial, ethnic, gender, economic, and religious communities are normally asked from the ideological position of the institution (the voice of authority) and of the dominant forces (values, assumptions, beliefs) at play in the classroom (Fish 1980). It is crucial that a curriculum in teacher education work to enhance students' understanding of the social and political nature of the curriculum and the classroom. If the curriculum is approached as a representation, a text to be experienced, rather than as a window to the world, the student can then begin to ask, "Whose world, whose reality?" In doing so, the student can leave the positivist functional notion of a single reality for a notion that situates texts as representations of multiple, constructed realities to be interpreted and deconstructed, and unpacked—multiple realities (Goodman 1978; Muffoletto 1990). In this manner, the student will be not the passive receptor of knowledge but a critical constructor. Moving the student to see educational texts "as symbolic systems or signifying practices which deal in representations rather than reflections of reality, is to understand the necessity for 'reading' the media rather than passively accepting them as substitutes for experience" (Masterman 1985, 38).

Accepting and confronting the notion of diversity requires the vision of multiple interpretations and constructions of what may be called reality. Breaking away from the functional objective paradigm and moving to the interpretive subjective arena requires those who move not only to be reflective but also to reconstitute their own position in relationship to others and self. A first step in this process may be to confront the notion of representation and the construction of meaning by acknowledging and inquiring into the nature of paradigms and representation.

A teacher education curriculum that reveals the constructed nature of paradigm as singular and reveals representations as paradigmatic constructions begins to move students into an acceptance of their active and social role of maintaining or constructing meanings. When students (and faculty members) divorce themselves from naturalism and realism, they can see all forms of communication as representative of ideological and paradigmatic constructs. Breaking from realism and objectivity is a difficult step to take. The interpretive/subjective paradigm offers no solid ground from which to speak or view the world. The world is no longer natural, language and image do not simply correspond to reality, the sign is not fixed, and what may have seemed simple is recognized now as complex.

Moving from the positivist, structuralist view of semiotics to a post-semiotic interpretative position requires individuals to begin viewing themselves as socially constructed entities, holding membership not in one but in many interpretative communities. Understanding the notion of interpretive communities (Belsey 1980; Fish 1980; Hall 1980) requires individuals to recognize alternative and oppositional meanings to the ones emerging from the realist authoritative tradition. Such recognitions preclude returning to the realist dream to *one*'s reality.

Moving students from a functional position to an interpretative one is no easy task. For too long they have been subjected to stories and beliefs about the world they live in. For example, it is not a quick or simple task to engage students in the subjective framework assumed by a history text and presented behind the mask of neutral science and instrumentality, then to engage them in what their analysis has missed. Students must analyze closely the signifying practices and their social and political effects. Such analysis is students' means to recognize the possibility of unpacking texts. Once students recognize the possibility, they can experience the value of decoding and recoding texts' messages about diversity, race, class, ethnicity, religion, and gender. This experience in turn helps them to recognize all sign systems as texts to be read. Such texts emerge from education as well as popular culture and they "construct representations of the world and serve as socializing agencies, providing young people with beliefs about behaviors and the world" (Considine and Haley 1992, 2).

Transforming students' perceptions and beliefs about something they called 'the reality' to the notion of "a reality" makes possible discussions about the representation and misrepresentations of various economic, gender, and racial communities. The requirement here is students' and teachers' recognition that something is missing, that the story in not quite right. This requires inquiry into and deliberation about the inclusion and exclusion of social and cultural codes in the material being considered (Goffman 1974). Seeing the text as something to be read, something to be experienced, frames a discourse analysis that considers whose voice(s) is being heard, who is to hear it, what is and is not being said, and what are the possible implications for social justice (Cherryholmes 1988)? From this perspective, questions regarding diversity, multiculturalism, gender, class, power, and social justice can be layered upon the curriculum representations found in teacher education as well as the K-12 curriculum. The results of this process may lead to a different definition of critical thinking. As Considine and Haley (1992) suggest, "If our schools intend to develop students who are literate and critical thinkers, they must teach students to comprehend the form and content of information in all media, including news, advertising, television, and motion pictures" (x). I would add to that list textbooks, computer programs, educational television and films, instructional packages, bulletin boards, classrooms, school buildings, school and classroom management procedures, and forms of student and teacher assessment. All of these social objects are mediated symbolic forms that refer to a social world where struggles over the control of meanings are played out daily in the lives of individuals and communities. To strive for diversity and social justice at all levels of education requires participation in that struggle.

CONCLUSION

To teach about diversity, to promote and struggle for equal and fair treatment in education as elsewhere, first is to recognize diversity, and second, is to recognize how it does or does not become real in the minds of individuals and communities.

This chapter presents criteria that are important for understanding the relationship between representations that reveal or mask diversity and something called reality. Analysis of the functional and the interpretive paradigms enables individuals to understand themselves and others. Localizing semiotics and post-semiotics within that objective-interpretative construct provides a model for understanding representational meanings. This chapter then situated *thinking* about diversity within an interpretive, subjective, and critical model. And finally, I suggested, that if we are to engage our students in critical thought about diversity, multiculturalism, and social justice, they as well as ourselves must move out of a realist functional paradigm into one that positions truth and knowledge as social and historical constructs that benefit some and not others.

NOTES

1. This is a fictitious account. I also realize that I have constructed the teacher's gender. I did this knowing fully well that the great majority of teachers in the K-6 environment are women. I also could have constructed race, age, and cultural background. It was not necessary for my example. Oregon Trail is a real program used broadly throughout the country and has been criticized for its cultural and gender messages.

2. This discussion will be concerned with realism and realistic representations—the photograph—even though the importance of all forms of representations is recognized. Numerous developments have occurred lately in virtual reality. Virtual reality must be submitted to the same questions faced by other representations.

3. The terms *man* and *his* in Berger and Luckmann's (1966) text refer to the notion of mankind. I realize the gender bias in this use of language, but I wanted to maintain the quote as written. Since a number of other authors use the term *man* to refer to the more general understanding of mankind, I will use it in that sense when it appears in other quotes. I have made efforts to remove any biased gender-related terms whenever possible within my own narrative.

4. I use *reconstructed* to refer to the cognitive process of collecting data and constructing the notion of the experience. In this manner we do not *hear* the doorbell; we organize sense data until we recognize it as something learned. Thus, we say we hear the doorbell, or the toaster popping up. I believe this is an important point to consider. We create the world as we know it and understand it. The dialectics between our inner and outer realities become more interesting in light of current advances in the field of virtual reality.

REFERENCES

Apple, M. W. 1979. *Ideology and curriculum*. London, Boston, and Henley: Routledge & Kegan Paul.

——— . 1982a. *Cultural and economic reproduction in education: Essays on class, ideology and the state*. London and Boston: Routledge & Kegan Paul.

——— . 1982b. *Education and power*. Boston, London: ARK Paperbacks.

Apple, M. and L. K. Christian-Smith. 1991. *The politics of the textbook*. New York and London: Routledge.

Atkinson, P. 1985. *Language, structure and reproduction: An introduction to the sociology of Basil Bernstein*. London: Methuen.

Attridge, D., G. Bennington, and R. Young. 1987. *Post-structuralism and the question of history*. Cambridge, MA: Cambridge University Press.

Barthes, R. 1964. *Elements of semiology*. New York: Hill and Wang.

Belsey, C. 1980. *Critical practice*. London and New York: Methuen.

Berger, J., S. Blomberg, C. Fox, M. Dibb, and R. Hollis. 1972. *Ways of seeing: Based on the BBC television series with John Berger*. London: British Broadcasting Corporation and Penguin Books.

Berger, P. L. 1963. *Invitation to sociology: A humanistic perspective*. Garden City, NY: Doubleday & Company.

Berger, P. L., B. Berger, and H. Kellner. 1973. *The homeless mind: Modernization and consciousness*. New York: Vintage Books.

Berger, P. L. and T. Luckmann. 1966. *The social construction of reality: A treatise in the sociology of knowledge*. Garden City, NY: Doubleday & Company.

Burrell, G. and G. Morgan. 1979. *Sociological paradigms and organisational analysis: Elements of the sociology of corporate life*. London: Heinemann.

Cassirer, E. 1955. *The philosophy of symbolic forms*. New Haven and London: Yale University Press.

Cherryholmes, C. H. 1988. *Power and criticism: Poststructural investigations in education*. New York and London: Teachers College Press.

Considine, D. and G. Haley. 1992. *Visual messages: Integrating imagery into instruction*. Englewood, CO: Teacher Ideas Press.

Coward, R. and J. Ellis. 1977. *Language and materialism: Developments in semiology and the theory of the subject*. London: Routledge & Kegan Paul

Eagleton, T. 1984. *The function of criticism: From The Spectator to post-structuralism*. London: Verso.

Ellsworth, E. and M. H. Whatley. 1990. *The ideology of images in educational media: Hidden curriculums in the classroom*. New York and London: Teachers College Press.

Feenberg, A. 1991. *Critical theory of technology*. New York and Oxford: Oxford University Press.

Fish, S. 1980. *Is there a text in this class? The authority of interpretive communities*. Cambridge and London: Harvard University Press.

Freire, P. 1971. *Pedagogy of the oppressed*. New York: Herder and Herder.

————. 1985. *The politics of education*. Massachusetts: Bergin & Garvey, Inc.

Freund, E. 1987. *The return of the reader: Reader-response criticism*. London and New York: Methuen.

Giroux, H. A. 1989. *Critical pedagogy, the state, and cultural struggle*. Albany: State University of New York Press.

Goffman, E. 1976. *Gender advertisements*. New York: Harper & Row.

Goodman, N. 1978. *Ways of worldmaking*. Indianapolis and Cambridge: Hackett Publishing Company.

Gouldner, A. W. 1979. *The future of intellectuals and the rise of the new class: A frame of reference, these, conjectures, arguments, and an historical perspective on the role of intellectuals and intelligentsia in the international class context of the modern era*. New York: Seabury Press.

Habermas, J. 1968. *Knowledge and human interests*. Boston: Beacon Press.

Hamlyn, D. 1967. Empiricism. *The encyclopedia of philosophy*, 499-505. New York: Macmillan.

Hawkes, T. 1977. *Structuralism and semiotics*. Berkeley and Los Angeles: University of California Press.

Holub, R. C. 1984. *Reception theory: A critical introduction*. London and New York: Methuen.

Kliebard, H. M. 1987. *The struggle for the American curriculum 1893-1958*. New York and London: Routledge.

Kuhn, T. S. 1962. *The structure of scientific revolutions.* Chicago: University of Chicago Press.

Langer, S. K. 1942. *Philosophy in a new key: A study in the symbolism of reason, rite, and art.* Cambridge: Harvard University Press.

Masterman, L. 1985. *Teaching the media.* London: Comedia Publishing Group.

Muffoletto, R. 1990. Media education as critical pedagogy. In *Journal of Thought.* Edited by R. Robinson. Vol. 25, nos. 1 & 2.

———. 1991. Technology and texts: Breaking the window. *Paradigms regained: The uses of illuminative, semiotic and post-modern criticism as modes of inquiry in educational technology.* Englewood Cliffs, NJ: Educational Technology Publications.

———. 1993. Machine as expert. In *Computers in Education: Social, Political, and Historical Perspectives.* Edited by R. Muffoletto and N. Knupfer. Cresskill, NJ: Hampton Press.

Nichols, B. 1981. *Ideology and the image: Social representation in the cinema and other media.* Bloomington: Indiana University Press.

Norris, C. 1982. *Deconstruction: Theory and practice.* London and New York: Methuen.

Popkewitz, T. S. 1984. *Paradigm and ideology in educational research: The social functions of the intellectual.* London: The Falmer Press.

———. 1987. *The formation of school subjects: The struggle for creating and American institution.* New York and London: The Falmer Press.

———. 1991. *A political sociology of educational reform: Power/knowledge in teaching, teacher education, and research.* New York: Teachers College Press.

Postman, N. 1992. *Technopoly: The surrender of culture to technology.* New York: Knopf.

Rheingold, H. 1991. *Virtual reality.* New York: Summit Books.

Saussure, F. 1959. *Course in general liquistics.* New York: Philosophical Library.

Weedon, C. 1987. *Feminist practice and poststructuralist theory.* New York: Basil Blackwell.

Wollen, P. 1969. *Signs and meaning in the cinema.* Bloomington and London: Indiana University Press.

3

KATHLEEN S. FARBER ————————————————————————

Teaching about Diversity through Reflectivity: Sites of Uncertainty, Risk, and Possibility

INTRODUCTION

This chapter grew out of a concern for teaching concepts related to issues of diversity that were encountered in course work on critical psychological and social foundations of education. The focus of this chapter is to develop well-grounded and articulated pedagogy for engaging preservice teachers in an analysis of the formal attempts at socializing/educating youth into the culture. These preservice teachers have a great deal of experience in and with schools. They bring to its study a wealth of information, some of which is quite helpful and enlightening. Concepts from the psychological and social foundations of education that relate to issues of diversity can help these individuals analyze their schooling experiences. One critical concern, however, lies in the difficulty of teaching such concepts in meaningful ways to students who, while experienced in schools, are relatively inexperienced in the study of schooling.

This chapter provides a unique and potentially powerful pedagogical framework to study schooling with preservice teachers and collectively dismantle some of the mythology that has been perpetuated and preserved in teacher education institutions. Further, it challenges teacher educators to create alternative paradigms. However, dismantling or deconstructing schooling is no easy matter. We are all products of the schooling process and carry deep within us all manner of ideological baggage that, coupled with our formal studies of schooling, go a long way to perpetuate the educational status quo. If we are really to uncover the process of schooling and to seek alternatives that better serve the purposes of a multicultural, democratic society, then some ground must be laid for such an endeavor. My purpose in this chapter is to provide a pedagogical approach rooted in Dewey's (1933) notion of "reflective thinking," coupled with work in feminist (Belenky et al. 1986) and liberatory pedagogy (Freire 1970), as a vehicle for deconstructing and reconstructing our conceptions of teaching, learning, and schooling.

The pedagogy advocated here can be used to connect students to the content and concepts to be studied by a reflective analysis of schooling. It is a pedagogy, therefore, that uses as its reference point many concerns that are central to critical psychological and sociological studies of schooling. However, in this chapter I go beyond articulating those concerns in that I also explicate and illustrate a pedagogical approach to teaching the content.

The pedagogical approach presented uses a view of learning that differs from traditional views dominated by concepts such as behavior modification, control, management, reinforcement contingencies, and information processing. Drawing on the concepts of reflective thinking (Dewey 1933), tacit knowledge (Polanyi 1962), and intrinsic motivation (Meyer 1980), I present a model of teaching and learning that actively engages students in the reconstruction of their own experience. In this model, learning is seen as the reconstruction of experience (Dewey 1933), with teaching serving to "connect" (Belenky et al. 1986) student experience with the concepts and content to be taught through a form of "problem-posing" education (Freire 1970).

AN EXAMPLE OF LEARNING AS THE RECONSTRUCTION OF EXPERIENCE

As an illustration, consider teaching preservice teachers about the structure and function of youth culture as it relates to teaching and learning in schools (Bennett and LeCompte 1990). One approach might initially ask students to think back to their schooling experience with different groupings of students and to list those groups and their characteristics on the chalkboard. Given the listing and descriptions, they might then be asked to consider the relative status of each group, who valued each one, and for what reasons. As the discussion unfolds, students might be led to consider how factors such as race, ethnicity, gender, class, special abilities, or perceived disabilities might have affected both the composition of groups and the status afforded each group.

An activity of this sort illustrates a number of elements key to the pedagogical approach that follows. First, the activity is designed to establish interest on the part of students (intrinsic motivation) by tapping into their repertoires of tacit knowledge (past experience that is accessible and available for use). In this example, students' experience with youth culture is the starting point for an analysis of the dynamics of sociological factors such as race, ethnicity, class, gender, and status relative to group formation and functioning. The motivation for taking part in the discussion is *intrinsic* in that students are engaged in the conversation as a means to resolve some perceived incongruity or question with respect to their own experience, that is, how they were or were not affected by the dynamics of youth culture. They are not likely to be engaged merely to gain some reward external to and divorced from their own curiosity and interest.

As the discussion progresses to the point at which psychological and sociological concepts begin to be introduced and discussed with respect to the groups, students can begin to reflect on the connections between the information made available through these concepts and their own current level of awareness and understanding of youth culture. Through the reflective process, students begin to develop insights regarding their experiences in school in light of new experience gained in the college classroom. That is, the instrumental value of psychological and sociological content is illustrated by using it to resolve problematic situations faced by students. Further, by engaging reflectively in a dialogue, students' ability to conceptualize so called youth culture is transformed and reconstructed in a more elaborate and potentially powerful way, in that they will now be better equipped to understand the structure and function of youth culture in the schooling environment. They have begun to understand youth culture in its complexity and multiplicity through conceptual lenses such as race, ethnicity, class, gender, and status as they relate to other concepts such as power, ideology, culture, and knowledge.

The necessary impetus for this reconstruction of experience is the establishment of a motive state, a sense of incoherence in students such that they will be interested in resolving that incoherence via reflective thinking. Feminist and liberatory educational practices are integral in a variety of ways to the approach illustrated. First, validation and valuing of student experience is central to the method. Second, conversation and dialogue, not didactics, form the foundation of classroom interaction. Third, the purpose of the lesson is growth and empowerment in the sense of enhanced ability to act consciously and intelligently in and on one's world. Exploring how such empowerment can be used to serve the democratic ideal and not serve as a form of manipulation and imposition is the overarching purpose of this mode of instruction. Finally, the relationships among culture, power, knowledge, and ideology are explored explicitly in the lessons such that students will gain a higher level of sophistication regarding these concepts as they relate to schooling in a democracy.

By using a model of teaching and learning based on these ideas, students' and teachers' personal knowledge is valued and validated, with new meaning constructed through critical reflection. Dialogue is necessary to implement this model, for teachers must come to know students' tacit knowledge in order to create a motive state and a problematic situation that relates to students' lived experiences. The next section presents a graphic representation of the model of teaching and learning, and an explanation of its components.

A MODEL OF REFLECTIVITY FOR TEACHING AND LEARNING

The model illustrated in figure 3.1 was developed and elaborated through an ongoing collaborative effort by several colleagues.[1] Any number of ways might exist to present in schematic fashion the interplay of elements and processes that make up instruction. The figure presented here, however, has proven quite useful for teaching a variety of preservice teachers, graduate students, in-service teachers, and professors about the teaching/learning/schooling process, and most generally about education as a life process. For further discussions of the use of this model in teacher preparation in this volume, see the articles by Armaline and Lock.

The various elements of this model must be viewed as being interactive, with learning occurring through the purposeful interaction of these elements.

FIGURE 3.1
A Model of Reflectivity for Teaching and Learning

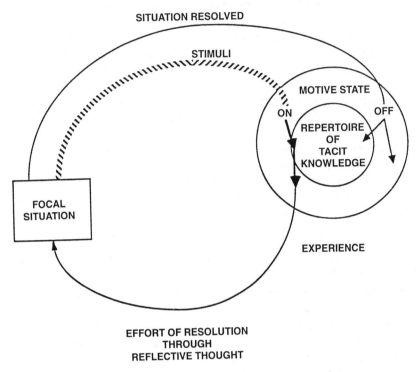

Initially, some transaction occurs between the self and the environment external to the self as one brings to bear past experiences on what is presently being experienced. In the model, tacit knowledge is an example of past experience and is schematically represented as a circle within the sphere of experience. The repertoire of tacit knowledge (RTK) refers to the nature, quality, and sum of accessible experience that students bring to the classroom, which is affected by factors such as cognitive style and abilities, race, class, gender, age, ethnicity, and special needs. Tacit knowledge is the knowledge with which one can think to resolve a problematic situation.

THE CREATION OF A FOCAL SITUATION AND THE MOTIVE STATE

The focal situation is the event of present interest and attention. Examples of focal situations include the tasks, content, and activities of the classroom. Focal situations are what one is paying attention to at the moment, the source of one's interest or incoherence. For example, the preceding focal situation involves the students' harkening back to their high-school experience to list and discuss the social grouping of their peers. Their attention and interest is focused on their past such that they might begin to analyze more deeply the nature and dynamics of that set of experiences in light of their beliefs, or their tacit knowledge, about schooling and society. In particular, they will begin to reflect on the degree to which aspects of their tacit knowledge, especially the ideology of individual achievement, merit, equality, and choice, actually play themselves out in secondary schools.

If incongruity exists between the focal situation (present experience of listing and discussing the peer groups in high schools) and tacit knowledge (past experience and beliefs regarding schooling and equal opportunity, merit, achievement, and choice), incoherence is perceived. When facing something one perceives to be incoherent, one feels unsettled and wants to act in order to resolve the incoherence. The perceived incoherence results in a motive state; one is motivated to reorganize or reconstruct what one is experiencing. That is, students are in a state of incoherence in that their beliefs are called into question by the very nature of their actual experience in schools.

Before experiencing this focal situation, students for the most part never really examine their belief systems. They take for granted that schools and the society within which schools operate, function according to the espoused ideals of freedom and equality. Once their taken-for-granted assumptions are viewed as problematic, students experience incoherence and are therefore in a motive state. Being in a motive state is used interchangeably with *being interested* and *being motivated*. Interest and incoherence involve the motive state of the student. If there is no motive state, no interest, then there is no desire to act and to think.

Once students are in a motive state and experience a feeling of incoherence, there are a number of ways that they might try to resolve that feeling. They might act impulsively, engage in denial or distortion, or simply ignore or avoid the classroom focal situation. In this way, nothing educative is accomplished, as students' realms of knowledge and experience are in no way enhanced or expanded. The task of the teacher becomes to engage students in a process that will enable them to draw from their tacit knowledge and to think with the content that is being taught in their efforts at resolution. That is, the teachers must create a focal situation that is likely to be perceived as incoherent and hence is interesting to students. However, the teacher must also engage with the students in a reflective resolution of the incoherence by using the content to be taught.

Two key questions have emerged so far for the teacher to consider:

How do I create a focal situation that relates to students' life experiences, taps their repertoires of tacit knowledge, and engenders a motive state?

How do I use the focal situation to facilitate critical and reflective thinking as the vehicle for students to reconstruct their experience?

REFLECTIVE THINKING

In this model, reflective thinking is the process by which the problematic situation (the focal situation that engenders a motive state) is most likely to be resolved, thereby establishing a sense of coherence and satisfaction. Dewey states that the function of reflective thinking is "to transform a situation in which there is experienced obscurity, doubt, conflict, disturbances of some sort, into a situation that is clear, coherent, settled, harmonious" (Dewey 1933, 100-101).

Reflective thinking begins when habit or routine action is disrupted and one experiences a feeling of doubt or conflict. One then must pause and consider alternatives to the routine. One examines these alternatives with respect to one's perception of the facts in order to define the problem more clearly. With the problem in better focus, hypotheses or guiding ideas are generated and their ramifications examined. The culmination of the reflective process is acting on one of the hypotheses in an attempt at verification. Should the hypothesis that is tested be verified, the state of perplexity is resolved and coherence reestablished. Action can proceed with new and deeper understanding of one's situation. It is important to note that the process of "verification" is not one that is personally removed or objectified, disconnected from the self. Rather, for verification to be meaningful, it must be connected both to the outer world, or the context of one's experience, and to one's inner world. Reflectivity begins and ends with one's subjectivity. Reflective thinking is an intentional act of creating meaning, grasping the previously unrecognized relationships between and among elements of problematic situations. One is consciously trying to make sense of a confusing, vague, and/or ambiguous experience.

AN EXAMPLE OF REFLECTIVE THINKING

As an illustration of a problematic situation that may be resolved reflectively in a classroom setting, imagine providing a teacher education class with data from various local high schools on performance levels for a particular battery of state-mandated competency tests (focal situation). Among other things, the results show a wide variation in the percentage of students who pass the entire battery of tests, from an 89% pass rate to a 6% pass rate. Further, the rate varies inversely with the percentage of "minority" and poor students enrolled. The highest rates of success occur in nearly all-white, middle- and upper-class schools and the lowest in schools that are nearly all "minority" and poor. The students are then posed with the problem of accounting for this occurrence.

The incoherence encountered by the students might result from a variety of sources. The degree to which the problem is close to home plays a role, and it is advantageous to use data from real schools involved in districtwide testing. (The preceding example, for instance, comes from results in the city schools of Toledo, Ohio for the first administration of statewide ninth grade competency tests in math, civics, reading, and writing.) Nonetheless, students will have to grapple with the fact that poor and minority students did not perform as well as their more affluent, white counterparts, and they will have to explain this phenomenon. When they experience incoherence regarding the data, they are said to be in a "Pre-reflective State" (Dewey 1933, 106-18).

Once in the Pre-Reflective State, students might do a number of things to resolve their incoherence. They might impulsively act on the first possibility that occurs to them, especially if they hold strong beliefs that mirror cultural stereotypes and prejudice regarding the intelligence and work habits of poor and minority students. They might gloss over the event and minimize the situation, denying that any problem even exists, by explaining that the data merely reflect the success and failure of schooling in the community.

Suggestion Phase

Independent of their initial reaction, the key to a reflective approach is that the students engage in a dialogue regarding the merits of each possible explanation generated. In other words, the explanations are to be treated as suggestions that represent the first phase of reflective thinking. These suggestions emerge from the students' repertoires of tacit knowledge. Some possible suggestions include the following:

- "poor and minority students are not as smart as affluent, white students;"
- "poor and minority students do not work as hard as affluent, white students;"
- "poor and minority parents do not value education as much as affluent, white parents;"
- "schools try intentionally to harm poor and minority youth;"
- "the background experience and culture of poor and minority youth is less congruent with schools and schooling than is that of affluent, white youth;" and
- "poor and minority youth are culturally deprived."[2]

Intellectualization Phase

As suggestions are generated, they need to be examined in terms of the context, circumstances, and perceived facts of the matter under investigation. In this instance, students must consider how well each suggestion accounts for what is known about children's performance on tests of the kind administered in the district. Is it the case, for example, that minority parents do not value education as much as white parents? Students might be encouraged to examine the research on parental attitudes regarding schooling, especially the work of people such as Annette Lareau (1989), who shows clearly that minority and poor parents value education a great deal. They just do not feel invited to participate in their children's education in the same ways that white, middle-

and upper-class parents do, nor do they feel as confident of their abilities to deal with teachers and school administrators. The same can be done for all of the suggestions that students generate. In this way, background knowledge that students have becomes connected with text concepts and information regarding the effects of race, class, gender, and ethnicity on student achievement.

This examining of suggestions in light of the relevant information is called *intellectualization* and represents the second phase of reflective thinking. Moreover, the movement back and forth between suggestion and intellectualization serves two important functions. First, it allows the students literally to construct and define the problem that they face. The nature and special features of the problem are brought into focus as information is contextualized and inspected by considering (intellectualization) ideas generated in the suggestion phase. Second, intentionality needed as a part of the guiding idea? Is it not more likely that poor and minority youth might be put at a disadvantage in more subtle ways that do not involve a conspiracy? Might a more likely explanation incorporate the insights that tests can be culturally biased and that poor and minority youth do not get from schooling the knowledge that they need, insights that might outweigh the interpretation of failure as the result of some intentional effort on the part of some individual or group?

Testing Phase

The same process might be applied to a number of guiding ideas, until one emerges as a strong candidate for resolving the incoherence. Once this occurs, what is left is to test the hypothesis. The nature of the testing phase, the fifth phase of reflective thinking, depends upon the particular problematic situation and the context within which it operates. In the preceding example, the test might be a public statement of explanation to a policy-making body or to some other so-called knowledgeable group who then might be able to react to the student resolution. To the extent that students receive positive feedback from their own group, and perhaps from outside evaluators, they will experience a sense of coherence and enter the "Post-Reflective State." I must emphasize that for Dewey (1933), the progression from the pre-reflective to the post-reflective state is one of degree and occurs on a continuum. It is not an either/or matter. The students resolve their problematic situation to a greater or lesser extent, and they are free to pursue new avenues of inquiry with expanded and reconfigured repertoires of tacit knowledge.

According to Dewey, reflective thinking is the process by which a problematic situation is most reliably resolved. It is most reliable because reflectivity involves a conscious, directed effort to establish belief by sooner or later one suggestion or a synthesis of several suggestions that will emerge as a likely candidate for resolving the incoherence. Once this occurs, the students move to the third phase of reflective thinking, the generation of guiding ideas or hypotheses.

Hypothesis Phase

In the third phase, one guiding idea or hypothesis emerges that will serve temporarily as a plan of action. This guiding idea represents the most likely explanation for the data presented at the beginning of the process. It should take into consideration what students know about testing and student achievement, as well as their knowledge of the effects of class, race, gender, and ethnicity on such performance. Once students construct a guiding idea, the results that are likely to accrue from acting on that idea become the focus of attention.

Reasoning Phase

The fourth phase of reflective thinking, the reasoning phase, involves students imagining the consequences or ramifications of accepting the guiding idea as an explanation for the phenomenon of test scores varying inversely with the number of poor and minority students. For example, suppose that the guiding idea chosen is "schools try intentionally to harm minority youth." If this were the explanation for the pattern of test scores that represents the problematic situation, what else must also be true? There someone must be involved in intentionally holding back minority youth from learning, in creating tests that put minority youth at a disadvantage, in preventing minority youth from learning what they need to know in order to succeed on the tests, and so on. Is it likely, one might ask, that such a conspiracy is possible, and if it were possible, would it be likely not to have been exposed? In other words, is the condition of integrating the subjective and the objective, by reconstructing experience with information, from the self and the external environment? For Dewey, learning results from a transaction between the individual and the environment. The primary agent is the learner who must actively reorganize and reconfigure incoming information by reflective thought.

REFLECTIVE THINKING AND WARRANTABILITY

Suppose again that a student is posed with a problem related to reasons for the pronounced variations in achievement levels for students of differing racial groups or class backgrounds. A nonreflective approach might allow a student to jump to a conclusion based upon prejudicial attitudes, common sense knowledge such as "some students just do not care to try," "their parents do not care about or value schools," or "they come from a 'deprived' home environment." A reflective analysis would accept these as suggestions to be evaluated in terms of the available relevant evidence on student achievement relative to factors such as race and class. When one examines such evidence and the bases for the first set of suggestions elicited, the probability increases for eliminating erroneous suggestions and generating different, more promising ones is increased. Further, as one develops guiding ideas in the form of hypotheses to be reasoned through and tested, the likelihood increases of arriving at a warranted conclusion. Thus, Dewey claimed that while reflective thinking does not guarantee anything, it does offer one the greatest probability of resolving a problematic situation in a satisfactory manner (1933).

Dewey distinguished between *learning* and *training* in that learning occurs when the individual is the reorganizing agent of experience. Training occurs when the experience is controlled or managed by an external force, such as in behavioristic theory. Dewey's idea of learning is tied inextricably to thinking and reflectivity. By contrasting in the teacher education classroom behavioristic training with Dewey's notion of learning, teacher education students must confront questions that are omitted or obscured by mainstream pedagogical instruction. The nature of subjectivity in recognizing, formulating, elaborating, and resolving problems never is a central issue in a traditional, behavioristic framework (Dewey 1916; Hullfish and Smith 1961).

In the context of the model here employed, Dewey's notion of learning as the reconstruction of experience by reflective thought allows teacher educators to seat the act of learning within the control and agency of students, beginning with their own experience and reconfiguring that experience in light of new and different experience engendered through classroom interaction. Students' own knowledge is valued, validated, and brought forth through classroom focal situations. Through the process of reflective thinking, students are encouraged to seek connections between their experience and new information and experience. Knowledge is given birth when tacit knowledge is called forth through the classroom focal situations and is provided an opportunity for rebirth when past and present experience is reconstructed into some coherent or meaningful form through reflective thinking. In this way, students reconfigure, elaborate, and expand their repertoires of tacit knowledge. This reconstructed knowledge thus becomes a part of their inner worlds and lies in wait, ready to be used when they are faced with another problematic situation.

CRITICAL QUESTIONS, PUZZLEMENTS AND CONCLUSIONS

The preceding ideas may lead the reader to believe that I view the pedagogy of schooling and diversity as a process that can be neatly packaged. This is certainly not the case, and in this section I would like to begin to address some of the concerns and cautions I have when using the pedagogy as described in this chapter. The method itself is not without problems. The situations created by using reflectivity for teaching and learning need to be analyzed more deeply if we are to succeed in our attempts to reconstruct our ideas about schooling and issues of diversity.

As we begin to address schooling and issues of diversity through the reflective process, often potentially disturbing realizations occur for both student and teacher. Commonly held beliefs are challenged, and tacit knowledge is called into question as new and surprising information unfolds about school, ourselves, and others. In my classes, I cling to the idea that reflecting on the injustices and inequities of marginalized populations would spur students to reconstruct their beliefs and tacit knowledge in light of this new information. Students, however, are often reluctant to engage in reflectivity and prefer to cling to the certainty of what they already know and have experienced. It was only until I began to examine this methodology as "high risk pedagogy" (Britzman 1992a) that I developed insight into the dynamics between teaching about diversity and the ideological and institutional nature of knowledge, identity, and opportunity. The following ideas have helped me to analyze the pedagogy discussed in this chapter, and they point to how teaching about diversity could be considered high risk pedagogy. Because my experience with and my understanding of high risk pedagogy is dynamic and ever changing, what follows is a beginning effort to address in writing the possibilities and risks that arise when teaching about diversity through reflective practice.

In their book *Testimony*, Felman and Laub examine the nature and function of testimony and witnessing in order to understand catastrophic historical events. They investigate the potentially educative force of the "process of testimony—that of bearing witness to a crisis or trauma" (Felman and Laub 1992, 1) and teaching through testimony as a way to enable change. Felman chronicles the story of her class-as it witnessed the testimonies and autobiographical accounts of survivors of the Holocaust. The testimonies did not just transmit facts about the events but introduced information that was strange and surprising to her students. She discusses her interest in the ability of her students to transform themselves in light of this information, and she comments that teaching "should make something happen" and "enable change" (Felman and Laub 1992, 53). Felman suggests that the strangeness and surprise of the testimonies create a state of crisis in the classroom whereby students often feel at a loss and disoriented because their commonly held worldviews are shaken. When crises occur in the classroom, teaching assumes a "position at the edge of itself, at the edge of conventional conception" (Felman and Laub 1992, 54).

Although I cannot equate teaching about issues of diversity and schooling to teaching about the horrors of the Holocaust, I can draw from Felman and Laub's insights regarding teaching for change through the witnessing of traumatic or disturbing events. When we teach with the explicit purpose of creating a more just and equitable society, we are asking students to see and be co-owners of the trauma engendered by the differential educational experiences and opportunities of the dominant culture as compared with microcultural groups. Teaching and learning then become living through crises because teachers do not just pass on information, but ask students to change and to deal with incongruity by pushing them beyond the limits of their knowledge (Felman and Laub 1992). Felman and Laub suggest that we should not only expect crises but also should create crises in the classroom. Reflecting on her own teaching, Felman states that she tries to create as much crisis as the students can stand without driving them crazy. In relating this to the model of reflectivity for teaching and learning in this chapter, teachers need to reflect on whether focal situations will create a crisis in class and what surprising and new information may come from the interaction with the focal situation. If crises occur, then we may have more opportunity to help students to look at things differently, to reconfigure their conceptions in light of new and different experience. Felman notes that within a crisis is a turning point, a breaking and changing of the "previous categories and previous frames of references" (Felman and Laub 1992, 54).

When we engender crises in the classroom by asking students to witness something surprising and to give up the safety of what they already believe, learning often occurs at what Erickson refers to as "the edge of risk" (1987, 344). Potential feelings of vulnerability and incompetence may arise because "to learn is to entertain risk, since learning involves moving just past the level of competence, what is already mastered, to the nearest region of incompetence, what has not yet been mastered" (Erickson 1987, 344). Students may experience feelings of incompetence when diversity is examined relative to issues of oppression because the very foundation of their experience is being shaken. The nature and limits of their knowledge is being called into question. Further, "risk in the form of a potential threat to positive social identity seems inherent" (Erickson 1987, 344-45) to learning about diversity when students begin to examine how they construct their own identities using the social markers of race, class, gender, ethnicity, and sexuality (Britzman 1992a). As the teacher I need to consider then what the students know about diversity and about how their socialization has affected their ability to understand issues of oppression and marginalization (Britzman 1992a). The risk for me as the teacher involves helping students to construct an understanding of diversity and oppression without imposing my construction on them. I must then begin to recognize what limits students' knowledge of these issues.

Sleeter, in her chapter in this volume titled "Teaching Whites about Racism" (1995), helps us to understand how white students' knowledge is influenced by social, cultural, and institutional interactions. She states that "Whites usually spend their lives in white-dominated spheres" and that they construct an understanding of diversity from this viewpoint (Sleeter 1993). She discusses Wellman's (1977) study of whites' perception of race and concludes "that a contradiction whites face is how to interpret racial inequality in a way that defends white interests in publically acceptable terms." Whites also often neutralize issues of diversity by, for example, "denying structural racism" (Sleeter 1995, 116). Teaching about issues of diversity is further compounded when we consider Wellman's suggestion: "Given the racial and class organization of American society, there is only so much people can 'see.' The positions they occupy in these structures limit the range of their thinking. The situation places barriers on their imaginations and restricts the possibilities of their vision" (1977, 235, cited in Sleeter 1995, 116).

The possibility of vision is made more complex when some of Britzman's (1992b) ideas regarding identity construction are discussed. In her article "Structures of Feelings in Curriculum and Teaching" (1992b), Britzman addresses the institutional structuring of students' thoughts, feelings, and identities. She suggests that students have been socialized to see themselves as "rugged individuals" who are "the sole authors of their identity" (1992b, 255). Their identities have been constructed around the idea of individualism and not the "social relations of their time and place" (Britzman 1992b, 255). Further, this is compounded when academic institutions perpetuate the conception of the "unconstrained and unmediated self" (Britzman 1992b, 255).

Britzman suggests that students' identities also are constructed by power relationships that are played out within social institutions. When I teach about diversity and schooling by using the model of reflectivity for teaching and learning, I create situations where my students must confront those relationships. In other words, they must begin to examine their race, class, gender, sexual preference, and so on in relation to oppression. Britzman suggests that often these situations create the victim and/or the victimizer but do not create space "to negotiate learning about other peoples' trauma" (1992a). Students may have glimpses of the inequities in their own experiences (they are victims) or hints of their participation in iniquitous practices (they are victimizers), but the feelings that these glimpses engender may compete with their efforts to make sense of the experiences of others. For example, when women students read about gender discrimination within the educational system, they may have difficulty accessing the dimensions of these experiences as they begin to recognize themselves as victims. The same may be true for male students as they begin to recognize sexism and their participation in sexist practice. "How can one acknowledge oppressive relationships without feeling a sense of responsibility and a sense of being implicated" (Britzman 1992b, 257)

Yet it is a sense of responsibility, not as victimizer, but as active members of a social community that I want to engender and build upon. An aspect of teaching about schooling and issues of diversity that needs to be considered is the issue of responsibility. As students begin to develop understandings of oppression, how do I, as the teacher, foster a sense of responsibility for or a commitment to reconstructing a more just and equitable society? I have often taught by using the ideas from this chapter and assumed that because students have begun to reflect on oppression they will automatically have the desire to transform oppressive conditions. However, as Britzman suggests, a linear or causal connection does not necessarily exist between forms of knowledge and action. What I find most difficult, then, is understanding the "commitments toward social life that [my] students already hold" (Britzman 1992b, 253).

In the process of trying to understand and hear my students' relationships to social life, however, I need to be aware that my own actions may be subjugating (Britzman 1992; Lewis and Simon 1986); that in my efforts at transformative practice, I actually may impose and oppress. I try to create situations in which students voice and expose how and whether they are using knowledge about diversity in their personal, professional, and (hopefully) political lives. For I find that if I try to create a space within which the students and I can negotiate, we all take more risks. Different forms of knowledge become unleashed (Britzman 1991a) and the classroom then becomes a cite of possibility and generativity.

I am frustrated and intrigued, confused and compelled by the possibilities and risks embodied in the pedagogical spaces created by using the model of reflectivity for teaching and learning about diversity. However, it is this uncertainty, this sense of incoherence, that motivates me to seek the personal, professional, and political possibilities inherent in high risk pedagogy.[3]

NOTES

1. Randy L. Hoover has been especially influential in the construction, explication, and use of the model employed in this article. For a more detailed rendering of the model, and for supportive theoretical and empirical material, see Kathleen S. Farber, *Thought and Knowledge: A Neurophysiological View*, unpublished doctoral dissertation, The Ohio State University, Columbus, Ohio, 1987.

2. I recognize that the term "culturally deprived" is pejorative. Because students and teachers unwittingly use it, however, I employ it to show frequently encountered responses and to indicate areas within those responses in need of additional analysis and reflection. In this case, the students and I might reflect upon the assumptions embedded in such a term and to reflect on the concept of culture and the ways in which power influences representation.

3. As Britzman (1991b), Bakhtin (cited in Britzman 1991b), O'Loughlin (1992), and others suggest, we are always in the process of becoming, of constructing knowledge and our identities in a social context. The ideas and beliefs in this chapter have not been constructed without help. I want to thank Bill Armaline, Pam Bettis, Deborah Britzman, and Renée Martin for helping me to continually construct and reconstruct my ideas and my identity.

REFERENCES

Bahktin, M. 1981. *The dialogical imagination.* Edited by Michael Holquist. Austin: University of Texas Press.

Belenky, M., B. Clinchy, N. Goldberger, and J. Tarule. 1986. *Women's ways of knowing: The development of self, voice, and mind.* New York: Basic Books.

Bennett, K. and M. LeCompte. 1990. *The way schools work.* New York: Longman.

Britzman, D. 1991a. Decentering discourses in teacher education: Or, the unleashing of unpopular things. *Journal of education* 173(3):60-80.

———. 1991b. *Practice makes practice: A critical study of learning to teach.* Albany: State University of New York Press.

———. 1992a. Gaps and silences in curriculum theory and their consequences for our work: A conversation. Presentation with M. Orner, E. Ellsworth, and J. Miller at the annual meeting of the American Educational Research Association, San Francisco.

———. 1992b. Structures of feeling in curriculum and teaching. *Theory into practice* 31(3):252-58.

Dewey, J. 1916. *Democracy and education.* New York: Macmillan.

———. 1933. *How we think.* Lexington, MA: D. C. Heath.

Erickson, F. 1987. Transformation and school success: The politics and culture of educational achievement. *Anthropology and education quarterly,* 18:336-56.

Farber, K. 1987. Thought and knowledge: A neurophysiological view. Ph.D. diss., Ohio State University.

Felman, S. and D. Laub. 1992. *Testimony: Crises of witnessing literature, psychoanalysis, and history.* New York: Routledge.

Freire, P. 1970. *Pedagogy of the oppressed.* New York: Continuum.

Hullfish, H. and P. Smith. 1961. *Reflective thinking: The method of education.* New York: Dodd, Mead and Co.

Lareau, A. 1989. *Home advantage: Social class and parental intervention in elementary education.* New York: Falmer Press.

Lewis, M. and R. Simon. 1986. A discourse not intended for her: Learning and teaching within patriarchy. *Harvard Education Review* 56:457-72.

Meyer, D. 1980. The biological bases of motives and emotions. Columbus, OH: Ohio State University, unpublished manuscript.

O'Loughlin, M. 1992. Rethinking science education: Beyond Piagetian constructivism toward a sociocultural model of teaching and learning. *Journal of research in science teaching* 29(8):791-820.

Polanyi, M. 1962. *The tacit dimension.* Chicago: University of Chicago Press.

Sleeter, C. 1995. Teaching whites about racism. In *Practicing what we teach: Confronting diversity in teacher education.* Edited by R. Martin. Albany: State University of New York Press.

Wellman, D. 1977. *Portraits of white racism.* Cambridge, MA: Cambridge University Press.

4

RENÉE MARTIN _____

Deconstructing Myth, Reconstructing Reality: Transcending the Crisis in Teacher Education

In her chapter "Teaching Whites about Racism," Christine Sleeter has encouraged teacher educators to create a "template for thinking about diversity." In response, this chapter will assert that as teacher educators we must reconstruct our own pedagogy to be inclusive of the following ideas. First we must identify ways to deconstruct biographies, ours and the biographies of those whom we teach, in order to examine, integrate, and reconstruct their own experiences with the experiences of people from microcultural groups (Sleeter 1994). Second, we must find ways to critically analyze and construct opportunities for the realization of democratic ideals and liberatory pedagogy in all classrooms.

This chapter will argue that in order for students in teacher education to engage in transformative, liberatory pedagogy, they must be taught to recognize the structural inequities that permeate schools and they must be educated to understand their roles as individual teachers in the perpetuation of those inequities. It further asserts that recognition can only occur when students gain insights into the ways in which power, culture, knowledge, and ideology intersect in a democratic society to produce academic outcomes that empower some and impede others.

Causing students to reflect upon their realities and the realities of those who are culturally different from them means creating an environment in which they can experience and eventually resolve cognitive dissonance engendered by the alternative paradigms they encounter. The goal is to challenge them to teach from a pedagogical foundation that liberates them from restrictive, hegemonic ideological practices. Such liberation is possible when we create classroom discourse that encourages teachers to assess their own race, class, and gender and the role that each plays in the perpetuation of privilege.

CREATING AN UNDERSTANDING OF THE NATURE OF POWER AND IDEOLOGY

Central to understanding the intricacies of issues of oppression in a democratic society is that students come to recognize the imposition of ideology upon school practice. Many students are unaware of how culture imposes various values, norms, and standards upon them as they grow into adulthood. Therefore I employ several activities that demonstrate the difference among the terms *cultural bias, individual prejudice, and institutional discrimination* (Vega 1978). Since most prospective teachers attended schools dominated by middle-class white teachers and other white students, many of them enter the university oblivious to issues of diversity. Whiteness, heterosexuality, being middle class, and the accompanying norms and standards of the dominant culture are viewed as a legitimate foundation for conceptualizing the world and ultimately for constructing pedagogy. Teacher education students are afforded few opportunities to critique prevailing functionalist perspectives or to assess their implications for diverse populations of learners. Most approach teaching with little knowledge of the impact of their own race, class, or gender upon the pedagogies that they will develop or with few incentives to realize the problems inherent in traditional pedagogy.

As noted by other authors in this volume (See Koppelman and Richardson, McCain-Reid, and Sleeter), for the most part, white students who enter teacher education institutions appear to be unaware of the dynamics of racism, sexism, and classism in their own lives and in the society at large (Martin and Koppelman 1991; Martin and Lock 1991). The failure of most teacher education institutions to link what happens in the classroom with what occurs in the larger society inhibits prospective teachers from creating the conditions to critically analyze and possibly alter the social construction of teaching and learning. There is a tendency for students to rely primarily upon their own individual experiences when formulating ideas of how schools should function. Fuller (1992) points out that the composition of teacher education faculties exacerbates this tendency since "the shortage of women among teacher education program faculty means pre-service teachers' search for role models requires them to rely on recollections of teachers they have had in grade school and high school. These recollections, accurate or inaccurate, are based on their perspectives as children rather than as young adults learning to become teachers" (193). In addition, the lack of faculty of color in teacher education institutions forces students to rely on impressions of professional people of color that emanate from the culture at large as portrayed, for example, by media. "The implication of this reduced exposure to diversity is the increased likelihood that pre-service teachers will have difficulty understanding and appreciating students whose culture and socioeconomic backgrounds are different from their own" (Fuller 1992, 193).

Students whom I teach in an entry level course entitled Education in a Diverse Society, a course designed to fulfill the NCATE criteria for multicultural education, are often confused and frustrated when they encounter minority students in public school field experiences. The biographies and experiences of the students whom they meet vary markedly from their own; consequently, the lenses they use to analyze what occurs in these public school settings are those of white, middle-class, privileged, heterosexual students who have benefitted from the structural oppression that exists in schools. The following excerpts from the writings of white students in field experiences illustrate this point. "I am in a junior high school which is predominantly African American. I've never felt so strange in all my life. I've never even heard of some of the people the history teacher is talking about, and all of the stuff on the walls and in the hallways is about Black events and Black people. It's like these kids aren't really even getting an education. They never seem to learn about anyone who was really important in history."

Another writer commented, "The little Black kids in the school I'm in are on the road to failure. They come into class and sleep and the teacher doesn't seem to care. She told me that a lot of them are in poor homes where the parents may be fighting and stuff, or they live in neighborhoods where there's lots of gangs and violence. I don't care. I still think it's her job to educate them and not make excuses for their home life. My parents weren't exactly rich, and we had fights, but I've always done pretty well in school."

Or, "Today my cooperating teacher was reading some journals that her sixth graders wrote. One of the boys said that kids in the school were always calling him a "Spic" and he was really hurt by it. First she asked me how to spell "Spic," and made a comment in his journal that he needed to work on his spelling. Then she gave him some advice. She told him that that's just the way this school is and that he should get used to it and try to ignore it and do his work. I've been thinking about this and I guess I agree with her. I mean she is only one person and the advice she gave him is pretty good because what she's really telling him is that he has to grin and bear it—something my mom always says to me."

These students have learned to deny or ignore the historical patterns and systemic nature of oppression in American society, and in particular, in American schools. Research indicates that prospective teachers carry dominant ideological notions of success, meritocracy, and individual agency into their careers as practicing teachers. Ashton and Webb note that "The life experiences of most teachers demonstrate their allegiance to the ethic of vertical mobility, self-improvement. hard work, deferred gratification, self discipline, and personal achievement. These individualistic values rest on the assumption that the social system works well, is essentially fair, and moves society slowly but inevitably toward progress" (1986, 29-30).

Progress toward understanding the complexities of teaching and learning in a culturally diverse society can be achieved when students understand their roles in the institutional dynamics of power in which issues of diversity are rooted. Such comprehension is gained when students learn to analyze the impact of their own biographies upon the teaching and learning processes and when they can come to grips with their own vested interests in maintaining or challenging the status quo. It is therefore important to create alternative explanations and approaches to diversity by challenging teacher education students' shared assumptions and mutual affirmations.

Central to an understanding of the intricacies of oppression within schools in a democratic society is that students learn to recognize the imposition of ideology upon school practice. For teacher educators, this means cultivating among their students an awareness of the hegemonic nature of the educative process and harvesting their power as potential agents for change in schools. Most teacher education students are not cognizant of the ways in which the culture imposes functionalist perspectives in the form of dominant cultural values, nor do they recognize how those values are incorporated into institutional practices and policies when they become teachers. Illustrations of taciturn assumptions that underscore relations of power between students and teachers are often captured by the hegemonic practices employed to manage classrooms. For example, most teacher education students believe that being on time is important to the smooth functioning of the classroom. Teachers invoke all sorts of penalties, such as detentions for students who arrive late to class. In some cases, students who compile enough detentions are suspended or sent to the principal's office. This often results in loss of actual learning time, and it further disenfranchises students, particularly those who are from microcultural groups where time is valued differently than it is in Anglo American culture. In some Native American groups, time is relative and flexible. Many indigenous languages contain no word for time which is in dramatic contrast to the dominant cultural perspective that views time as linear and fixed. Consequently, the way in which a Native American child may interpret the necessity to be on time may be very much different from the way a middle-class Anglo American or African American child will regard this cultural phenomenon.

The practice of raising one's hand, thus deferring power to the teacher to designate who will and who will not speak is another manifestation of classroom hegemony. My students argue that opportunities to learn are increased when such behaviors are strictly followed and that when they are not, chaos ensues. When I ask them how many times they have observed truly chaotic behavior that is the result of too many students trying to engage in a discussion, most admit that seldom does such behavior occur. More important, when asked how they have come to understand notions of being on time, that there is a singular view of time, that raising one's hand or that there is only one view of how verbal interaction occurs, most admit that they have unconsciously incorporated the behaviors and value structures of the dominant culture. Seldom do any of them realize how these values infiltrate schools and how they affect learning. Even fewer recognize the inherent power accorded a teacher who promotes these values.

The following example is also illustrative of students' pervasive, unquestioning acceptance of dominant ideology. I ask students to rise and say the pledge of allegiance to the flag, and I observe them as they dutifully stand and recite the pledge in unison with some students symbolically raising their right hand or placing it over their heart. After they have finished I tell them to be seated and I ask them a series of questions: Did all of you attend the same elementary school? If not, what accounts for each of you reciting the pledge of allegiance using virtually the same inflections, meter, and tone? At what age did you learn to recite the pledge? What did the terms *republic, allegiance* or *pledge* mean to you at five or six when you learned it? This exercise elicits several points for discussion. To begin with, only a handful of students can recall ever having discussed the significance of the pledge of allegiance to their lives as citizens in a democratic society. While a few recollect that, on rare occasions, individual students of various ethnic or religious groups might have requested exemption from recitation, none recall a substantive discussion about why the option existed or whether or not they had the right to exempt themselves.

Developing a clear understanding of the dynamics of power by beginning with something as familiar to them as the pledge of allegiance or classroom activities designed supposedly to "maintain order" helps to establish a framework in which to contextualize issues that are less familiar to them. These exercises challenge basic assumptions about relationships of power between teachers and students. They also set the stage for discussions that investigate notions of hegemonic reproduction, cultural capital, and functionalist views of education.

MAKING MEANING OF RACE, CLASS, AND GENDER

It is important to clarify that although the exercises presented here may appear to isolate singular variables such as race, it is neither possible nor desirable to disregard the impact of other elements such as class or gender upon people's lives and their academic achievements. Students must become aware of the overarching dynamics of oppression and of the ways in which race, class, and gender intersect and overlap. Otherwise, some will rationalize the subjugation of women or the oppression of homosexuals and fail to see the interconnectedness of all issues of oppression. The activities presented here are not comprehensive; rather, they are meant to illustrate simple, effective ways to begin to address complex issues.

Issues pertaining to social class are difficult to teach because students seem to have the least personal awareness of them. Although many students recognize the existence of the homeless population, they continue to harbor false impressions that people are homeless because they simply haven't worked hard enough, thereby subscribing to a meritocratic, bootstraps mentality. In order to challenge their perceptions, I ask students to analyze critically two institutions in different socioeconomic areas of the city and then to gauge the impact of each institution's services upon people in the community and to discuss the implications of that impact. They have compared libraries, grocery stores, various branches of chain stores and hospital and mental health facilities. Their findings in combination with course readings, which they recount in a 3 to 5 page reaction paper, often are shocking to them. For example, one student observed in an urban area populated primarily by low-income African Americans a grocery store stocked with moldy donuts, rotting fruit, meat that was an "odd greenish/gray color," and shelves of baby food that were exorbitantly priced. The store, owned by white people, was "poorly stocked, dimly lit and generally dirty." Service was rendered on a "cash only" basis. She noted that even though the area was a residential one, there were five liquor stores within a block of the grocery store, and the parking lot of the store was riddled with broken glass, beer and wine bottles, and other trash. In marked contrast was a store in a predominantly white, upper-middle-income suburb where fresh produce, meat, and numerous varieties of all types of food including gourmet and ethnic items were pleasingly displayed in abundant supply. The store was clean and equipped with modem conveniences such as grocery carts with calculators, automatic credit card payment devices at each cashier's stand, and baggers who carried groceries to her car.

In another example, a student compared two building-supply stores. The one located in an urban area required customers ordering kitchen cabinets to measure and bring the dimensions for cabinets to the store. The store offered a limited range of four cabinet designs and a small price range, and it would only deliver and install the cabinets for an additional fee. The student then visited the suburban store owned by the same company and noted that store customers there were offered a wide range of prices and options. The clerk informed him that the store would gladly send someone to his home to take the necessary measurements, whereupon they offered him a range of about thirty-five designs from which to choose. Delivery service was free and installation was to be performed for a fee.

Other course activities are designed to evoke an understanding of race by acquainting students with their own racial identity and its centrality in the creation of a power structure that serves the interests of the dominant culture. Students are asked to write, in class, about the first time that each of them recalls being from the racial group to which she or he belongs. White students who are asked to engage in this activity often experience perplexity and confusion. They ask questions such as "What do you mean? You want me to write about being white?" Others volunteer remarks such as "Well, I'm white and I guess I never really thought about it." Those who are able to recall the first time they remember being white inevitably recount an experience they had in college when they were the only white person at a social event, such as being a guest at an African American fraternity party. In my experience, no white student has ever viewed being white as an impediment to their success as a student or as a member of the society at large.

Conversely, students of color are usually able to begin the exercise immediately. Most recall racial slurs and epithets that they encountered as very young children, and all are acutely aware of the impact that their racial identity has had upon their experiences as students. In addition to asking students to reveal what they've written, I ask students whether or not they observed how many in the class were able to begin the exercise immediately. We discuss why some had difficulty writing about their experiences or the lack of them and what that implies. For many Anglo American students, this is the first time that they have been asked to think of themselves within the context of their own whiteness and privilege. Some feel uncomfortable, others want to rationalize or discount the importance of their racial identity. Actually calling attention to the fact that we are all raced, classed and gendered is an important first step in identifying the role of the individual in structural oppression.

Among the most controversial segments of the course are those that address issues of gender. In particular, young female teacher education students are often resistant to the realities of living in a sexist society. There are a number of reasons for this. Few have a sense of the history of the oppression of women in American society. Most take for granted daily events that their female ancestors had to fight to acquire. For example, a student in one of my classes once had this to say about sexism as a viable social issue. "Dr. Martin, I know that you think that sexism is a real problem in this society and maybe it was in your day, but it's just not a problem for women my age. I have my own Master card and everything." When a young man from the other side of the room responded by saying "Yeah, but did your dad have to co-sign for it?" she admitted that was the case but still refused to believe that women in contemporary society are subject to differentiated standards.

Some students have encountered tolerance of sexist language and behavior throughout their schooling, and teacher education institutions are no exception to this practice. Students in my classes routinely report that professors continue to use exclusive, androcentric language. Courses continue to be titled Man and the Environment or Man and Biology, and students report sitting in classes in nontraditional fields such as engineering where professors actively discourage the involvement of female students either by not calling on them or by making disparaging remarks about their ability to succeed.

In addition, some students engage in femiphobia, fear of and hostility against feminists and their perspectives. Students who have not previously been exposed to feminists in classrooms and who rely upon the impressions created by media ideologues such as Phyllis Schlafley or Rush Limbaugh have exaggerated and unrealistic impressions of feminism. For many students, feminism and lesbianism are inextricably linked. The rampant homophobia in the culture therefore undermines many initiatives that female professors may address relative to issues of gender. Feminist professors are seen as singular advocates for women's issues. The femiphobia combined with the broad-based homophobia and misogyny in the culture perpetuate negative attitudes about issues of diversity and specifically sexism in many female professor's classrooms. Exposing students to feminist writing throughout the teacher education curriculum and acknowledging it as an alternative pedagogical strategy can be crucial to the success of such courses (hooks 1989). However, most teacher education institutions actively discourage feminist pedagogy or relegate it to existence in isolated graduate courses.

It is also important to note that the structure of many courses prevents students from engaging in the kinds of reflection, reading, and course activity that would dispel femiphobia and other elitist, racist, sexist behaviors. For example, in my own institution the course that I teach occurs in a ten-week quarter with little or no follow-up to what is advocated. It is virtually impossible to alter attitudes in any significant way, far less change behaviors significantly, in such a brief period of time.

Combating sexism can therefore be a task of nearly insurmountable proportions. In order to begin to heighten awareness of sexism in the culture, I have students investigate their own beliefs and those projected about women in contemporary society through the media. In one activity I ask students to compile four lists: one of traditionally feminine behaviors that they have cultivated in their lives; one of traditionally feminine behaviors that they have avoided cultivating; and two similar lists for masculine behaviors. We share their lists by writing them on the chalkboard. Characteristics on the feminine list that are desirable include being polite, sensitive, nurturant, caring, gracious, ladylike, in control of their emotions, learning to cook, being able to sew, doing gardening or interior decorating, and being considerate. Characteristics they cultivate on the masculine list include assertiveness, leadership, physical strength, the ability to manage money, being athletic, knowing how to fix a car, being independent. Feminine behaviors to be avoided are being too emotional, moody, bitchy, acting like a sissy, being a dumb blonde, bad driver, independent, gossipy, timid, crying, unassertive, worrying too much about one's physical appearance. Masculine characteristics to be avoided are being macho, rude, using profanity, being aggressive, or engaging in physical exercise that builds too many muscles. This exercise elicits the obvious impressions of what they regard as appropriate masculine and feminine behaviors and has implications for their expectations of the students whom they will teach and for the people whom they choose to emulate as role models.

I also use Kilbourne's work, a video entitled *Still Killing Us Softly*, as a lens through which to comprehend popular cultural images of women in advertising. Students extend their investigations of images of women and men in various directions: observations of the ways that toys are packaged for girls and boys; of marketing strategies for various kinds of other products such as the sale of automobiles, lyrics of music videos, discussion of female and male characters in television dramas and situation comedies; and comparative analyses of salaries of women and men in a variety of professional arenas. When accompanied by readings and statistics that dispel myths about women, such as statistics about poverty, income levels, years spent in the workforce, distribution of resources, representation in government and the higher echelons of business, these activities can be powerful incentives to deconstruct stereotypic assumptions about gender.

RESISTANCE TO LIBERATORY EDUCATION

Many of the activities I have described may elicit anger or frustration among students. Unaware that inequities exist, unconscious of their impressions of members of microcultural groups and of the stereotypes that they harbor, students may find themselves traversing new cognitive and affective terrain. This may be the first time that many of them experience what Habermas and others refer to as "emancipatory knowledge" (McLaren 1994, 179) which McLaren explains as knowledge that attempts to reconcile and transcend the opposition between practical and technical knowledge . . . which helps us understand how social relationships are distorted by relations of power and privilege" (170). These exercises have the potential to create an initial awareness of the tension and dynamics inherent in issues of diversity, and they can act as a starting point for an exploration of the relationship between the language of critique and the language of possibility (Giroux 1992).

Creating contradictions within the framework of accepted practice can be tricky for teacher educators. Some students may misconstrue the intent of activities or discussion because it may be the first time that they have participated in a discourse that questions their traditional assumptions about issues of democracy and diversity. In an attempt to deflect some of these behaviors and set the stage for scholarly discourse I prepare the class by doing the following. At the outset I discuss the explicit statements on the syllabus that specify the course's focus on alternative pedagogy that I will model as an option to what teacher education students are being taught in other courses. I explain that because they have been exposed primarily to functionalist perspectives, the course will provide alternatives that challenge prevailing ideology. (Andrzejewski discusses this more fully in her chapter in this volume.) Students read from the two assigned texts, Bennett and Lecompte's *How Schools Work* and Gollnick and Chinn's *Multicultural Education in a Pluralistic Society*, and various other sources. The course provides numerous opportunities to engage in discussion and classroom activities. I use the first chapter in Bennett and LeCompte's text to explicate the differences between social transmission and social transformation theories, and I then use the examples mentioned earlier to illustrate the imposition of dominant ideology upon school practice.

One consequence of being exposed to alternative paradigms is that students may experience cognitive dissonance. I argue by analogy that the dissonance represents growth, and I encourage them to think of times in their lives, such as puberty, when they experienced growth that they may have found stressful or painful.

I have found that students commonly argue from their privileged positions against the historical patterns of systemic oppression. Therefore I discuss rationalizations such as denial, avoidance and "victim blaming" (Ryan 1971) to further underscore how individuals support their racist, sexist, homophobic, and elitist constructs in an oppressive society and how this attempts to validate their life experiences and foster dominant ideological value systems. Denial is a refusal to believe that systemic oppression exists. For example, a student in one of my classes once said, "I attended a high school that was all white. We decided to bus Blacks and the trouble began. We didn't have any problems with racism until they came in and upset the school. Suddenly they had to have stuff in the textbooks and curriculum about them; they weren't satisfied with the ordinary things that everyone is supposed to learn." Clearly, this student was unaware that systemic racism was prevalent in the school's failure to maintain a curriculum that was representative of women and people of color regardless of its minority population. He regarded the arrival of students of color whose consciousness had been raised about issues of diversity as troublesome, rather than as a potential new source from which to learn more about a marginalized group. Further, the needs of the African American students for greater inclusion held the oppressive conditions up to scrutiny. This forced the predominantly white student body and administration to assume responsibility for greater inclusion or to suffer the consequences of maintaining a racist institution. The response of the white student was to deny the existence of racism and place the solution for the problem with those who were the victims of exclusion.

The second method of discounting societal problems in which students sometimes engage is one of avoidance. This form of discounting acknowledges the existence of a problem but finds a way to deflect the primary focus away from the real problem to lesser issues that in turn delay finding actual solutions. Examples include those such as the following: "I don't know what minorities want. Don't they realize that these things take time. After all, Rome wasn't built in a day. It's going to take time for all things to become equal." Or "The real problem is that we all need to be more Christian in our attitudes. If we would all just treat everyone as if he were our brother, the problems of the world would be solved." Both examples overlook the real problem which is institutionalized racism and suggest that individual human agency is the key to resolution of this societal problem. The second, and I would argue, more ethnocentric statement overlooks the fact that the world is not comprised primarily of Christians or males, and it assumes a naive, simplistic view of the world in which all humans supposedly share the same value systems.

The third form of discounting is "victim blaming" described by Ryan (1971) as an "ideological process . . . (in which) we cannot comfortably believe that we are the cause of that which is problematic to us: therefore, we are almost compelled to believe that *they*—the problematic ones—are the cause and this immediately prompts us to search for deviance (68)." In my classes, victim blaming frequently occurs as statements regarding "reverse discrimination" in which students blame those who have been victimized by an unjust system and place the blame for the system with the very persons who have been victimized. For example, students will sometimes cite an individual experience in which they know of a woman or person of color who was admitted to an institution of higher education while a friend of theirs, a white male, was denied entrance. This phenomenon relies upon their singular experiences to discount historical patterns and practices of discrimination, and it implies that white males are "victims of the same discriminatory policies and practices visited upon people of color and women" (Andrzejewski 1990, 79). I introduce them to an article in which Andrzejewski has debunked the "myth of reverse discrimination." She writes that it is "designed to continue the protection of white male club privilege by the method of projection—that is projecting white male institutional discrimination practices onto the few minorities and women who gain entrance to any resource pool" (1993, 92). She further notes that reverse discrimination is "related to blaming the victim since feelings of anger, hostility, and fear are directed, not at those in power who create and maintain the discriminatory practices but at members of the groups who have been excluded from power" (1990, 79).

Over the years, I have kept track of statements of denial, avoidance, and victim blaming which I discuss with students as a way of illustrating how common these rationalizations are and as a demonstration of possible approaches for facilitation of the issues with their own students. I note that a person who is in a state of denial has quite a different perspective from one who admits the existence of a problem but has chosen to avoid it. To note this difference also is to suggest that the strategies to address issues of diversity vary and must begin with the individual's current place in a belief system rather than with where she or he ought to be.

IMPLICATIONS FOR PEDAGOGY

Lather writes that deconstructing pedagogy means that "pedagogy becomes a site *not* for working through more effective transmission strategies but for helping us learn to analyze the discourses available to us, which ones we are invested in, how we are inscribed by the dominant, how we are outside of, other than the dominant, consciously/unconsciously, always partially, contradictorily" (1991, 143). Giroux (1988) calls for teachers to position themselves as intellectuals who engage in critical pedagogy as a "deliberate attempt to construct specific conditions through which educators and students can think critically about how knowledge is produced and transformed in relation to the construction of social experiences informed by a particular relationship between the self, others, and the larger world" (Giroux 1992, 98). Such a position requires us now to broaden the discourse in teacher education classrooms to include discussions of power as relational between students and teachers and to culture as more than an artifact.

If the classroom is to be a place where traditional values are critiqued, teacher educators must create circumstances in which notions of power and hierarchy are interrogated. We must begin to aid prospective educators in the development of a discourse that addresses power and possibility and we must provide prospective educators with a climate that is conducive to critical analysis of schools in order to construct alternative foundations for teaching and learning. Multicultural social reconstructionist education can act as a conduit for such reform. However, reform will only occur if there is a comprehensive commitment by teacher education institutions to assess and analyze existing programs and if teacher educators recognize their roles an individuals in the reform process. As Purpel notes, "It is time for all of us to engage in this titanic struggle, and as educators we must accept our part of this struggle to seek to establish our commitment and reiterate our faith in what part the educational process can play in transcending the current crisis" (13).

REFERENCES

Andrzejewski, J., ed. 1990. *Human relations: The study of oppression and human rights. V. 1.* Needham Heights, MA: Ginn Press.

Ashton, P. T. and R. B. Weob. 1986. *Making a difference: Teachers' sense of efficacy and student achievement.* New York: Longman.

Bennett, K. P. and M. D. LeCompte. 1990. *How schools work: A sociological analysis of education.* New York: Longman.

Fuller, M. L. 1992. Teacher education programs and increasing minority school populations. In *Research and multicultural education: From the margins to the mainstream.* Edited by C. Grant. London: Falmer Press.

Giroux, H. A. 1988. *Teachers as intellectuals.* Massachusetts: Bergin and Garvey.

―――. 1992. *Border crossings: Cultural workers and the politics of education.* New York: Routledge.

Gollnick, D. and P. Chinn. 1994. *Multicultural education in a pluralistic society.* Columbus: Merrill-McMillan.

Habermas, J. 1972. *Knowledge and human interests.* London: Heinemann.

Lather, P. 1991. *Getting smart: Feminist research and pedagogy within the postmodern.* New York: Routledge.

Martin, R. J. 1986. A comparative analysis of the implementation of the human relations mandates in three selected teacher education institutions in the states of Iowa, Minnesota, and Wisconsin. Ph.D. diss., Iowa State University, Ames, IA.

Martin, R. J. and K. Koppelman. 1991. The impact of a human relations/multicultural education course on the attitudes of prospective teachers. *The Journal of Intergroup Relations* 23(1) (Spring):16-27.

Martin, R. J. and R. S. Lock. 1991. Confronting realities, cultural reproduction in physical education: An analysis of non-sexist teaching behaviors of student teachers. *Teacher Education Quarterly* 18(2) (Spring):45-55.

McLaren, P. 1994. *Life in schools.* New York: Longman.

Orner, M. 1992. Interrupting the calls for student voice in "Liberatory education: A feminist poststructuralist perspective." In *Feminism and critical pedagogy.* Edited by Carmen Luke and Jennifer Gore. New York: Routledge.

Ryan, W. 1971. *Blaming the victim.* New York: Pantheon.

Purpel, D. E. 1989. *The moral and spiritual crisis in education.* Granby, MA: Bergin and Garvey.

Sleeter, C. 1995. Teaching whites about racism. In *Practicing what we teach: Confronting diversity in teacher education.* Edited by R. J. Martin. New York: State University of New York Press.

Vega, F. 1978. The effect of human and intergroup relations education on the race/sex attitudes of education majors. Ph.D. diss., University of Minnesota, Minneapolis, MN.

5

CARL ALLSUP _____

What's All This White Male Bashing?

The study and subsequent instruction about issues of race, gender, and class pose the most significant challenge to the questions about the nature of higher education in the United States. This debate became most obvious in the late 1960s as ethnic studies, quickly followed by feminist or women's studies, established an albeit marginal presence in the university. As tendentious as their so-called reception by the traditional intellectual community proved to be, the separate place of these disciplines minimized their systemic impact. This is not to understate the value and contributions of feminist and multicultural scholars and educators and their curricular creations. But this is to distinguish between the then relatively isolated world of the eclectic, non-required, so-called radical department/program and a curriculum that today is required increasingly as a part of the general education core for a liberal arts, university education. Because of numerous factors (that will not be discussed or analyzed in this essay), teaching about race, class, and gender has now achieved this more global role in American universities. But the varying and established university authorities, have sought at least to "include" these items of inquiry in the learning of western society, the assumptions, presumptions, and "givens" have withered. The realization that even the questions, much less the answers about race, class, and gender are difficult and complex, and actually may be subversive to the institutional and private status quo, enervates the already resistant and recalcitrant academy.

This discomfit is most acute or becomes more actualized because the major proponents of the inquiry are women and men of color and white females. Indeed, almost apocalyptic is the specter (as in, "a spectre is haunting") of the nontraditional voice speaking from one of the most hallowed forums (the university lectern) while utilizing descriptive, analytical, and metaphorical terms such as *Dominant Center, Oppression, White Male, People of Color, Female,* and *Gender,* as central themes in the understanding of society is almost (almost?) apocalyptic. At least, one might suppose such calamity when one gives attention to the most scurrilous and blasphemous accusation by those who have witnessed these acts, that is, the tyranny of the politically correct. The opponents of the recent attempts to reconceptualize the paradigms by which we in fact do seek to understand human society absurdly accuse us of "imposing" political views, eliminating objective inquiry, and subverting the intellectual standards by which we come to "know" what we know or "should" know. More rational and sincere debate does underline the nature of knowledge and the role of its discourse in the articulation and perpetuation of education that replicates that dominance. Perhaps the most concise *location* for such an examination is the curriculum and classroom where it must live.

The focus of this essay is such ah examination. It will include the most obvious as well as the very subtle and critical elements of the classroom. They are instructor, students, and course content that combine to form a sometimes confusing but always dynamic interplay called the environment. Contrary to simplistic notions of the sum and its parts, this environment does not result in a clinically observable learning process, nor is it readily analyzed by the course or student evaluation methodology that is so prevalent in the academy today. When we consider the dynamics, of race, gender, and class curriculum, we find that the classroom environment is chaotic, cacophonous, and at moments quite disturbing for all of the participants. It is also an active opportunity for those participants to engage in an inclusive endeavor, to move beyond the narrow, dominant doctrines experienced by most students in American education. The common but not necessarily permanent response experience—What's all this white male bashing?—offers a serious reflection on the perceptions of a content and instructor that does not meet the expectations of the traditional white American student. I will outline what I believe to be the most intellectually honest and necessary approach to inclusive education. It has come to be described as liberating pedagogy, as the matrix of race, class, and gender influence. Certainly it is an attempt to incorporate and perceive the world with a discourse other than the tradition of the Western university.

RECONCEPTUALIZATION

All societies create a discourse that explains their ontology and dominance with cosmic, universal explanations. These explanations may be mythical concepts, or they may be organized *history*, but they will offer the members of the society a justifying rationale for what is, what should be, or a combination of the two. This discourse with its symbolic and concrete manifestation achieves the status of standards for behavior, institutionalized and private. In order to understand that goal and achievement, it is fundamental to recognize who are their creators and to ask who benefits from these myths, norms, and so forth and who does not.

In recent years, many liberatory scholars and groups have pursued these questions. This pursuit suggests that we come to a *location*, a cognitive place not of our choosing yet where all of us *begin* (hooks 1990). It is at a center that Gramsci calls a cultural hegemony and that others call the dominant center. It is not a speculative or theoretical center. It is reality: white, elite, and male, defined structurally and philosophically by race, class, and gender. All of us are raised and educated to believe and feel that white, elite, and male is central. However, those who are oppressed and who have sought a different vision unfetter themselves in the process of seeking a different location.

To bring this location and vision to articulation, to consciousness, initially we may search for a place within the hegemony of the traditional center. Inevitably, such attempts keep those who are *other* at the margins. Embracing hegemonic leadership endorses values, and doing so makes it difficult to reframe an inclusive understanding of the world. Consequently, we reconceptualize that margin ontologically and epistemologically as a site of resistance to that structure, ideology, and thought that have operated to define and maintain the dominant center (hooks 1990). This reconceptualization leads to a transformation from the margin and not from the center; it is not a reconfiguration that would renew dominance where the oppressed are the objectified subject. Instead, bell hooks suggests that we must enter this new and discursive endeavor with an understanding that our speech will be "troubled" that there exists no ready-made common language. As we draw from our "experiences," we recognize the "polyphonic" nature of this discourse, its cacophony, and its revelation. We invite students to enter this site of marginality and resistance where we then attempt to erase the imposed distinctions of colonized and colonizers (hooks 1990). We understand the doctrine and ideology that contain the conscious and unconscious power of the oppressor. We reconceptualize history, philosophy, literature, religion, and so forth that emanate from that center. We re-envision to learn, to understand, and to rethink the boundaries of that center. As a result, we have the possibility of a new location of radical openness.

While we must engage with the center, we also must confront severe obstacles and limitations created by it. The center's present discourse lacks a sense of human commonality and community but is hierarchial and describes a particular (white male culture) as generic. It contributes to a distorted sense of aesthetics, ideals, and heritage that focus on a Eurocentric, white male elite. It results in a treatment of gender differences and similarities as framed from an androcentric viewpoint. This perspective leads to an understanding of U.S. American history and culture wherein race and ethnicity are isolated as diversion from the so-called main story—the margin becomes an academic and social ghetto. Because we are all raised within this context, we approach the world grossly ignorant of a fuller range of human potential (Butler 1989).

To overcome these obstacles and to reconceptualize and re-envision, we must understand an even more troublesome aspect of this discourse. Language that seems to reject or even denounce such evils as racism, sexism, classism, heterosexism, and militarism also is used in their service. One such approach is to understand racism and/or sexism as an example of a common human condition where there is moral dysfunction. This dysfunction is understood or described as an alienation or digression from the deeper yearning for meaning and wholeness. On one level this is true. However, to pretend that the dysfunction has a similar effect on all people ignores the very power that is fundamental to racism, sexism, and other forms of oppression, and it obscures white racism and male sexism. This power is not what we can accurately describe in terms of material outcomes but expresses itself as authentic and transcendental values beyond reproach. They are above what we call history and beyond historical and epochal construction. Therefore, they are and by nature must be unchallenged (for example, by liberatory theory) in order to overcome history and provide a means for reconciliation with the true and good. This reconciliation as a resolution implies that there is an equivalency of dysfunction, that is, all human beings can be sexist, can be racist, as they fall away from a transcendental or metaphysical essence. As appealing and resonant as this approach is, it separates thoughts from things and projects spiritual alienation as responsible for the racism and sexism of oppressed and unoppressed alike. The primary solution then becomes a reconciliation with God, and in the end, with one another. This appeal is very problematic in its tendency to embrace the dominant metaphysical rationales of Western Christianity. It also is woefully inadequate because it dissembles the condition of the oppressed. For example, this framework suggests that the possible prejudice or hatred toward whites by people of color is responsible for or central to their own condition rather than a response to it. It implies that the radical and new location that would challenge the dominant center is a caricature inappropriate for serious consideration or as a locus for active change. This framework confirms its so-called "legitimacy" through a selective mining of history that may well include the experiences of those who are oppressed but as an echo, not as a critique of the tradition that participated in the original domination. Those mined experiences are refitted to reflect the authentic and unchallenged dominant perspective. Thus, the historical experience of the oppressed is separated from the context of their reality. The historical becomes ahistorical. Dominance, power, and oppression are obscured or even enhanced in its objectification.

Thus, we must exhibit great care when we identify the traditions of *others* that address these issues. For example, when we analyze the clash of Native American and European traditions and myths, we must understand the difference between them and why Christian principles, even at their most benign, would not tolerate Native American spiritual concepts. It is again problematic to impose the universality of historical or contemporary dominant centers on dissimilar perspectives created by very dissimilar experiences and contexts. For example, European genocide of Native American people and cultures has been explained as a misapplication of Western secular and/or spiritual principles. But such an explanation makes the so-called white man's values seemingly more important than the decimation of a people and value system that might have provided an alternative to what became the dominant way. It is to universalize the dominant myth of "in the beginning" without even taking into consideration different notions of time. To then equate the spiritual thoughts and words of the conquered with those of the conqueror (a marriage that most of the conquered would undoubtedly have rejected) is to once again embrace the dualism and bifurcation of the dominant culture. It is to adjust the dominant center to the site of resistance without relocation.

We should come back to the primary condition of *relocation* to its paradigm of reconceptualization. The process required by that paradigm is difficult but rewarding. Indeed it is an inclusive journey that opens our vision to the just society. Within the paradigm of reconceptualization, no institution, system, or body of thought is exempt from examination and reevaluation. Inclusion, therefore, is not accomplished only by the addition of a voice or an example that demonstrates the "contribution of the oppressed." Inclusion as reconceptualization also is the knowledge of those voices as they emanate from their location at the site of resistance. It is the recognition of the experience that is shaped by the relationship of the marginalized to the dominant center.

Inclusion also is an analysis of power both controlling and enabling because the shift to reconceptualization will occur only if our standpoint interrogates the *issues* of domination and power (hooks 1990). Such inclusion occurs at all levels and moments of *interaction*, be it secular, structural, or otherwise. It is the voice of Pizzan, de Zayas, King, Malcolm X, and others as they express *their* experience and philosophy in the context of their history without forcing a reconfiguration to that center from which they were excluded. It is the understanding of *all* parts of a society and the elements of human existence (hence commonality). When we permit that vision, we understand how a society will be severe in its patriarchy and chauvinism and also will construct its own philosophy of peace while designating reconceptualization as subversive to objective inquiry—one that is not separate from the other. To cite other examples in a typical American History survey course, we understand the Puritans who accept and practice genocide and also establish values accepted as paramount by their descendants—one is not separate from the other. We understand abolitionists who denounce slavery but not the moral evil of racism nor the controls of patriarchy; and we must come to terms with economic and social conflict as the major or first cause of the North opposing slavery to the point of Civil War—one is not separate from the other.

Reconceptualization for inclusive vision also compels us to reevaluate philosophical inquiry without exempting or presuming that there is some absolute truth that we have misplaced, that is, transcendent Western values. We ultimately conclude that such a truth exists. But it is quite problematic to denounce one mode of thought as secular and therefore unresponsive to the resolution of our problems, and to put forth another as above so-called history or human action and therefore removed from human challenge. Indeed it seems peculiar for one to describe, analyze, or project human behavior from a holistic concept while excluding a *complete* examination of the subtle (and not so sub-

tle), complex, and myriad factors that operate synergistically to produce
inequity and injustice. Denouncing social science as insignificant, irrelevant, or
subversive to our achieving this holistic knowledge is dismissive of the great
body of theory that has reexamined and is attempting to reconceptualize *all*
institutions. Repudiating the certain "traditions" that have sought a different
perspective promotes caricatures inappropriate in our mutual attempt to come to
more fully know our world. Societal structures reflect the interplay of values
that at least rationalize that those structures are reflections of the interplay of
secular and various moral ideologies of our culture. The conflicts and seeming
incongruities must be approached as reflections of all of the characteristics we
understand as common to human society.

INSTRUCTOR AS RECONCEPTUALIST

Among the most thorough efforts have been those of feminist and Marxist
theorists and their studies of race and ethnicity. Many of these have challenged elitist, Anglo-centric, male-dominated centers of power and have contributed new and fundamental knowledge of the dynamics of human society.
Each theoretical perspective, from its own emphasis, has explained human
interaction as much more than what the dominant center would insist.[1] As
each new paradigm has breached and then expanded the boundaries created by
dominant ideology and doctrine, its location has sometimes excluded as well
as included (for example, class is primary over gender which is primary over
race). While this process has demonstrated how imbedded ideology may be, it
has also proved the site of resistance, by its own paradigm, to be an inclusive
and transforming place. We are proceeding to a synthesis or matrix of theory
and experience. Virtually all of the authors in this volume have noted that
race, gender, and class are not independent of each other but are integral to an
individual and group's internal and external societal definition. Emerging
scholarship challenges all groups and individuals to understand, acknowledge, and be accountable for the reality of what we are and how we have
come to be. Along with other authors in this work, I offer a more inclusive perspective attempted in our world of ideas, because it does not exclude nor
exempt any idea from question.

   Appreciation of the traditions that have contributed to the form of our
world of ideas does not mean acceptance. Appreciation is the knowledge and
consideration of those values and ideas from the *site* of reconceptualization, a
site infused with the conviction that gender, race, and class define our world. It
is the knowledge of vulnerability and the search for the enabling power that
provides understanding and praxis. As each voice is less than complete, truth,
or at least authenticity emerges from the specific context of this conversation
among the marginalized at the site of resistance. Those in the dominant center
and those at the different margins must enter obliquely into the world of all *others* with the assuredness that our-commonality and difference will strengthen

our moral resolve. Hopefully we share that resolve equally because it may only come from dissimilar understandings. We become what we learn and we learn as we become.

CAVEAT AND WARNING

Within the site of resistance, the most dramatic examples of this obliqueness are the attempts by some feminist theories and analyses to include, or presume to include, women of color in their discussions of gender oppression. As Elizabeth Spelman (1988), Audre Lorde (1988), Nancie Caraway (1991), Johnnella Butler (1989) and others have written, there is no sisterhood if the most accessible voices of that sisterhood do not recognize the impact of race on both white women feminism and the experiences of women of color. While certainly emphasizing the incalculable contribution of feminist scholarship, most of those theoretical and concrete applications clearly have also been reductive to those who have lived the oppression of gender without the identifiable and concomitant oppression of race. White liberal feminists have too long minimized or ignored the fact of their membership in the dominant racial group and have subverted attempts by women of color to intersect race and gender in the "mainstream" feminist inquiry. A simple historical reconceptualization of white women's experience vis-à-vis slavery and segregation or the racial relationship between Anglo females and Latinas in the Southwest would (or should) engender at least a modest doubt about so-called sisterhood.

One could and should make the same critique concerning class; white, middle-class feminists again have overlooked or failed to identify the factor or agenda of class in their contemplation of gender. By generically concluding that male economic power is a characteristic of sexism, the location of the *woman* as *women* assumes an unmerited universality. White middle-class women undoubtedly enjoy economic advantage over white working-class women; many women of color have worked *for* white middle-class women without compelling evidence that the commonality of gender has produced economic empathy (Davis 1981). If reconceptualization and the search for matrix accurately describes feminist pedagogy, then the generic *woman* must be identified as her own combination of race, gender, and class experience, not as a singular representative of female history.

Similar critical focus on the ethnic studies variety of multicultural education reveals a *dominant center* in which race and class, but particularly race, emerge as the major explanation of historical experience and contemporary existence. The fetters of sexism prevent the inclusive, more accurate assessment of the historical parameters of people of color. Every group's racial history that has otherwise countered white supremist accounts is again more of a "universal" discourse of mostly male authorship that has subsumed or silenced the female voices of that community (with the notable exception of traditional, Native American society until the mid-nineteenth century).[2]

To correct this imbalance is a challenge to the heroic efforts of separate sites of resistance to the almost unapproachable and unrelenting white, elite, male, Eurocentric dominant center. That we must expand our own visions and learn about our own accountability is the most glaring testament to the power of oppression. This is the ultimate, most demanding, and (hopefully) enlightening aspect of the reconceptualist. The educator-instructor brings this questioning, reflective, and ongoing dynamic to the content of the curriculum on race, gender, and class. The effect on the student is overwhelming.

STUDENT PROFILE

Before describing that impact, I will attempt to present a "profile" of the student, including the resources (knowledge, facts, assumptions) that this generic creature brings to the classroom. Hopefully, the fictional status of this general person is apparent. The base from which I draw the following assessments and conclusions is twenty years' experience as a multiculturalist/reconceptualist practitioner in several universities with student populations ranging from 3,500 to 40,000, virtually all white, in Texas, Indiana, Illinois, Minnesota, Iowa, and Wisconsin. My most recent place is the University of Wisconsin, Platteville, whose degree/curriculum program is a mandate-of the University of Wisconsin System's *Design for Diversity* which requires organized instruction on race and ethnicity for every student's educational program. At UW-P, the faculty and administration expanded the mandate to include gender issues.[3] The required course for every first-year student is Race and Gender Issues in the United States of which I am the principal instructor. The course methodology combines three large lecture sections (160+) per semester with smaller discussion sessions (twenty-five maximum). The class evaluation consists of two essay exams and four student essays reacting to the discussion group dialogues. It is important to note that students must complete *all* essays but that the "grade" is only a notation of completion. Much of the contentions and profile described emanate from these essays and the discussion experience (to date, that means approximately 1,800 students and 7,200 student essays). The student demographics show a white, small middle class-large working class student-family background (144 students of color in 5,000 student population). Most are from central and southern Wisconsin and are often first generation college students. The male-female ratio is extraordinary; 63% white male due to the predominance of the schools of Engineering, Business, Industry, Communication, and the now declining school of Agriculture. If not for the College of Education, the UW-P would be even more imbalanced. The majority male demographic highlights even more the dissonance between the goal of an inclusive awareness and the reality of the exclusive nature of their so-called "education."

FIRST THE BAD NEWS

The first and indisputable characteristic of these students is that they "talk" about race and gender, racism, and sexism. Approximately 60% have discussed the issues with their families (mostly parents); approximately 88% dialogue with their friends. The primary source of the data that informs these exchanges is the popular media; that is, television news, infrequent reading of newspapers, and entertainment. Only 10% have experienced formal education in public schooling regarding race and gender, and that comes mostly from individual teacher-educator efforts, not from organized, ongoing curriculum based on even the tepid resources most accessible to the public school instructor (Student Survey, ES 101 Discussion Sessions, 1989-90). The content or framework described earlier is virtually absent in their past education (again, except for the *rare* public school instructor). The clear outcome of this experience is the absence of a discourse and paradigm by which they can even address the root explanations of race, gender, and class in the history of Western civilization and U.S. society.

Just as clear is students' assuredness that they are "not" racist or sexist. Their education has convinced them that racism and sexism are mute historical issues or are someone else's problem; this is often the KKK villain or the brutal misogynist, not their peer group. Interestingly, many students are convinced that their parents suffer from believed stereotypes but students feel/know they have moved beyond, as they express, this ignorance. Consequently, responsibility for racism and/or sexism does not rest within their moral expectations— except for the classic "American" reaction—"If I treat everyone fair, then I expect the same and everything will be good." Of course these views express an extremely limited understanding, not the least because the concept of fairness is an almost nonexistent perception of the conceptual notion of fairness. Dominant-center discourse forms their set of values and convinces them that their good society is freeing itself, where there is a problem, from the parameters of race, gender, and class oppression.

So, a third so-called certainty is that any person or group can be racist, and male or female can be sexist. Because racism and sexism are personal beliefs, an African American can be racist, a male can be sexist, and so on. The definitions of racism and sexism as created by the dominant center, those most responsible for racism and sexism (and class control), simply or insidiously eliminate power, particularly institutional power, as the critical dynamic of racism and sexism. The understanding of cultural hegemony, dominant thought, imposed morés, and structural perpetuation of the white, elite, Eurocentric male is, at best, described as a carping radical grievance.

One process toward the assumed solution of reciprocal fairness is to ignore a person's color or a person's sex when evaluating that individual. The suggestion that this is an example of unilateral, dominant-center discourse is a startling idea. I will never forget the terrible sincerity of a young, white female student at a small Wisconsin college, UW-River Falls, when she responded to my suggestion that she, as a resident hall assistant, should inform students of color about the opportunities in the Black Student Union or Latina(o) Student

Club. Her reply was, "I would no more call attention to the color of a minority than I would give food to a bulimic." The 'fair' or 'just' society for most of these students is, in reality, white culture, a white, male culture that labels its singular values as universal and the so-called obvious differences between groups as natural or resulting from irresponsibility of those labeled *the minorities* or *the women* or *the poor*. Moral mandates extend to a personal, but superficial, relationship that utilizes the dominant discourse: "I will ignore your color—I will be colorblind" (a male); or, I will respect you as a woman but question any attempts to transcend the universal (my imposed) barriers.

Most of the white students in this course have great difficulty in realizing the paradigm of their culturally and racially dominant group. As Gainen-Kurfis (1988) notes in the discussion of Peary's model, the students' dualism obliterates the complexity of their indoctrination. They recoil from the "possibility" that a person can hold more than one truth. That is, one can be racist and be against racism, one can be sexist and be against sexism. This rather simple example of critical thinking is quite contrary to most of the students, and unfortunately, evidence suggests that they will not arrive at a more relativistic level or ability in their university experience (Gainen-Kurfis 1988). So, in my experience their most resilient "answer" is equivalency. At the superficial level, such answers sound like the following: "I am called Honkey and that is as bad as me saying racial names"; "I tell racial and sexist jokes but so do women and minorities"; "If women were not subordinated then they would dominate me."

The most serious and/or intense reaction to the reconceptualist approach and content is by young white males. Most are not accustomed to "their" group being depicted as active agents in historical or contemporary analysis. There is no untoward discomfort in identifying people of color as groups active in their white perception of history as long as such action is categorized as abnormal or as marginal to such white males' center of experience. Nor is any significant critique offered to the dominant-center discourse of universality *until* it is described as imposed and authoritarian. Many young white males display the most amazing anger at the seemingly obvious connotation of the label *mankind*. This innocuous explanation (given the more horrific examples of patriarchy) of symbolic and domineering language is received as a shattering threat to the security of their civilization. I am caricaturing, obviously, but not to the extent one might expect if one had not witnessed this agony. As the educator proceeds with more complete analysis, including the concept of choice and accountability, the tension is palpable and it is most visceral when the issue is sexism.

Students defend and rationalize their perception of such discussions as attacks on their heretofore assured virtue and superiority by judging them to be "white male bashing." When the content of the curriculum of reconceptualization deconstructs the codified discourse of power, those who never questioned the assumed affirmation of their perceived dominance find solace in blaming the messenger who reconfigures the message. As Lana Rakow has astutely pointed out, the instructor becomes and is a major target for the dissatisfied (Rakow 1990). If the instructor is a person of color or a white female, a bond is broken, the bond of unstated but understood affirmation between white male student and white male instructor. The intrusion of the *Other* or the nontraditional teacher disturbs the race and gender partnership. There is no "acceptance" from the perceived authority figure, or at least the young white male perception is that of dissonance. The contract of gender and race identity is violated, and the party of the first part often feels betrayed. Then, as the content and instructor are merged in the interpolation of the student, the historical analysis becomes a *blaming* and *political opinion*. As one white male student put it, "if he [Mexican American instructor] were white, he would agree with us [the male white student]" (Discussion Session 1992).

The manifestations of these reactions are varied. They may be disruptive questions designed to detract or dissemble the classroom-course focus; they may be loud whispers to depict dissatisfaction and/or dismissal of issues being discussed; or they may be body language to convey dismay or anger. When the instructor is female, the challenge is to authority *and* credibility. The concepts and content of education about oppression, power, and hegemony are themselves played out by the group that must be historically described and by members of that group that are contemporaneous beneficiaries. It makes for a stormy environment.

NOW THE GOOD NEWS

The preceding depiction of white student values, knowledge, and beliefs might seem to represent a rather bleak opportunity for the understanding of the curriculum of reconceptualization. The harsh impact of this curriculum on classroom environment may appear (and does to many white teachers) as negative and counterproductive. This perception is often expressed as, "How can they be willing to learn if you are trashing their cultural values and sense of well-being" or "It seems this curriculum is judgmental." Of course I will refrain from suggesting the hidden meaning from those statements (as in, perhaps white educators do not wish to question their own accountability) although I will address this issue later. Just as the paradigm and the discourse of reconceptualization should be perceived as cacophony, so should the epistemology of white students not be viewed as homogenous. Without negating the previous contentions, I would now suggest other dimensions.

Many white female students express (written or verbal) discontent with male gender attitudes only when an opportunity is presented, such as a language that can describe their perceptions. They bring with them a vague uneasiness about their status (self-perceived and otherwise) as female. As the course content begins to convey the historical parameters of patriarchy and sexism, the discourse of the oppressor becomes more clarified. For some, it is the first moment of unnegotiated accountability in their own learning experience. (That is, the creation and perpetuation of patriarchy is presented as a generalized, intentional Eurocentric, male act.) The conflict of their own epistemologies, the paradox of so-called ideal learning as an independent agent with the reality of being indoctrinated through the patriarchal prism is suddenly validated. The positive reaction by many of the white females is obvious and, at times, breathtaking. This revelation gives impetus to the bridge (or leap) to the matrix of race, gender, and class. If men are more likely, indeed, are sexist by the imposed values, structures, and benefits of patriarchy, then perhaps white persons, including women, are susceptible to the same benefits of white racism, white supremacy. So, those who are oppressed by one mode (women by patriarchy) can be the oppressor by another (white women by white racism).

Another learning dynamic now intersects or, more candidly, invades the customary educational environment of the white male student. The glimmer of the matrix by white female students underlines Belenky's analysis of women's way of knowing and collides with Peary's schemata and (to some extent) Kohlberg's thesis of male epistemology and moral reasoning (Gainen-Kurfis 1988). The language of connected knowing and separate knowing are clearly evident as male and female students discuss, argue, and shout about the history of their histories. The volatility of the exchanges illuminate the very issues that the content and curriculum attempt to reveal. Some students literally grope for more secure moorings as others are determined to move away from and beyond the Eurocentric bastions. The discourse of reconceptualization, of the matrix of race, gender, and class provides that direction and alters the obviously more appealing, but also lethargic, terrain of the traditional American culture. An exchange in one of the discussion groups poignantly illustrates the dilemma.

> *Discussion Leader:* Who is the usual perpetrator of sexual violence?
> *White Male Student:* Oh, here we go again with the white male bashing.
> *White Female Student:* You mean, you call fact and truth, 'white male bashing'?
> *White Male Student:* [No answer]

In that same discussion group, and with the same (and to his credit) young white male, another exchange:

> *Discussion Leader:* If we want to understand opportunity, how do we discuss it?
> *New White Male Student:* Everyone has the same opportunity.
> *Discussion Leader:* So, history has no impact and if we eliminate that, then we can only evaluate others by our own experience—if you are a white male then . . .
> *White Male Student from Previous Exchange:* Then we might blame others or judge others as failures without understanding the limits we [white males] impose.

A very valuable and encouraging moment emerges from the conflict and resistance that would not have occurred without that confrontation.

THE INSTRUCTOR AND THE CLASSROOM

Christine Sleeter (1991) has eloquently informed us about the capacity of multicultural education to empower, "to develop the [ability] and power to construct their [students] own understanding of themselves and the world . . . to question why things are as they are, and how they might be different, and to hear and value the voices of those whose life histories have been very different from theirs" (Sleeter 1991). The radical educator obviously comes to the classroom with a conceptually different epistemology and understanding of race, gender, and class but must meet most students at their own dramatically different location. Freire emphasizes that the teacher must begin at that place and work with students in a dialogic process to achieve a coalition of mutual understanding of the reality of the human experience (Freire 1969). The conflict or conundrum for the instructor is glaring: we cannot permit the acceptance of racism and sexism with the cliché that a balanced education should allow choice, but we surely must avoid so-called indoctrination.

However, the radical instructor with the curriculum of reconceptualization is not a robotic calculator to assure balance, avoid politicalization, and/or to maintain an equilibrium of truth and harmony. Members of dominant groups benefit from their position. That fact is a political certainty; and the absence of such clarity in the paradigm of American education is just as certain. The numbing discourse of patriarchal, white supremacist, and elitist rhetoric cloaked as objective inquiry governs the process by which students learn and evaluate. The presentation of a different knowledge, of a more inclusive understanding is a threat, of course, to those who have been assured that they deserve the authority they utilize. It is a devisive and political act to suggest otherwise; it is also subversive for the subject of that authority to consider rejection of the unearned privilege of being white, or male, or white male, or elite white male, or middle-class white female, or male of color vis à vis female of color. It is also a shocking revelation for the student to share the confusion of the instructor. As Johnnella Butler (1989) charges us:

> All the conflicting emotions, the sometimes painful movement from the familiar to the unfamiliar, are experienced by the teacher as well. We have been shaped by the same damaging, informed view of the world as our students. Often, as we try to resolve their conflicts, we are simultaneously working through our own. Above all, we must demand honesty of ourselves before we can succeed (160).

So, we must be focused and unyielding in our determination to establish the discourse of liberatory pedagogy and to bring that language to the classroom. We do not negotiate the historical and contemporary "presence" of race, gender, and class in American society. We do not engage in *blaming* but we also do not avoid the description or *naming* of the actors and their roles in the play.

CONCLUSION

The hope and the basis for understanding and addressing the issues of race, gender, and class as imposed and perpetuated modes of oppression is to establish the paradigm and discourse of reconceptualization. This analysis of the intersection of race, gender, and class can inform the goal of education as social reconstruction (Sleeter and Grant 1988). The classroom then becomes the location for an experience that must be volatile and conflicting by the very nature of the curriculum content. To avoid or dissemble that content is to deny the reality of the issues addressed; and that denial is the unspoken but accepted value that power is not willingly surrendered or even shared. Most white students (and definitely most white male students) will recoil at the suggestion that they are members of a dominant group; most will reject the suggestion that they are accountable for the benefits of their history that includes oppression in their society; most will express dismay when the opinion and what they consider to be the knowledge they utilize are exposed as the discourse of the oppressor. The result may be anger, resentment, and confusion toward the instructor, toward each other, and possibly toward the idea of resolution itself.

That moment is the opportunity to challenge the authoritarian, ironclad canon of their learning experience. It is the moment to dissemble the "paradigm of thought by which children are taught not to see what they see" (Williams 1991). It is the moment to offer a persuasion that begins by voicing of the site of resistance that seeks to embrace the difference within our history and the truth of that difference. It is the moment to present a real choice between the possibility of an inclusive society that endorses the power of enablement or the existing values that depend upon the power of dominance and control. We should not be dismayed that many will choose the latter, and we should not therefore fear that outcome. We should be just as positive that many will recognize their opportunity to make new choices and pursue new understanding. The new understanding emerges from that paradigm whose power to transform matches the passion and energy that will sustain its vision.

NOTES

I wish to acknowledge the contributions of Lisa Peck (Ph.D) toward the narrative on Reconceptualization.

1. There are many authors whom one could cite. A very selective list would include: bell hooks, Angela Davis, Elizabeth Spelman, Allison Jaggar, Andrea Nye, Mary Field Belenky, Nancie Caraway, Maxine Baca-Zinn, Paula Gunn Allen, Dexter Bell, Paula Rothenberg, Vicki Ruiz, Elizabeth Higgenbotton, Christine Sleeter, Patricia Williams, James H. Cone, Leonard Harris, Mario Barreta, Arnulfo de Leon, Ronald Takaki, Patricia Hill Collins, Margaret Anderson, Johnnella Butler, Cornel West, Peggy McIntosh, Bonnie Anderson, M. E. Hawkesworth, Judith Zinsser, Catherine McKinnon, Audre Lorde, and Paulo Freire.

2. Multicultural inquiry, including its most well known subfield, ethnic studies, has been informed primarily by male scholars of color with primary emphasis on race as the fundamental center of historical understanding. While feminists of color have recently produced a much needed critique of multicultural studies with emphasis on the matrix of race, gender, and class, the patriarchal/racial theory imbalance remains. A relatively recent concept of multiculturalism, social reconstruction, does attempt a more substantive reanalysis with race, gender, and class as interrelated components. This raises the question of whether social reconstructionism is by definition apart from multiculturalism rather than a new version.

3. The state of Wisconsin educational system requires that every student receiving a degree in elementary/secondary education fulfill the "human relations" mandate. This includes curriculum and field experience specifically on designated groups, such as African Americans, Native Americans, the physically disadvantaged, etc. and et al. There is no certain or emphasized organizing principle; each college of education constructs its own program to fit under a very large, vague umbrella. The curriculum may be any strain of multiculturalism, from "ethnic food festivals and heroes of history" to timely social reconstructionist perspective. The programmatic relationship between the Design for Diversity and the Human Relations Mandate is haphazard and problematic.

REFERENCES

Allsup, C. and T. Russo. 1989, November. Teaching diversity through pluralism: A model for teaching about racism. Paper presented at University Teaching Improvement Council Conference, The Challenge of Diversity: Curriculum Development For the 21st Century, Madison, Wisconsin.

Andersen, M. and P. H. Collins. 1992. *Race, class, and gender, an anthology*. Belmont, CA: Wadsworth.

Belenky, M. et al. 1986. *Women's ways of knowing: Self, voice, and mind*. New York: Basic Books.

Butler, J. E. 1989. Transforming the curriculum: Teaching about women of color. In *Multicultural education; issues and perspectives*. Edited by James A. Banks and Cherry A. McGee Banks, 145-63. Boston: Allyn and Bacon.

Caraway, N. 1991. *Segregated sisterhood: Racism and the politics of American feminism*. Knowsville: University of Tennessee Press.

Davis, A. 1981. *Women, race, and class*. New York: Vintage Books.

Freire, P. 1969. *Pedagogy of the oppressed*. New York: Continuum Pub.

Gainen-Kurfis, J. 1988. Critical thinking: Theory, practice, and possibilities. In *Developmental Foundations of Critical Thinking*. Edited by Jonathon D. Fife. Washington, DC: Association for the Study of Higher Education.

hooks, bell. 1990. *Yearning: Race, gender, and cultural politics*. Boston: South End Press.

Lorde, A. 1988. Age, race, class, and sex: Women redefining difference. In *Racism and sexism, an integrated study*. Edited by Paula Rothenberg. New York: St. Martin's Press.

Rakow, L. 1990. Gender and race in the classroom: Teaching way out of line. In *Teaching Forum*. Edited by Marilyn Annucci. Madison, WI: University Teaching Improvement Council, University of Wisconsin System.

Sleeter, C., ed. 1991. *Empowerment through multicultural education*. New York: State University of New York Press.

Sleeter, C. and C. Grant. 1988. *Making choices for multicultural education: Five approaches to race, class, and gender*. Columbus, OH: Merrill Publishing Company.

Spelman, E. 1988. *Inessential woman: Problems of exclusion in feminist thought*. Boston: Beacon Press.

Williams, P. 1991. *The alchemy of race and rights*. Cambridge: Harvard University Press.

IMPACT AND IMPLICATIONS
OF BIOGRAPHY FOR PEDAGOGY

6

<small>Carmen Montecinos</small> ───────────────

Multicultural Teacher Educ
for a Culturally Diverse Teaching ⌐ ⌐⌐⌐

> [T]he habit of ignoring race is understood to be a graceful, even
> generous, liberal gesture. To notice is to recognize an already dis-
> credited difference. (Toni Morrison, from *Playing in the Dark*, 10)

At the core of multicultural approaches to schooling are two related premises. First, it is believed that the development of pedagogical practices must take into account students' cultural background. Second, it is believed that a student's cultural background mediates the way in which he or she comes to understand, interpret, and respond to school curricula. While these two premises have been well acknowledged in regard to the schooling of a culturally diverse K-12 student population, they are less apparent when one turns to multicultural teacher education. More often than not, empirical studies describing teachers' participation in multicultural education courses tend to ignore the salience of ethnicity as a basis for teachers' participation in these courses. When teachers' ethnicity is considered, by only making *whiteness* problematic, these studies leave the impression that they are confined to the education of white teachers who will then work with ethnic minority children. As a consequence, the needs and perspectives of minority preservice and in service teachers have been largely ignored.

My concern is that multicultural teacher-education research has failed to advance a discourse that is committed to the education of a culturally diverse teaching force. As an educational reform movement, multicultural education will fail if the cultural backgrounds of all the members of the teaching force are not considered (Dilworth 1990). If the current efforts of schools and colleges of education across the United States to recruit and retain minority teachers are to be successful, researchers in teacher education cannot continue the "habit of ignoring race."

In this chapter, I first quantitatively summarize the ways in which a core of eighteen empirical studies on multicultural teacher education described the ethnic background of the participants. Since these studies described multicultural education courses, I assume that this body of research reflects multicultural teacher education practices. Next, I attempt to explain multicultural teacher tion's inattention to teachers' ethnicity by arguing that it stems from an overly technical view of teaching that has permeated much of teacher education. The problem is that a technical model of teaching, one that by definition attempts to negate the fundamentally social character of teaching, the teacher, and the student cannot in any serious way encompass multicultural education.

In the last three sections of the chapter I will discuss some implications of making teachers' ethnic group membership a significant factor in the development of multicultural teacher education curriculum and pedagogy. The first implication is that given concrete differences that exist between ethnic minority groups educators should not take for granted that minority teachers, in contrast to their nonminority colleagues, *do* know how to teach children who are culturally different from themselves. A second implication is that the selection of content for multicultural education programs needs to be undertaken in relationship to the ethnic backgrounds of *all* course participants. If indeed students' cultural backgrounds matter, then the fact is that multicultural teacher education must, at some level, differ for minority and nonminority teachers (Sleeter 1992). A third implication is that researchers need to make participants' ethnicity an important aspect of the interpretation of data. If indeed students' backgrounds matter, then we cannot expect minority and nonminority teachers to respond in exactly the same way to the curriculum.

EMPIRICAL STUDIES IN MULTICULTURAL TEACHER EDUCATION

Through an ERIC database search and leads from references in related articles, I searched for studies that described how preservice and in-service teachers responded to their participation in a multicultural education course, workshop, immersion program, or staff development. I was able to identify and obtain a complete copy of eighteen empirical studies that described multicultural teacher education practices (see table 6.1). All of these had been published either in professional journals or, in one case, as a book chapter. Obviously, these studies do not exhaust the literature but they can, collectively, help illustrate some of the weaknesses of current discourse on multicultural teacher education that stem from its ambiguous attention to teachers' ethnic/social identities.

Table 6.1 presents data on the number of teachers who participated in each study and these participants' ethnic/racial backgrounds. Sixteen of these eighteen studies provided data on sample size, comprising a total of 1,194 teachers: 80% preservice ($n=960$) and 20% inservice ($n=234$). Ten (55%) of the studies did not provide any reference to their participants' ethnicity. One study indicated that all participants were white (Ross and Smith 1992), and a second referred to participants as being monocultural (Fuller and Ahler 1987). Three studies included participants from various ethnic backgrounds but authors did not disaggregate data by race/ethnicity (Burstein and Cabello 1989; Larke 1990; and Sleeter 1992). In one study the authors emphasized multicultural education for nonnative Alaskan American teachers but did not clarify whether all of their participants were nonnatives (Noordhoff and Kleinfeld 1990). Only two studies (11%) that included minority and nonminority teachers located trainees' responses to training in terms of their ethnic backgrounds (Washington 1981; Cochran-Smith and Lytle 1992).

Eighty-seven percent (n=1042) of the teachers studied were constructed as "ethnicless" when authors failed to indicate participants' ethnicity. Participants' ethnic identities were more often described in studies that included in-service (four out of seven studies) as compared to preservice teachers (two out of twelve studies). Cochran-Smith and Lytle (1992) included both in-service and preservice teachers; however, they only identified the ethnic backgrounds of in-service teachers. The ethnic backgrounds of those 13% or 152 teachers identified were as follows: white, 73%; black, 19%; Hispanic, 6.5%; Asian < 1%; Other < 1%; and Native American 0%.

Researchers can be seen as constructing a reality of multicultural teacher education that can be defined both in terms of what has been made explicit and what has been omitted. Ostensibly, authors have particular intentions or motivations for including and excluding information gathered in a study. As a reader, however, I am not privileged to their unstated intentions or rationale for excluding data related to their participants' ethnic identities. I can comment on the consequences of such a practice.

THE SOCIAL CONSTRUCTION OF MULTICULTURAL TEACHING

The Limits of a Technical View of Teaching

An overly technical view of teaching has permeated much of teacher education (Liston and Zeichner 1987). From this perspective, teaching is conceptualized as a process of solving classroom problems by applying correct, research-derived techniques (Noordhoff and Klienfeld 1990). From this perspective, knowledge resides in the hands of experts who have a claim to authority. This claim rests on two premises: ownership of a domain of a morally neutral set of facts and the belief that those facts represent lawlike generalizations that can be applied to particular cases (MacIntyre 1984). Teacher education is, therefore, concerned with constructing an abstract teacher whose expertise is defined by the possession of knowledge created and transmitted by experts. The extent to which teachers can successfully acquire expert's knowledge, and therefore engage in multicultural practices, is related to the adequacy of the teaching techniques employed by teacher educators. Ignoring the salience of teachers' ethnic identities in their construction of multicultural practices is congruent with this technical view of teacher education.

McDiarmid (1992) has noted the paradox of asking teachers to rid themselves of stereotypical thinking about minority groups while at the same time asking them to learn about the cultural patterns of these groups. The inclusion of course content that emphasizes generalizations about an ethnic group is

TABLE 6.1

Number of Participants by Race/Ethnicity in Eighteen Empirical Studies on Multicultural Teacher Education

Study	Year	Preservice/ Inservice	Race/ Ethnicity	African American	Asian American	Latino/a	White American	Other	Total
Baker	1973	Preservice	No data						299
Baker	1977	Preservice	No data	Of these teachers, 229 were the participants in her 1973 study.					520
Cross & Deslonde	1978	Inservice	No data						82
Bennett	1979	Preservice	No data						39
Washington	1981	Inservice		24			25		49
Henington	1981	Preservice	No data						73
Fuller & Ahler	1987	Preservice	References are made to the training of monocultural students and their Northern European ancestry.						?
Burstein & Cabello	1989	Inservice		2	1	4	8	1	16
Grottkau & Nickolai-May	1989	Preservice	No data						122
Cooper, Beare & Thorman	1990	Preservice	No data						103
Larke	1990	Preservice				5	46		51

(continued on next page)

TABLE 6.1 (continued)

Study	Year	Preservice/ Inservice	Race/ Ethnicity	African American	Asian American	Latino/a	White American	Other	Total
Larke, Wiseman & Bradley	1990	Preservice	No data						22
Noordhoff & Kleinfeld	1990	Preservice	References are made to the training of non-native students. It is not clear if all of their participants are non Native American.					24	
Mahan & Rains	1990	Inservice	No data						45
Cochran-Smith & Lytle	1992	Both	Does not provide explicit information on sample size. They quoted 6 teachers (3 white, 2 African American, 1 Puerto-Rican). They also mentioned the work of five African-American teachers. Two student teachers are quoted without locating their ethnicity.						
McDiarmid	1992	Inservice	No data						12
Ross & Smith	1992	Preservice					6		6
Sleeter	1992	Inservice		3		2	26		30
TOTALS		Preservice n=960 (80%) Inservice	No data n=1042 % Total=87	n=29 % Total=2.4 % Identifed=19	n=1 % Total < 1 % Identified < 1	n=10** % Total=0.8 % Identifed=6.5	n=111 % Total=9.2 % Identifed=73	n=1 % Total < 1 % Identified < 1	n=1194*

* There is overlap of 299 students in both of Baker's studies. They are counted only once. Participants in the Cochran-Smith study are not included since their numbers could not be clearly established.

** Six were described as Mexican-American and four as "Hispanic."

consistent with the technical approach's belief that social life in general, and teaching in specific, can be reduced to lawlike generalizations. These types of generalization serve the purpose of giving the illusion that the expert, in this case a teacher who possess that knowledge, is in a better position to predict and control the learning of the ethnic minority child.

As noted by Liston and Zeichner (1987), within a technical perspective teachers are not encouraged to interrogate critically the social arrangements that shape their lives and the lives of their students. From a technical perspective, the purpose of multicultural teacher education becomes one of helping trainees acquire technical mastery of knowledge and practices that will meet the needs of diverse learners. Issues such as racism, higher dropout rates among ethnic minority students, and other social problems that must be redressed by multicultural education are thought capable of resolution by the application of correct techniques. Students then become subjects on which teachers apply these techniques. Students are expected to respond to these techniques in uniform and predictable ways. The multiplicity of ways in which racism is constructed and enacted by situated social actors is, thus, negated. The racism of the oppressed and the racism of the oppressor are then assumed to be the same, negating the social-structural basis of racism.

As Ferdman (1990) noted, attending to ethnic diversity in education involves attending to the role of culture in the individual's transaction with the social world. If it fails to interrogate the social forces that shape these transactions, how can a technical view of teaching in any serious way encompass multicultural education? Even in its most conservative form, the contributions approach described by Banks (1991), multicultural education cannot be fully accounted for by a technical view of teaching. Banks (1991) states that the contributions approach is characterized by the addition of ethnic heroes into the curriculum. There is no technical knowledge that teachers can appeal to in deciding who is a hero for an ethnic group since there is no so-called essential hero that we can speak of. Rather, teachers' choices of people to be included in the curriculum are inextricably entangled with their values, interests, and intentions. For example, what technical knowledge can teachers use to decide whether to include Martin Luther King and/or Malcom X in their curriculum? None, because such a choice stems from political considerations, not technical ones.

Giving Centrality to Teachers' Social Locations

Banks (1991), Sleeter and Grant (1988), and others have proposed approaches to multicultural education that seek social transformation. From such a perspective, Ladson-Billings and Henry (1990) defined culturally relevant teaching as that which "uses the students' culture to empower students to be able to critically examine educational content and process and ask what role they have in creating a truly democratic and multicultural society" (82). Such a view of multicultural teacher education gives centrality to teachers' voices in the con-struction of meaning rather than seeing teachers as spokespersons for the experts. From this perspective, multicultural education gives centrality to pro-cesses for interrogating the formation of particular forms of social relation-ships, such as racism.

Recognizing the role that teachers' social identity plays in the construction of knowledge involves recognizing its prominence in the teacher educators' own construction of knowledge. It exposes experts' knowledge as embedded in particular social interests and intents. The authoritative voice of the teacher educator can no longer rest in his or her claim to a morally neutral set of facts he or she has generated. To understand teachers' social identities as mediating their understanding of teaching is to understand research-produced knowledge as one more voice in a conversation about teaching, not as the only authoritative voice.

Multicultural education that seeks social transformation involves social actors who understand and challenge the social construction of racism, sexism, difference, et cetera. This can happen when teacher educators recognize the plu-rality of meanings that can be constructed in their courses. The heterogeneity that multicultural education seeks to foster, however, is negated when teacher educators transmit knowledge of teaching practices that promote a research-based normative stance toward teaching. As noted by Cochran-Smith and Lytle (1992), teacher educators who posit monolithic solutions to complex social problems contradict the concept of diversity. As stated by Heshusius (1991) teaching, in this case taking a multicultural approach to teacher education, has more to do with recognizing, respecting, and trying to make explicit teachers interests, struggles, and intentions than with denying their collusion in the choices teachers make about teaching.

Teachers' Identities

I chose to examine these research studies' descriptions of the participants' identities by focusing on ethnic identity for two reasons. First, multicultural teacher education is, most often, understood as preparing teachers who can meet the needs of an ethnically/racially diverse school age population. Concerns with the preparation of teachers who address diversity that result from factors such as social class, gender, abilities, and their interactions are less frequently dealt with in this literature (Sleeter and Grant 1988). Second, I was interested in ascertaining the extent to which the experiences and perspectives of ethnic minority teachers were being addressed. I am aware, however, of the limitations of searching for identity by just looking at ethnicity.

A teacher's background is defined and continuously redefined along a multiplicity of dimensions other than ethnicity. In fact, I contend that given the diversity found within an ethnic group, research and practice in multicultural teacher education need to consider the broader concept of teachers' social identities. Social identity involves "those aspects of an individual's self-image that derive from the social categories to which he perceives himself as belonging" (Tajfel and Turner 1986, 16, cited in Ferdman 1990). According to Ferdman (1990), ethnic identity is that part of the individual's social identity that is linked to membership in an ethnic group. Educators must not ignore the salience of ethnicity as a basis for students' participation in social life. They cannot, however, see ethnic minority students as unidimensional individuals defined solely on the basis of their ethnic group membership. Educators who do so risk prejudging these students and further contributing to stereotypical thinking.

Minority voices, as white voices, are polyphonic. As noted by Ladson-Billings and Henry (1990), not all African American teachers are committed to what they call "liberatory pedagogy" for African American children. Some African American teachers have low expectations of African American children and see their roles as preparing them to adapt to existing social arrangements rather than to challenge them. A study by Ross and Smith (1992) is one of the many examples that show diversity in the ways white educators view the teaching of children culturally different from themselves. The views of the six white preservice teachers they interviewed ranged from denying the impact of ethnicity on students' school achievement to expressions of concerns about the impact of societal inequalities upon the achievement of minority children.

These findings suggest that understanding how teachers construct the teaching of the *Cultural Other* involves understanding their social location beyond an ethnic dimension. Rather than constructing an *ethnicless* teacher, a generic white or ethnic minority teacher, teacher education needs to examine how a teacher's social identity frames her or his understanding of multicultural education. It is by attending to teachers' social identities that we can further our understanding of how multicultural teaching is constructed by situated social actors.

In this chapter, I use the term *minority teachers* to avoid an enumeration of the diverse ethnic/racial groups comprised under that social category. By using this term, I am not essentializing ethnic minority teachers. My intention in using the term is to make the writing more clear. The reader is invited to interchange the term for African American, Mexican American, Puerto Rican, Cuban American, Navajo, Hopi teacher, and so forth. The same rationale holds true for my use of the term *white teacher*. Nor am I essentializing "whiteness" or implying that all white people are alike.

BICULTURALISM IS NOT MULTICULTURALISM

The Marginalization of Minority Teachers

According to Grant and Secada (1990), minority teachers represent 12-14% of the U.S. teaching force. They represent, nevertheless, only about 3 % of all participants of the studies I reviewed for this paper and 27% of those whose ethnic status was identified: 71% were black, 25% were described as Mexican Americans or as "Hispanic," none were Native Americans, and only one teacher was identified as having a Filipino ancestry.[1]

The scant empirical attention given to minority teachers in the multicultural education literature is consistent with the general paucity of empirical evidence on the development and practices of minority preservice and in-service teachers (Dilworth 1990; Foster 1990; Grant and Secada 1990). Multicultural teacher education research has contributed to minority teachers' invisibility through three related practices: (1) by considering that teachers' ethnic backgrounds are irrelevant, (2) by only problematizing *whiteness*, and (3) by saying very little about the views of minority teachers.

The limited attention given to minority teachers could stem from the fact that they represent a small portion of the teaching force. It could also reflect a variety of misconceptions, such as: (a) unless explicitly trained, white educators do not know how to teach children who are different from themselves whereas minority educators do; (b) white educators will practice in culturally diverse environments, and minority educators will practice in homogeneous environments; and (c) white educators have biases and prejudices that need to be unmasked, and minority educators are free from such things.

Making Minority Teachers' Experiences Problematic

The impact of a white teacher's limited experiences with cultural diversity upon his or her ability to teach ethnic minority children has been discussed at length in the multicultural teacher education literature. What has not been mentioned is the nature of minority teachers' cross-cultural experiences with cultures other than white-European. A minority's biculturalism, however, should not be equated with multiculturalism.

The literature available on minority teachers' practices is more revealing of single-ethnic group pedagogy than of multicultural pedagogy. For example, the works of Ladson-Billing and Henry (1990), Foster (1990), and Delpit (1988) provide insight into African American school teachers' understandings and practices. What remains to be investigated is whether aspects of culturally relevant pedagogy for one ethnic group can be transferred to the teaching of children from other minority groups. In other words, the fact that an African American teacher can effectively work with African American children should not lead to the foregone conclusion that she can, therefore, effectively work with children who are members of other ethnic minority groups.

In her discussion of the disjuncture between the school and the community, Sleeter (1992b) noted that none of the twenty-six white teachers who participated in a multicultural staff development program she investigated lived in racial minority communities. She neglected to mention, however, where the four minority teachers lived.[2] I find these types of descriptions problematic because they fail to acknowledge differences that exist within members of one minority group and between minority groups. They assume, therefore, that a minority educator has a privileged understanding of the positions of others who might come from his or her same ethnic group but who differ from him or her in terms of social class, religion, gender, sexual orientation, region of the country, and so forth. They also assume that the politics of a common minority experience will outweigh the politics of national origin, race, class, assimilation, gender, and so forth.

The so-called Latino population in the United States represents a good example of the concrete differences that exist among members of an ethnic group. Shorris (1992) notes the cultural distinctions between "the quiet formality of the Mexicans and the aggressiveness of the Caribbean" (24). Socioeconomic data show differences among Latino subgroups from various national origins; median family income ranges from $19,933 for Puerto Ricans to $31,262 for Cubans (Shorris 1992). Discrepancies in political attainment among the various subgroups are exemplified in the following comment by Stepick (1992): "Cubans in Miami . . . have appropriated political power more quickly and more thoroughly than any other first-generation immigrant group in U.S. history" (40). This diversity, however, does not preclude communication: "So there are no Latinos, no Hispanics. There are only Mexicans, Cubans, Puerto Ricans, Dominicans, Salvadorans and so forth. Each is different and alike . . . they are not so different that they cannot communicate and not so alike that they have nothing to say to each other" (Shorris 1992, 24). This diversity does suggest that a descriptor such as "Latina" conveys very little information regarding the social background of the teacher so described or about her ability to effectively teach "Latino" children.

One could assume that because of the concern that multicultural education has with minority students' cultures, minority teachers would show greater commitments to its implementation than their nonminority counterparts. Establishing this, however, can be difficult because there are different versions of multicultural education and because teachers may be committed to some and not others. Swisher (1984) compared the attitudes of Native American teachers toward multicultural education to those of nonnative teachers. She found that the two groups did not differ. The definition provided to them, however, was one that primarily reflected what Banks (1991) labeled the "contributions approach": "learning about the language, diet . . . and code of ethics of many different groups. The purpose . . . understand, accept, and appreciate differences" (4). If, as Sleeter (1993) suggests, minority teachers are more likely to address issues of racism, then I wonder whether Swisher would, have found differences among groups if the definition of multicultural education given to the teachers had more explicitly addressed questions of racism, as in Banks's (1991) social transformation approach. The point to keep in mind is that understanding how minority and nonminority teachers respond to multicultural education cannot be divorced from an understanding of the specific version of multicultural education they are taught in teacher education.

In the only study I reviewed that statistically controlled for teachers' race, it was found that teachers' race was strongly related to their attitudes toward multicultural education (Washington 1981). African American in-service teachers had a more positive attitude than their white counterparts. After participating in a multicultural training program, African American teachers increased their use of multicultural material, whereas white teachers didn't. There were no differences between groups on measures of multicultural classroom behaviors.

Demographic data on immigration patterns undoubtedly show that minority teachers, as well as white teachers, will work in classes populated by children from diverse cultural backgrounds. Minority teachers' backgrounds, like white teachers' backgrounds, influence the expectations they hold for students. Attending to how minority educators construct the Cultural Other and the teaching of children culturally different from themselves is, therefore, critical. Researchers and teacher educators must acknowledge that white and ethnic minority teachers' ethnicity is intertwined with the construction of knowledge for multicultural education. At this point, however, we have a minimal understanding of issues related to the preparation of minority teachers who can take multicultural approaches. In the next two sections of the paper I will explore areas of inquiry that can help reverse this situation.

ADDRESSING TEACHER DIVERSITY IN THE MULTICULTURAL TEACHER EDUCATION CURRICULA

Recently, a friend and colleague of mine was describing to me her efforts to get a mentorship program underway that would give student teachers under her supervision opportunities for meaningful interactions with adult members of the local African American community. I asked her if all the student teachers were white, to which she responded that one of them was African American. When I asked her what she understood this African American student's participation in this project to be, she was startled, she had never thought about it! She recognized that not only had she taken for granted that this student would know how to engage in multicultural education, but also in planning course activities, she had marginalized him.

From my readings of these research studies on multicultural teacher education I get the impression that my friend is in good company. Advocates of multicultural education recommend that the curriculum relate to and draw from the experiential backgrounds of the learners (Sleeter and Grant 1988). More often than not, however, the multicultural teacher education curricula seems to have an all-white audience in mind. For all practical purposes, much of the current literature on multicultural teacher education seems to address the question, "What can we do for white teachers to prepare them to work with children different from themselves?"

Interrogating Course Content

In order to develop a multicultural teacher education curriculum that is concerned with the education of a culturally diverse teaching force, teacher educators need to ask themselves: To what extent does the curriculum offered reflect educational needs of teachers from diverse cultural backgrounds? I will draw from three studies to illustrate how this issue can be investigated.

Burstein and Cabello (1989) described the various components of a course designed to help teachers develop awareness, knowledge, and skills for teaching diverse learners. These authors did not discuss the extent to which course activities were culturally responsive to the diverse backgrounds of course participants. For example, 38% of the teachers in this study prior to training explained minority students' school performance from a cultural deficiency point of view and 50% understood it as a mismatch between the home culture and the school culture. Were these different understandings related to teachers' ethnicity? Since the author did not disaggregate the data, this question cannot be the answer. Previous research has shown that the primary difference between white teachers and minority teachers who participated in staff development on multicultural education was that the latter rejected conservative explanations of racial inequality (Sleeter 1992). These findings pose an important curricular question. How can these differences be translated into teacher education practices?

Noordhoff and Kleinfeld (1990) noted that the nonnative Alaskan American preservice teachers whom they worked with have to contend with deciding what aspects of the Western culture are worth teaching to Native Alaskan American children. Is this a dilemma unique to nonnative teachers? Do Native teachers have a monolithic view concerning the balance between teaching the local culture and the Western culture, or do they also have to struggle with this issue? More generally, what are the similarities and differences among native and nonnative teachers' approaches to issues related to multicultural education? How can our understanding of these approaches improve current discourse on multicultural teacher education?

McDiarmid (1992) described some of the content covered in the multicultural education workshop that the Los Angeles Unified School District offers to its teachers. In this program, as in several others studies I reviewed, a group of sessions were devoted to the presentation of information on specific minority groups (e.g., Grottkau and Nickolai-Mays 1989). Knowing about the large population of Mexican Americans in the Los Angeles area, I wondered whether there were any members of this ethnic group in the cohort of 110 teachers he followed. If there were any Mexican American teachers, did they benefit from attending those sessions that described them? Would it have been more productive for them to have the presenters address issues such as social, political, and economic differences among the various Latino subcultures in their school district?

More generally, research needs to examine whether, and under what circumstances the ethnic composition of course participants influences the selection of specific cultural groups to be described in the curriculum. The research also needs to examine what types of knowledge should be included by presenters who talk about these groups. For example, what cultural patterns, diversity stemming from social class, gender, or level of acculturation within groups, or interactive processes among groups occurs? Additionally researchers need to focus on whether a teacher's ethnic identity has an impact on the approach to multicultural education that one embraces.

Current demographic trends indicate that schools and colleges of education are required to teach an increasingly homogeneous, white and female teaching force (Grant and Secada 1990). This fact, however, should not translate into privileging the needs of white teachers in courses that also enroll ethnic minority teachers. Giving primacy to the education of white teachers is a way that multicultural teacher education maintains the asymmetry of power/knowledge that defines white-color social relations in the United States.

Delpit (1988) has described minority teachers' sense of alienation and frustration with the ways that their white colleagues talk to them and about them. She quotes a black woman teacher who says: "When you're talking to White people they still want it to be their way. You can try to talk to them and give them examples, but they're so headstrong, they think they know what's best for *everybody*, for *everybody's children*. They won't listen, White folks are going to do what they want to do *anyway*" (280). This quote clearly emphasizes the importance of giving voice to the experiences, perceptions, and aspirations of minority teachers who participate in multicultural teacher education courses. To do otherwise invalidates the ways in which their cultural backgrounds permeate their classroom practices and their responses to teacher education. To do otherwise is to talk *about them* not *with them*. Cochran-Smith and Lytle (1992) reported the experiences of preservice and in-service teachers who participated in two different programs that emphasized inquiry into cultural diversity. By describing the interactions among participants of various ethnic groups, differences and similarities in the struggles to develop culturally responsive pedagogy emerged. It is this kind of cross dialogue that can enrich the discussion on multicultural education.

Educating Minority Teachers

Failing to examine course content as a function of a participant's ethnicity could stem from the belief that the tasks of multicultural teacher education are the same for minority and nonminority educators. Sleeter (1993) has suggested that multicultural education has somewhat different purposes for each group. White people, she argues, have a vested interest in maintaining a racist social structure that privileges them: "Faced with the paradox of liking and helping students of color, and at the same time explaining the subordination of people of color and adhering to social structures that benefit themselves and their own children, the White teachers I studied responded in patterned ways. Many simply refused to see color. . . . Discussing race or multiculturalism means discussing 'them', not the social structure" (27).

According to Sleeter (1992, 1992b) multicultural education for white teachers involves activities that would help them examine their privileged status and uncover the various strategies they use to avoid restructuring their thoughts about race and education. Minority teachers, she argues, bring life experiences that make them more likely to challenge racist institutions. Instead of helping them understand white privilege, multicultural teacher education should help them politicize their understandings of racism so that they can engage in the reconstruction of schooling.

Minority teachers' commitments, however, should not be taken for granted. As noted by Paulo Freire (1970) and others, oppressed people learn to internalize the oppression and learn to engage in practices that serve the purpose of maintaining oppressive, racist institutions (hooks 1989). In my own research with prospective minority teachers, I have found them to be strongly committed to multicultural education (Montecinos, in press). These students, however, tended to equate multiculturalism with curricular inclusion and could not, spontaneously, articulate social transformation as a goal of multicultural education. This is not surprising since social transformation was not a goal espoused by the kind of formal schooling they had, so far, experienced.

At this point I can only speculate on what could be some of the specific areas related to the preparation of multicultural minority teachers. First, teacher educators cannot assume that teachers who are members of a minority group can translate their cultural knowledge into culturally relevant pedagogy and content (Grant and Secada 1990; Dilworth 1990). One of the tasks of multicultural teacher education for minority teachers is to help them translate their cultural and pedagogical understandings into culturally responsive pedagogy. As noted earlier, single-ethnic pedagogy cannot be confused with multicultural pedagogy; therefore, the task cannot stop there.

I would also advocate that attending to the needs of minority teachers involves moving away from understanding multicultural education solely in terms of white-color relations. Given that not all minority groups have an equal economical or political status in U.S. society, I would argue that the preparation of minority teachers involves an understanding of the processes of conflicts and alliances among minority groups. One needs to look no further than the recent Los Angeles riots or the evening news reporting conflicts among various minority groups in New York City to realize the importance of addressing questions of interracial relations between the various minority groups.

Although calls to increase the number of minority teachers have become commonplace in the teacher education literature, there is little evidence of any serious discussion concerning how the teacher education curricula will address this much needed diversification of teacher education students. Instead of serving the purpose of homogenizing teachers' practices, how can teacher education foster and nurture cultural diversity in teachers' practices (Grant and Secada 1990)? Addressing this question is critical if increased teacher diversity is going to have a positive impact on the academic and social achievement of a diverse school age population.

ADDRESSING TEACHER DIVERSITY IN THE EVALUATION OF MULTICULTURAL TEACHER EDUCATION

Proponents of multicultural education argue that what the student actually learns from the school curriculum is mediated by his or her cultural background. Cultural beliefs influence such things as what seems important to learn, what makes sense to us, how we interpret information received, and what we do with that knowledge. For example, some researchers have found that students from minority cultural groups resist learning what the school has to offer because they see it as "becoming white," as a way of giving up their own cultural identities (Ogbu 1992; Ferdman 1990). The impact of race on how teachers respond to an antiracist education program has been illustrated by Washington (1981) and Sleeter (1992). For example, Washington (1981) found that whereas white teachers understood the content of an antiracist workshop as an "attack on Whites" and got angry, African American teachers got annoyed at white teachers' apparent resistance to "see" their own prejudices.

Despite the role that multicultural education attributes to the home culture and its impact upon school learning, the majority of the studies reviewed did not make teacher trainees' home culture an important aspect of their analysis of training outcomes. I will describe two ways in which this literature tended to treat teachers' ethnic identity when evaluating program impact.

Ethnic Children, Ethnicless Teachers

As mentioned earlier, 55% of the studies reviewed did not mention the ethnic backgrounds of the participants; thus, 87% of the teachers who participated in these studies were constructed as ethnicless. In addition, in three of the studies that did mention participants' backgrounds (*n*=97), ethnicity was not made a significant aspect of data interpretation.

For example, McDiarmid (1992) concluded from pre-post interview data that, to a large extent, the multicultural curriculum offered to a group of Los Angeles Unified School District's teacher trainees had little impact in changing participants' views on teaching culturally different students. Since McDiarmid (1992) did not report information on his participants' ethnicity, we cannot ascertain whether teachers' lack of change was primarily a result of inadequate pedagogy and content. If it is true that a learner's cultural background is relevant to learning, one must wonder whether this apparent resistance to change was somehow related to these teachers' ethnic locations. By dislocating teacher trainees' ethnic identities or including only white participants, we fail to examine whether minority and nonminority educators are equally impervious to the type of multicultural education described by McDiarmid (1992). The same holds true for other types of programs. For example, immersion programs such as those described by Mahan and Rains (1990) and by Cooper, Beare and Thorman (1990) should examine the interactions of teachers from diverse cultural backgrounds with their host communities. If a Puerto Rican teacher goes to live with a Navajo family, are his or her experiences comparable to those of a white teacher, a black teacher, and so forth?

Sleeter (1992b), for instance, described the structural, as opposed to individual, constraints that teachers face when attempting to implement multicultural education. Even though her sample consisted of white and nonwhite teachers, she did not indicate whether or not teachers' backgrounds made a difference relative to the ways in which they conceptualized these problems. Lack of time, for example, was described by twenty out of thirty participants as an impediment to a greater engagement in multicultural education. Does this constraint impact minority and nonminority teachers' commitments and practices to multicultural approaches in the same manner?

When data is not desegregated in quantitative analysis, the ethnic identity of teachers is assumed to be unrelated to how they understand and respond to multicultural education. By not socially locating the voices of the teachers who are quoted in qualitative studies, these authors construct generic teachers who bring to their educational experiences, to borrow from the title of Nagle's (1986) book, a "view from nowhere." If it were true that teachers' ethnic identities are irrelevant to how they respond to multicultural education, what is the rationale for linking the multicultural education project to the diversification of the teaching force?

I am not necessarily arguing that teachers' ethnic identities are central to every aspect of Sleeter's, McDiarmid's, or other researchers' analyses. What I am arguing is that researchers in this field need to publicly ask the following questions: When does considering teachers' ethnic location enrich the analysis of multicultural teacher training efforts? When does attending to ethnic differences among teacher trainees impoverish the analysis, for example, by deflecting attention from the structural as opposed to the individual conditions of teachers' work? More generally, paraphrasing Toni Morrison (1992), a critical question to be addressed by multicultural teacher education is: What does positing teachers, in the wholly racialized society that is the United States, as unraced and students as raced entail?

Ethnicless White Teachers

As noted by several of the authors whose studies I reviewed, one of the goals of multicultural teacher education is to help teachers analyze and evaluate their own ethnic backgrounds and to help them become aware of their own beliefs and their origins (e.g., Baker 1977; Bennett 1979; Cross and Deslonde 1978). Fuller and Ahler (1987) have described the difficulties white preservice teachers have in defining themselves as cultural beings. The importance of disrupting the view that whiteness is not an ethnicity is exemplified by the insights of a preservice teacher quoted by Larke et al. (1990) who said: "Being reared with White values and attitudes, (I didn't know Whites had their own attitudes, I thought they were characteristics of all Americans) I supposed I just took culture for granted. Now that I am aware of the differences I feel that I am able to teach children according to their needs without imposing my own beliefs upon them" (9).

I am concerned that while some of the research studies in this field make whiteness problematic (i.e., Fuller and Ahler 1987; Sleeter 1992, 1992b), other studies contribute to maintaining the invisibility of the dominance that white European culture has had in teacher education. This happens in studios that do not mention participants' ethnicity if the sample is all white. This happens in studies that use ethnic identifiers in the title of the article only when participants are ethnic minorities.

I am concerned when authors fail to describe the ethnic background of the participants if the sample is all white. When teacher educators do not make explicit how white ethnicity affects teachers' responses to multicultural courses, the social reality of whites is universalized. The constructed and arbitrary character of the dominant culture of teacher education schools is then given an essential character that prompts the kind of marginalization of minorities teachers described by Delpit (1988).

SUMMARY

Multicultural teacher education has, so far, been concerned with the education of the *monocultural* teacher, neglecting to examine the processes by which a bicultural teacher becomes multicultural. Throughout this paper I have noted areas of research that need to be undertaken in order to develop a multicultural teacher education project that is committed to the preparation of a culturally diverse teaching force. Our understanding of multicultural teacher education can be advanced by taking into consideration the fundamentally social character of teaching, the teacher educator, and the teacher trainee.

NOTES

I am grateful to Leander Brown, Renée Martin, Christine Sleeter, John Smith, and Barry Wilson for their helpful comments on earlier drafts of this chapter. I also wish to thank the Graduate College of the University of Northern Iowa for a summer research grant that supported the preparation of this manuscript.

1. Assuming that some of the "ethnicless" teachers were members of minority groups, the actual percentage of minority participants is likely to be higher than 3%.

2. This article comes from a larger study in which the biographies of these minority teachers are described in more detail (Sleeter 1992). All four grew up in segregated environments and currently lived in various kinds of neighborhoods.

REFERENCES

Baker, G. C. 1973. Multicultural training for student teachers. *Journal of Teacher Education* 24(4):306-7.

————. 1977. Two preservice training approaches. *Journal of Teacher Education* 28(3):31-33.

Banks, J. A. 1991. *Teaching strategies for ethnic studies.* 3d ed. Needham Heights, MA: Allyn and Bacon.

Bennett, C. T. 1979. The preparation of pre-service secondary social studies teachers in multiethnic education. *The High School Journal* 62(5): 232-36.

Burstein, N. D. and B. Cabello. 1989. Preparing teachers to work with culturally diverse students: A teacher education model. *Journal of Teacher Education* 40(5):9-16.

Cochran-Smith, M. and S. L. Lytle. 1992. Interrogating cultural diversity: Inquiry and action. *Journal of Teacher Education* 43(2): 104-15.

Cooper, A., P. Beare and J. Thorman. 1990. Preparing teachers for diversity: A comparison of student teaching experiences in Minnesota and South Texas. *Action in Teacher Education* 12(3):1-4.

Cross, D. E. and J. Deslonde. 1978. The impact of teacher inservice programs on attitudes toward multicultural education. *Educational Research Quarterly* 2(4):97-105.

Delpit, L. J. 1988. The silenced dialogue: Power and pedagogy in educating other people's children. *Harvard Educational Review* 58(3):280-98.

Dilworth, M. E. 1990. *Reading between the lines: Teachers and their ethnic cultures.* ERIC Teacher Education Monograph, no. 11. (ED322 148).

Ferdman, B. M. 1990. Literacy and cultural identity. *Harvard Educational Review* 60:181-204.

Foster, M. 1990. The politics of race: Through African American teachers' eyes. *Journal of Education* 172(3):132-41.

Freire, P. 1970. *Pedagogy of the oppressed.* New York: Herden and Herden.

Fuller, M. L. and J. Ahler. 1987. Multicultural education and the monocultural student: A case study. *Action in Teacher Education* 9(3):33-40.

Grant, C. A. and W. G. Secada. 1990. Preparing teachers for diversity. In *Handbook of research on teacher education,* 403-22. New York: Macmillan.

Grottkau, B. J. and S. Nickolai-Mays. 1989. An empirical analysis of a multicultural education paradigm for preservice teachers. *Educational Research Quarterly* 13(4):27-33.

Henington, M. 1981. Effect of intensive multicultural, nonsexist instruction on secondary student teachers. *Educational Research Quarterly*, 65-75.

Heshusius, L. 1991, February. Curriculum-based assessment and direct instruction: Critical reflections on fundamental assumptions. *Exceptional Leadership* 57(4):315-28.

hooks, b. 1989. *Talking back*. Boston, MA: South End Press.

Ladson-Billings, G. and A. Henry. 1990. Blurring the borders: Voices of African liberatory pedagogy in the United States and Canada. *Journal of Education* 172(2):72-88.

Larke, P. J. 1990. Cultural diversity awareness inventory: Assessing the sensitivity of preservice teachers. *Action in Teacher Education* 12(3):22-30.

Larke, P. J., D. Wiseman, and C. Bradley 1990. The minority mentorship project: Changing attitudes of preservice teachers in diverse classrooms. *Action in Teacher Education* 12(3):5-11.

Liston, D. P. and K. M. Zeichner. 1987. Critical pedagogy and teacher education. *Journal of Education* 169(3):117-37.

MacIntyre, A. 1984. *After virtue*. 2d ed. Notre Dame, IN: University of Notre Dame Press.

Mahan, J. M. and F. V. Rains. 1990. Inservice teachers expand their cultural knowledge and approaches through practica in American Indian communities. *Journal of American Indian Education* 29:11-24.

McDiarmid, G. W. 1992. What to do about differences? A study of multicultural education for teacher trainees in the Los Angeles Unified School District. *Journal of Teacher Education* 43(2):83-93.

Montecinos, C. In press. Will a diversification of the teaching force result in the multiculturalization of schooling? *Equity and Excellence in Education*.

Morrison, T. 1992. *Playing in the dark: Whiteness and the literary imagination*. Cambridge, MA: Harvard University Press.

Nagel, T. 1986. *A view from nowhere*. New York: Oxford University Press.

Noordhoff, K. and J. Kleinfeld. 1990. Shaping the rhetoric of reflection for multicultural settings. In *Encouraging reflective practice in education: An analysis of issues and programs*. Edited by R. T. Clift, W. R. Houston, and M. C. Pugach, 163-85. New York: Teachers College Press.

Ogbu, J. G. 1992. Understanding cultural diversity and learning. *Educational Researcher* 21(8):5-14.

Ross, D. D. and W. Smith. 1992. Understanding preservice teachers' perspectives on diversity. *Journal of Teacher Education* 43(2):94-103.

Shorris, E. 1992. Latinos: The complexity of identity. *Report on the Americas* 26:19-26.

Sleeter, C. E. 1992. *Keepers of the American dream: A study of staff development and multicultural education.* London: Falmer Press.

————. 1992b. Restructuring schools for multicultural education. *Journal of Teacher Education* 43(2):141-48.

————. 1993. How White teachers construct race. In *Race identity and representation in education*, 157-71. Edited by C. McCarthy and W. Crichlow.

Sleeter, C. E. and C. A. Grant. 1988. *Making choices for multicultural education: Five approaches to race, class and gender.* Columbus, OH: Merrill Publishing Co.

Stepick, A. 1992. Miami: Los Cubanos han ganado. *Report on the Americas* 26:39-45.

Swisher, K. 1984. Comparison of attitudes of reservation parents and teachers towards multicultural education. *Journal of American Indian Education* 23(10):1-10.

Tajfel, H. and J. C. Turner. 1986. The social identity theory of intergroup relations. In *Psychology of intergroup relations*. Edited by S. Worchel and W. Austin, 7-24. Chicago: Nelson-Hall.

Washington, V. 1981. Impact of antiracism/multicultural education training on elementary teachers' attitudes and classroom behaviors. *The Elementary School Journal* 81(3):186-92.

7

Christine Sleeter _____

Teaching Whites about Racism

As student populations become increasingly diverse in racial and cultural composition and as the teaching force becomes increasingly white, interest in training teachers in multicultural education is growing. Many educators conceptualize this task as helping white teachers and preservice students replace negative attitudes about race with positive attitudes, and as helping them acquire a knowledge base about race and various racial groups. I see the task as more complex than that: as white women, many of whom have worked themselves up from working-class origins, these teachers already have considerable knowledge about social stratification in America, but it tends to be fairly conservative. Part of the task for teacher educators is to help them examine and reconstruct what they know. Otherwise, they simply integrate information about race into the knowledge they already have and in the process distort it. This chapter describes a process I have used with white preservice students to help them recognize the limits of what they know about social stratification so that they can begin to reconstruct what they know.

How White Teachers Think about
Social Stratification and Race

Anthony Giddens (1979) advanced his analysis of social theory on the premise that "every social actor knows a great deal about the conditions of reproduction of the society of which he or she is a member" (5). Regardless of how little experience with racial or cultural diversity white teachers have had, they enter the classroom with a considerably rich body of knowledge about social stratification, social mobility, and human differences based on their life experiences. The analogies they draw between racism and what they know about sexism, class mobility, and the white ethnic experience tend to minimize the importance of race as they see it.

Race is one axis of oppression in America; social class and gender are equally important axes. About 90% of the teaching population is white, and most teachers, as whites, are members of the dominant racial group. As such, most never have been victims of racism in America nor have experienced racial minority communities in the same way Americans of color do. Whites draw on their own experience to understand inequality, and their interpretation of that experience usually upholds their belief that the rules of society apply roughly the same to everyone. Haves and have-nots rise or fall by their own merit or effort, for the most part.

White Americans and Americans of color grow up in different locations in the racial structure, although Whites usually deny that there is a significant racial structure. Based on his study of white perceptions of race, David Wellman (1977) argued that a contradiction whites face is how to interpret racial inequality in a way that defends white interests in publically acceptable terms. Generally, sociobiological explanations for inequality are not acceptable today, so whites construct alternative explanations, resolving "the contradiction by minimizing racism. They neutralize it" (219), viewing racism as individual prejudice and inequality as due mainly to cultural so-called deficiencies."

While denying structural racism, whites usually spend their lives in white-dominated spheres, constructing an understanding of race and social equality from that vantage point. According to Wellman (1977), "Given the racial and class organization of American society, there is only so much people can 'see.' The positions they occupy in these structures limit the range of their thinking. The situation places barriers on their imaginations and restricts the possibilities of their vision" (235). Consequently, they assume the opportunity structure works the same for all Americans.

A large proportion of teachers are women, and a large proportion have also worked their way up from lower or working-class origins. In that regard, they are members of oppressed groups, and their experiences with social class and gender provide teachers with a perspective about how they believe social stratification works.

Historically, teaching has provided members of the lower- and working-class entrée into middle-class status; many teachers have experienced working their way up by attaining education (Lortie 1975). For example, Patricia Ashton and Rodman Webb (1986) noted that, "The life experiences of most teachers demonstrate their allegiance to the ethic of vertical mobility, self-improvement, hard work, deferred gratification, self-discipline, and personal achievement. These individualistic values rest on the assumption that the social system . . . works well, is essentially fair, and moves society slowly but inevitably toward progress" (29-30). For example, I interviewed twenty-three teachers about their parents' occupations (Sleeter 1992). Four of their fathers had held jobs that normally require college education, two had owned small businesses, and the fathers of the other seventeen had worked as laborers of various sorts. Some of the teachers had experienced the stigma of being poor. But they had raised their own social class standing by earning college degrees and becoming teachers. Education had served them as an effective vehicle of upward mobility and personal betterment. Several teachers also talked about their European ethnic backgrounds (or those of their spouses). Their parents or grandparents had come to America very poor and had worked hard; gradually the family had moved up the social ladder. These life experiences taught teachers that the social system is open to those who are willing to work, regardless of ethnicity (a view that equates white ethnicity with race). Many Americans regard their own social standing as higher than that of their parents. While most social mobility has been due to an expansion of middle-class jobs and widespread improvement of the living standard of Americans in general, people tend to attribute their own improved status to their own individual efforts (Kluegel and Smith 1986).

Teachers' experience with sexism also provides them with an experiential basis for thinking about social stratification. As women, many teachers have experienced prejudice and stereotyping. Therefore, they perceive themselves as knowledgeable about how discrimination works. They locate sexism (and classism) mainly in biased attitudes of individuals who limit the opportunities of others by treating them stereotypically. The main solution to discrimination from this perspective is to try to eliminate stereotyping so that all may strive as individuals.

Most teachers' understanding of sexism and social class is cast within a conservative framework that emphasizes individual choice and mobility within a relatively open system. One's progress may be hindered by prejudices and stereotypes, as well as by meager economic and cultural resources from home. However, these blocks can be compensated for by hard work. Structural bases for gender and social class oppression are rarely studied in school in any depth, so most teachers' understanding of their personal experience stays rooted within a naive individualistic framework. But it is important to recognize the power of personal experience in reinforcing this framework.

When concerned white teachers define classism, sexism, and by extension racism as a matter of individual prejudice, they then strive to keep racial prejudices and stereotypes from coloring their interactions with individuals. I interviewed twenty-six teachers over a period of time as they participated in a two-year staff development project in multicultural education. How to think about race, color, and culture was a major issue they grappled with and often discussed in interviews and in the staff development sessions. Many of them upheld the "colorblind" perspective, believing that one is not participating in racism if one learns to ignore color and feel comfortable around children of color. Yet most white teachers had an unresolved dilemma: how to accept all children regardless of race while explaining their difficulties in school without seeming racist. Some blamed the "culture of poverty," asserting that race was not the issue. Several tried to ignore explanations that "blamed the victim." But they unconsciously used such explanations anyway for lack of means to explain children's classroom behavior and achievement. First, they mentioned the racial and socioeconomic composition of their students; then they immediately described those students (for a complete report on the study, see Sleeter 1992).

Those who attempt to teach white teachers about racism commonly encounter defenses that are difficult to penetrate. Convinced that individual attitudes and stereotypes form the basis of racism, whites try very hard not to see color and therefore not to hear race-related information; whites also experience guilt when confronted with information about racism. Reducing social organization to individual relationships, many whites define "getting along" in face-to-face interactions as the solution to racism, then maintain that they already do this well. Many whites equate race with what they know about white ethnicity, drawing on what they know about their own ancestors' experiences pulling themselves up "by the bootstraps." The European ethnicity analogy assumes that every group faced difficulties but that most overcame those difficulties through hard work; it ignores the importance of skin color in perpetuating racial discrimination. However, drawing parallels between racism, sexism, and classism, many whites resentfully interpret civil rights laws and social interventions as people of color wanting "special attention and privileges."

The European ethnic immigrant experience provides a template for thinking about diversity that white teachers commonly use to try to construct race in what they construe as a positive rather than negative manner. According to the ethnicity paradigm, members of diverse groups voluntarily came to America to partake in its freedom and opportunity; while systems were not always fair in the past, opportunity has gradually been extended to everyone. In his study of how Euro Americans think about ethnicity, Alba (1990) found them to view it as voluntary participation in a group, in which the meaning of ethnicity is tied mainly to family history and expressions of so-called old-world culture, especially cuisine, holidays, and ethnic festivals. Among Euro Americans, ethnic differences no longer define opportunities or social participation: marriage, housing, employment, education, and so forth are almost unrelated to European ethnic background. So, it makes sense for Euro Americans to view their own ethnicity as voluntary and to define it as they do. However, colonized groups as well as immigrant groups who are visibly identifiable have not had the same history; the European ethnic experience does not provide an appropriate framework for understanding non-European groups (Omi and Winant 1986; Ringer and Lawless 1989). Trying to apply it to everyone, in fact, is another defense Whites use.

One approach to penetrating these defenses is to affirm to whites that their beliefs are valid—for whites, but not necessarily for people of color. Since whites tend to deny that a racial structure locates them differently from people of color, one can begin by helping them recognize structural racism and the importance of visible differences among people when defining access. This shifts attention away from feelings of guilt, reliance on the White ethnic experience, or the possibility of being colorblind.

In what follows, I describe a process I have used to help white preservice students articulate some of what they know about the social system, recognize that what they know may be true for white people but does not necessarily generalize to Americans of color, and develop some sensitivity to how the rules of American society work differently for people of color than they do for whites. It is significant to my teaching that I am white. I deliberately use my race and my background to try to relate to the white students, for example, by telling them that I used to think X until I experienced Y, that "we as whites" experience advantages we are often aware of, or that I have made some big mistakes that whites commonly make.

Professors of color can draw on different advantages than white professors to teach about race. A lifetime of personal experience with a group and with racial discrimination arms a professor of color with a rich repertoire of experiences and examples (as an African American friend put it to me once, "I've been black all my life and taking notes"). Students may attempt to dismiss professors of color as advocating a cause (as well as women professors who teach about gender); this avoidance technique should be pointed out directly, and students should be redirected to the information the professor is attempting to teach.

ANALYTIC FRAMEWORK

Before describing some specific teaching strategies, I will present a framework that structures how I teach about race and other axes of oppression. I share this framework with students, referring back to it repeatedly. The framework directs them to analyze social institutions rather than characteristics of individuals and groups, and to examine how institutions work differently for different groups; it is based on conflict theory.

In a fair social system individuals generally get what they strive for according to predictable rules that apply equally to everyone. This is a tenet of U.S. society that most citizens, regardless of race or any other ascribed characteristic, believe ought to be the case. Figure 7.1 represents this visually, in which "Reward" refers to whatever an individual is striving for (such as a job, or a decent place to live, or food), and the arrow indicates the social rules governing distribution of that resource.

However, in reality the rules do not work the same way for everyone. Conflict theorists postulate that dominant groups make the rules in order to retain control over the resources of society. Different groups actually experience society's rules differently, and as a consequence, view society and *have not*

FIGURE 7.1
How Do We Explain Who Gets What?

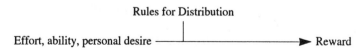

Rules for Distribution

Effort, ability, personal desire ─────────────────────────────▶ Reward

groups differently. Figure 7.2 illustrates this. Since it repeats what has been said thus far in this chapter, I will not elaborate on it here. But the figure helps orient students visually to a major idea of the course: that society operates differently for different groups, and consequently different groups construct opposing explanations for inequality.

Most Americans analyze who gets what only in terms of individual effort and ability. Figure 7.3 illustrates two additional levels of analysis that explain group differences in status: the institutional level and the cultural level. At the institutional level, one examines both written and unwritten rules and procedures that are used to regulate human behavior; one can also examine the degree to which any given reward (such as housing or higher education) is actually available to everyone who works for it. At the cultural level, one examines beliefs people have about society and diverse groups, how and by whom those beliefs are encoded, and how and to whom they are transmitted. The relationship between cultural beliefs and individuals, and between cultural beliefs and institutions is reciprocal; both levels influence one another.

FIGURE 7.2
Different Perspectives

	Dominant Groups	Oppressed Groups
Nature of society	Fair, open	Unfair, rigged
Nature of *have not* groups	Lack ambition, effort, culture language, skills, education	Strong, resourceful work to advance

FIGURE 7.3
Levels of Analysis of Oppression

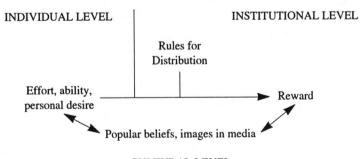

INDIVIDUAL LEVEL | INSTITUTIONAL LEVEL

Rules for
Distribution

Effort, ability,
personal desire ————————————→ Reward

Popular beliefs, images in media

CULTURAL LEVEL

When teaching whites about racism, my main goal is to help them ask and begin to answer questions about racism at the institutional and cultural levels, those levels that people of color generally direct their attention toward to explain racial disparities. Such analyses are foreign to the way most white people think about racial disparities, and it takes a good deal of practice to be able to think in institutional and cultural terms. As whites gain practice in doing so, however, they begin to understand (sometimes for the first time) what people of color are saying about racism. Below, I will describe some specific strategies I use to help students learn to ask and answer questions at the institutional and cultural levels.

HELPING WHITE PRESERVICE TEACHERS RETHINK RACE

I begin the semester by having students describe and discuss some of their beliefs about teaching and about how society works. They do this first in writing, then in small group discussions, addressing questions such as the following. What is proper student behavior in the classroom? What does it mean to be late, and how do you interpret someone who is late? Why do most people live in racially homogeneous neighborhoods? What do you consider to be the greatest works of literature? I also have students fill out a questionnaire examining how much contact they have had with members of other racial groups and social class backgrounds in various areas of their lives, including school, college, work, neighborhood, and church.

Students generally approach this task puzzled by the obviousness of it. On the one hand, their beliefs have a transparently "obvious" character. For example, they believe proper classroom behavior consists of students showing respect and interest by attending to the teacher, asking questions politely, obeying, sitting quietly, and so forth. Most believe people live in relatively homogeneous neighborhoods because they prefer to do so. In small group discussions about their beliefs, there is usually so much agreement (especially when groups are all white) that they are unclear why they are doing this. On the other hand, the questionnaire about their backgrounds shows the extent to which the great majority have had fairly little contact with people of a different background; this, too, has a certain obviousness about it. Some students at this point maintain that they are not prejudiced; others admit that their beliefs are limited by their backgrounds, though they do not know to what extent.

I then tell the class that all of their answers are correct, but also that multiple correct answers exist for every question they have been discussing, ones that vary by race, culture and other factors. At this point, I introduce two related but somewhat different ideas that subsequent class sessions will develop.

First, all social behavior is culturally constituted, often differently across cultural groups. One example of how something that seems obvious can be viewed differently across cultures is interpretation of time. I ask students what time they would arrive someplace if told to come at 9:00. Even within an all-white class, students suggest different appropriate arrival times. Someone always asks whether the event is an appointment or a social gathering, which leads to consideration of time as culturally interpreted. I provide examples of correct arrival times in contexts that do not surface in the discussion, such as on an Indian reservation, for a black as opposed to white party, or in Switzerland. I then discuss the concept of code-switching, emphasizing that they (and everyone else) have learned a set of correct cultural codes in their own environment, that the codes they know are not the only correct ones, and that anyone can learn another set of codes if taught.

Second, I suggest that a color line exists, in addition to gender and social class lines, that differentiates those who make the rules of society and for whom the rules operate fairly consistently from those who do not make the rules and for whom they do not operate consistently. I point out that we all see color and that visible differences become important social marks of who belongs on which side of the line. The line is socially constructed, although we may associate it with biological features. Over time (and in different cultures), the line may be positioned differently. For example, southeastern Wisconsin (where I teach) was a popular destination for eastern and southern European immigrants historically, and some of their descendants usually are in the class; I ask students whether Italians are white or not. Those who are familiar with the history of discrimination against Italians locally can point out that they were not considered white for a long time but generally (although not universally) are now. When Latinos are class members, we discuss whether class members view Latinos as white; students usually emphasize the importance of visible characteristics, especially to white people, in making this determination. I then comment that education is supposed to pay off equally for everyone and show statistical information illustrating that it actually pays off (in terms of income and employment) differently based on race and sex. Students' main reaction at this point is that this is not fair, and they begin asking why.

I then assign students to read the book *The Education of a WASP* (Stalvey 1988), which traces the experience of a white middle-class woman as she relearns how race in America works for African Americans. The book is autobiographical. It opens with Stalvey's description of her growing up in Milwaukee during the 1940s and 1950s and of her naive beliefs about the essential fairness and justice of American society. At this point, most of my students can identify with her. The book then chronicles her life and the change in her perspective over a four-year period as she became increasingly involved with struggles within the black community. She describes how she learned about institutional racism in a variety of areas: housing, schooling, media coverage, job opportunities, and so forth. Over the four years, Stalvey crossed a color line that most white Americans never cross, and she learned firsthand how African Americans experience America, from the other side of a color line that Stalvey earlier had believed did not exist.

When I first assigned the book, I was afraid my white students would find it too offensive, too angry, or even too dated to take seriously. Generally, this is not their reaction, and many of them cannot put it down once they start reading it. Overwhelmingly, they tell me that it is very interesting and eye-opening. Some say it made them cry, some say it was the first textbook they had read cover-to-cover, a few confess they are not reading assignments for other classes because they want to finish it. Some loan it to friends and neighbors; one class commented that there will probably be few used copies in the bookstore because this is one book no one would want to sell. One student who had studied about racism in high school, wrote later:

> I must admit now that I have received this education with my eyes and heart closed. For example, I know how blacks were historically forced into slavery and about the black inventors who made many contributions for American society. . . . I am sure that I can go on with more historical knowledge, but the point is that even though I have been taught these accounts, I have never experienced any of them. This is because I am white and have never really had any contacts with people outside of my race until after I entered college.

The Education of a WASP provokes a strong reaction from most White readers. Many students find themselves emotionally-engaged in a struggle against racism for the first time in their lives. The engagement is vicarious but strongly felt. Students of color also find the book worth reading, commenting that it made them think about issues they had not thought deeply about for a while and that it gave them a better idea of how white people think. As one African American student put it, "I knew white people were naive, but I didn't know they were *that* naive."

The book focuses on institutional racism as well as media production of imagery that rationalizes racist actions. It provides a very different template for thinking about race than the European ethnic immigrant experience does. But it also describes one woman's experience, almost three decades ago. Subsequent activities engage students in examining the same factors the book describes, here and now, focusing on institutional processes and on cultural beliefs and images.

I have found two simulations very helpful. The one I use first, because it is the less threatening of the two, is BaFa BaFa (Shirts 1977). In this simulation, the class is divided into two groups in two different rooms where each learns and practices a different culture. After each group has mastered its culture, observers and visitors are exchanged for a few minutes at a time and are encouraged to share with members of their own culture what they saw. The simulation is followed by a discussion. During the simulation itself, which lasts about one hour, contact experiences with the other culture invariably produce a set of stereotypes, antagonisms, and feelings of confusion. Members of each culture rather quickly learn to view theirs as best and most sensible, and they use it as a benchmark to judge others negatively. After discussing their reactions to each other, we draw parallels between the simulation and real-life denigration of members of other groups. The example I provided earlier about cultural differences in time orientation is helpful again here. Often, white students comment that this was the first time they experienced feeling left out and confused by encountering a different set of cultural rules and that now they have a sense of what code-switching means.

The other simulation I use, usually two or three weeks later, is Star Power (Shirts 1969). In this simulation, participants are divided into three groups to play a trading game, the purpose of which (they are told) is to compete in the accumulation of points. The trading game in the simulation is rigged so that one group continues to accumulate more than the rest, but they are led to believe their success is due to their skill. Part way through the simulation, the top group (Squares) is given power to make rules for the rest of the simulation. The Squares invariably use this power to further their own advantages (e.g., they restrict membership, impose taxes, make rules for themselves that differ from rules for everyone else, and sometimes establish a welfare system to keep everyone else playing). The other two groups react in a variety of ways to their powerless position; sometimes they stop playing, usually they find ways to subvert the rules, sometimes they revolt. The discussion that follows the simulation helps participants move from their own particular experiences with the simulation to broader issues of power and social structure. In the discussion, I try to draw from the group as many real-life examples that parallel the simulation as possible. I have also found the simulation helpful in providing the class with a common vocabulary and set of experiences I can use throughout the semester to make points (such as, Why might this set of parents be behaving like Triangles?). Typically students need help connecting both simulations to racial issues around them; some draw parallels easily, but others need to have me walk them through specific examples (such as race relations in the university) before they start to make connections.

Some students dismiss the book as outdated and the simulations as unreal. Therefore, I also ask students to investigate some aspect of racism for themselves, locally. We use the framework in figure 7.3 to generate questions, brainstorming questions one could ask at each of the three levels of analysis; I instruct students to focus on the institutional or cultural levels. For example, they can interview a realtor to find out if color is taken into account when selling a house, investigate whether there is a relationship between racial composition of neighborhoods and accessibility of voting places, ask university students of color why students at the university are disproportionately white, and so forth.

For example, in one class recently a white student interviewed a family friend who is a realtor. This individual explained to her that he does not care who he sells a house to, but the neighbors often do, believing that blacks do not keep up their houses and do contribute to neighborhood crime. Therefore, although he personally does not agree with this view, he honors it. Another student telephoned several local industries and banks to find out how many people of color they had hired in management positions. Most of the individuals he tried to talk to refused to answer his questions or gave him a runaround; he interpreted their refusal to discuss this with him as indication that few if any people of color occupy management positions. Still another student asked a black university student about obstacles he encountered to getting into college and was told that a major one was money. The part-time jobs that paid most were located in the suburbs (near where this white student lived), too far away from him and most other blacks to be accessible. The white student realized that he held a part-time job that the black student did not have access to. Yet another student counted the racial representation of people on cereal boxes, then shared his findings with an African American friend. She found his figures interesting, but suggested things that were more important, from her perspective, such as the preponderance of white women used to portray beauty.

I encourage students to share what they find out. I also supplement their sharing with a barrage of statistical information on distribution of income across racial lines, unemployment, housing discrImination, life expectancy, access to health insurance, and so forth. By then, they are usually willing to listen to me, especially if their own personal investigations have validated the idea that society's rules operate differently for people of color than they do for whites, just as Stalvey found out.

I also show a videotape of Dr. Charles King talking about racism on the Phil Donahue show several years ago. In the videotape, Dr. King (who is black) deliberately shows his anger and impatience toward white racism and white denials of racism, and he attempts to direct viewers away from blaming blacks for their condition toward examining the racist structures that are responsible for the condition in which blacks find themselves. Since Dr. King does not mince words with the audience and shows his emotion, most whites find the videotape offensive unless they have been prepared for it. Having prepared students with the above activities, most are able to listen to him fairly non-defensively. In a follow-up discussion, one of the main points I stress is the difficulty we as whites experience listening to people of color talking honestly about racism but our need to listen nonetheless in order to learn, just as Stalvey did.

In May of 1992, I showed a class Dr. King's videotape shortly after the riots in Los Angeles following the acquittal of white police officers accused of police brutality and after we had completed the rest of the activities above. Many class members told me that the idea of racism finally made sense: they were for the first time able to see what people of color were angry about. The combination of the book, the class activities, and the videotape—so very directly connected to a current issue—finally came together.

I teach a two-course sequence in Multicultural Education; this describes only the beginning. In subsequent sessions I have students examine how schools institutionalize racism, as well as classism and sexism, and then explore things they can do differently. I also direct students to find out more about students of color from people of the students' own racial background, including community members, teachers, and scholars. (White preservice students are often very resistant to seeking information from anyone other than teachers they encounter, the great majority of whom are white.)

I also try to help students move beyond their understanding of sexism and classism as matters of individual stereotyping. Discussion of these areas is beyond the scope of this paper, but I will note that most students are quite resistant to examining institutional sexism or the social class structure outside the school itself. To many of them, questioning the class structure sounds like what they call "socialism" or "communism," which they have been trained to regard as anti-American. Questioning sexism leads to an analysis of family roles and structures; young women who are preoccupied with establishing their own families resist this tenaciously. Further, many young women have learned to associate a gender analysis with "feminism," a term they perceive as militantly anti-male.

TEACHING WHITES ABOUT RACISM

I have found the process described above to be fairly effective, although it does antagonize a few students to a point where some drop out. I judge its effectiveness based on connections students make in papers and class discussions and on receptivity to ideas that build upon this foundation over the two-course sequence. I believe the approach is effective with many students for several reasons.

First, I begin by having students articulate some beliefs, and then I attempt to validate that what they know is correct for themselves but at the same time not correct for all Americans. Students often become angry and defensive when told their experience is wrong; they are much more receptive when shown that it is right but limited. While it is difficult for many people to accept that there are multiple perspectives and multiple experiences, it is even more difficult for an individual to accept that she or he is completely wrong. Multicultural education is about multiple realities, not about one "correct" reality.

Second, I direct students' attention toward barriers to access, rather than characteristics of people of color, which is where whites normally direct their attention; and I encourage them to investigate some barriers for themselves. I try to show them how stereotypes arise from the consequences of barriers, then are used to justify the barriers. The books, the simulations, and their own investigations help to reinforce this point and help keep their attention directed toward access barriers. A student's paper about *The Education of a WASP* illustrates the focus: "We learned that the black people learn at a very early age just where their place in society is, and the consequences for stepping over that line. Their reactions are a form of self preservation." Later I explore strengths and resources among oppressed groups (such as community self-help groups, or linguistic resources in one's first language or dialect, upon which a second language or dialect can be built), and I contrast this view with the *cultural deficiency* view.

Third, I try to involve students actively in constructing a sense of how discrimination works, drawing ideas out of their experience with the simulations and their investigations rather than imposing ideas on them. Again, this approach validates their ability to construct for themselves an understanding of how society works, but it introduces a different set of questions and materials on which to draw than most have used previously.

The approach I have described is not a panacea. I strongly suspect that many white students continue to regard it as an academic exercise, giving me what I want but not taking it very seriously. Some who are actively interested and engaged at the time shift their attention to other things later on in their preservice program; whites have the luxury of being able to forget about racism, and my students are no exception. A variation of the forgetfulness is that many students learn the vocabulary I have used to examine racism without connecting it with much in their own lives; instead they revert to blaming "cultural deficiencies" of students of color when they get into schools and are confronted with behavior they do not really understand.

However, I also believe that the emotional impact of the book, and the experiential basis of the simulations and their own investigations, interpreted through a vocabulary and set of concepts I try to provide, equip many white preservice students with a foundation on which they can continue to rethink how racism works and their own participation in racist institutions. (Contact I have had with some former students who are now teaching supports this belief.) As a student concluded in a paper: "After having some exposure to the harsher realities of life, I now hope that I will not be as blind to them as I was before, and that my education never stops, for my sake and the sake of others."

REFERENCES

Alba, R. D. 1990. *Ethnic identity.* New Haven: Yale University Press.

Ashton, P. T. and R. B.Webb. 1986. *Making a difference: Teachers' sense of efficacy and student achievement.* New York: Longman.

Giddens, A. 1979. *Central problems in social theory.* Berkeley: University of California Press.

Kluegel, J. R. and E. R. Smith. 1986. *Beliefs about inequality: Americans' views of what is and what ought to be.* New York: Aldine de Gruyter.

Lortie, D. C. 1975. *Schoolteacher.* Chicago: University of Chicago Press.

Omi, M. and H. Winant. 1986. *Racial formation in the United States*. New York: Routledge and Kegan Paul.

Ringer, B. B. and E. R. Lawless. 1989. *Race-ethnicity and society*. New York: Routledge.

Shirts, G. 1969. Star Power. La Jolla, CA: Western Behavioral Sciences Institute.

────── . 1977. BaFa BaFa. La Jolla, CA: Western Behavioral Sciences Institute.

Sleeter, C. E. 1992. *Keepers of the American Dream*. London: Falmer Press.

Stalvey, L. M. 1988. *The education of a WASP*. Madison: University of Wisconsin Press.

Wellman, D. T. 1977. *Portraits of white racism*. Cambridge, MA: Cambridge University Press.

8

KEITH OSAJIMA ⎯⎯⎯⎯⎯⎯⎯⎯⎯⎯⎯⎯⎯⎯⎯⎯

Creating Classroom Environments for Change

For four semesters, between Spring 1988 and Spring 1991, I taught a course entitled Race and Education at a small, elite, liberal arts institution in the Northeast. The course typically enrolled thirty-five to forty students, generally 80% of whom were white. While the class was offered out of the Department of Education, most of its students were not preparing to teach. The majority were concentrators in the college's Educational Studies program or were majoring in departments from across the campus.

The main purpose of the course is to have students think reflectively and analytically about the nature and impact of racism in the United States. I use an examination of educational institutions and students' own educational experiences as the vehicle for this endeavor. The course is organized around three interralated questions: 1) How have educational institutions served as both a vehicle in the oppression and liberation of people of color in this country? 2) How have white and minority students been miseducated about the nature and history of racism in the United States? 3) What strategies and actions can students adopt to address the ways racism impacts on their lives? The course appeared in the curriculum during a time of increasing racial tensions and polarization on campus. A fraternity "jungle theme party" in fall 1988, where three students dressed in blackface, brought to the surface many people's dissatisfaction with and harsh criticism of the college's efforts to address issues of diversity. These views were countered by those growing numbers who believed the college's African American-oriented residential unit fostered separatism and reverse racism.

The general campus conflicts invariably entered the classroom. The tensions and heated emotions that often obstructed students' ability to talk, listen, and think, which made Race and Education an extremely challenging course to teach. From the outset, I realized that any success in teaching about racism hinged on understanding the nature of and reasons underlying the emotion-laden tensions and on applying that analysis to the development of effective teaching strategies. This chapter presents lessons I learned from my teaching of Race and Education. I begin with a brief discussion of how the chapter is situated in relation to the literature on multiculturalism and critical pedagogy. I then turn to an analysis of the pedagogical challenges that appeared within the class

131

and describe teaching strategies I have used to address those challenges. Finally, I present an assessment of the course's impact based on student evaluations.

SITUATING REFLECTIONS ON CLASSROOM PRACTICE

The chapter's focus on classroom dynamics complements and extends the ongoing efforts to develop antiracist and multicultural practices in higher education. To date, much of the effort of multicultural or ethnic studies proponents has been directed toward issues of inclusion. These encompass the late 1960s battles to establish ethnic studies courses and departments (Umemoto 1989) and the current struggles to maintain or establish programs in the hostile, so-called politically correct climate. Considerable energy has also been focused on building a body of scholarly research and materials to be included in the curriculum of such courses (Banks 1991; Gollnick and Chinn 1990). To augment these efforts, attention must also be directed toward understanding the process of teaching antiracist courses. We must know not only what to teach but also how to effectively reach students by the ways we teach. The chapter and this volume join a growing body of literature that examines the dynamics of teaching multicultural and antiracist courses (Ellsworth 1989; Tatum 1992; *Teaching Education* 1991).

The chapter's focus on teaching is also situated in relation to the literature on critical pedagogy. I have long been influenced by the work of critical educators, such as Paulo Freire (1970, 1985) and Henry Giroux (1985, 1990), and have sought to incorporate their visions into my courses. For Race and Education, that meant wanting to create a learning environment where students could develop an understanding of the complex interrelationships between their personal life histories and the surrounding sociopolitical and historical contexts of race relations in the United States. It also meant wanting to empower students to take actions against racism in their lives.

Transforming these desires into classroom reality, however, has proven to be a continual and difficult challenge. The critical pedagogy literature, while supplying general theoretical visions, often fails to provide adequate guidance for transforming theory into practice. For Elizabeth Ellsworth, the problem is that much of the critical pedagogy literature "operate(s) at a high level of abstraction" that is more suited to philosophical discussion than to actually planning classroom practice (1989, 300). Researchers who write about critical pedagogy often "strip discussions of classroom practices of historical context and political position" (300). Ellsworth also notes that the literature on critical pedagogy is problematic because it privileges reason and rational argument as the basis for understanding and political action. She argues that the ideal of the rational person may, in itself, be an oppressive myth—excluding, obscuring or delegitimizing the experiences and knowledge of women and people of color (304).

The following discussion of my Race and Education class is made with these critiques in mind. The chapter assesses the limits and potential of transforming the conceptual goals of critical pedagogy into concrete classroom practices. The analysis pays particular attention to how surrounding sociopolitical and historical forces affect student identities and teaching situations. It also examines how affective, seemingly nonrational factors affect classroom dynamics. By situating the chapter within debates on critical pedagogy, I seek to move beyond the particularities of my small liberal arts college experience to address issues relevant to educators in a range of educational settings.

PEDAGOGICAL CHALLENGES—DIFFERENCE AND CONFLICT

Bob Suzuki (1984), in outlining principles for developing multicultural education, argues that the first step is to "start where students are at." Indeed, students bring to class an array of identities, perspectives, and experiences shaped within the context of American race relations in the post-civil rights period (Hall 1989; Kellner 1992; Omi 1991). The different starting points have a profound impact on classroom dynamics. Based on the experience of my four classes, the most challenging aspect of teaching about racism involves understanding and managing the tensions, differences, and emotions that students bring to class and what often position students in conflict with each other (Tatum 1992).

In my classes, the most glaring conflict has been between well-intentioned white students and politically active students of color who are often perceived as militant. A large portion of my white students start from a point of genuine interest and concern about race relations. They are troubled by campus racial tensions, and they want to learn more and to do something about those problems.

Good intentions aside, these white students are generally naive and uninformed about racial issues. Their life experiences have left them unprepared, tentative, and unclear about how to proceed. The majority of white students have lived racially isolated lives. They were raised in predominantly white neighborhoods and attended predominantly white schools. Many have never had close contacts or friendships with people from other racial groups. These students begin class with an uncritical acceptance of the rhetoric of racial progress that emerged in the post-civil rights movement period.

They believe, for example, that the legislative and legal victories of the 1960s effectively removed all structural barriers to equality. America, in their eyes, is a color-blind society that is based on meritocratic ideas. They see themselves in that light, firmly believing that they are not racists and confident that they treat people as individuals. They can honestly claim they do not use or condone the use of overtly racist language and actions. Racial relations are understood as problems of attitude, interpersonal relations, and communications. Racial inequalities can be overcome by assimilation and hard work. Tensions can be resolved if people come together, talk to each other, and come to some common ground.

Their sincere desire for racial harmony by improved attitudes and interpersonal relations is admirable, but it comes into direct conflict with most students of color who begin the class at a different starting point. Many African American, Latino, and Asian students closely identify with the collective struggles of the 1960s, particularly with the activist black, Chicano/Latino, Native American and Asian American movements of that period. They also are influenced by the Afrocentric arguments of the late 1980s. They see white supremacy and institutionalized racism as the key problems, not interpersonal attitudes and interactions. They are frank about their anger and are easily frustrated by the attitudinal orientation of the liberal white students.

The presence of politicized students of color coming into conflict with white students in my class is a direct outgrowth of changes in higher education since the 1960s. Many of the students of color, for example, are beneficiaries of expanded educational opportunities for minorities, such as Head Start, compensatory education programs, desegregated schooling. A Better Chance, and affirmative action programs. Their knowledge of racial issues often is cultivated in African American or ethnic studies courses, which reflect the expansion of the curriculum to meet the demands of so-called "Third World" students in the late 1960s.

The division between well-intentioned white students and politicized students of color is the most common starting point of conflict. It is not, however, the only source of difference and conflict that students bring to class. Not all students neatly fall into these two categories. I have had students of color, for example, who know little about racial issues. They tend to be more assimilated, fitting into the mainstream campus community. They find themselves at odds with and often criticized by the more politicized students of color.

Some white students, on the other hand, are extremely knowledgeable about racial issues. They have taken advantage of the expanded, inclusive curriculum and learned a great deal about racism in the United States. They clash with conservative white students who echo the widespread critiques that affirmative action constitutes reverse racism and dilutes educational standards. These students do not hesitate to express their impatience with students who "constantly complain" about racism and rally behind the cries of "political correctness."

It is important to emphasize that the differences and conflicts between students are intricately connected to the terrain of American race relations that has unfolded over the past three decades. Defining student conflicts only in personal terms or dismissing their emotions as overreactions and oversensitivity is dangerous. These views discount the intellectual understanding of racism that can be gained by examining how one's feelings about race are shaped by and reflect the surrounding social and historical forces.

WALKING FINE LINES

The different starting points and conflicts I encounter give rise to and shape other pedagogical challenges. As in any teaching situation involving diverse student bodies, the differences in experience, knowledge, and perspective that students bring to class raise difficult questions regarding the appropriate content of the curriculum. Where should the focus of the course be directed? At what level and to what audience does one organize topics and materials? If I teach to meet the needs of the large group of white students, is that in the best interests of the students of color?

What I have discovered is that no single solution exists to the issues raised by the myriad questions, no single set of materials and strategies can resolve the differences and conflicts. Instead, when I move to address one question, reverberations invariably extend to other areas, and new pedagogical problems arise. Teaching about racism involves walking a number of fine lines, between curricular and instructional decisions to maximize learning for the largest number of students and management of potential negative effects and tensions that may emerge in response to those decisions. In this section, I describe some of the common pedagogical challenges I faced in teaching the course, particularly in the early classes. These problems are best illuminated by a discussion of my specific efforts to incorporate historical dimensions into the class.

Because most of my students are white and come to class with limited knowledge of racism in the United States, I spend time on the historical relationship between racism and education. Several weeks are devoted to an historical overview of the experiences of Native Americans, Latinos, Asian Americans, and African Americans in relation to education. The primary objectives are to contextualize the contemporary manifestations of campus racial tensions, to impress upon students that campus tensions are not simply a problem of interpersonal relations, and to extend the analysis of American racism beyond black/white relations.

The decision to focus on history was made to fill what I perceived to be a significant gap in the starting point of the majority of students. For many, my class was the first in their course of study to deal directly with racism. The ambitious scope and limited time available, however, made it difficult to cover history in any depth. I simply could not, in a few short weeks, make up for the voids and deficiencies in their school experiences. Feeling the need to impress upon white students the depth and seriousness of American racism, the section tended to highlight those harsh, most dramatic instances of discrimination. For many students of color, who were already familiar with the history of American racism, this decision did not necessarily expand nor deepen their existing knowledge.

Two pedagogical challenges emerged from this curricular decision. First, it unintentionally reinforced a simplistic, dualistic analysis that underscores many people's popular understanding of racism in the United States. It fueled the students' tendency to view the issue in either/or, dichotomous terms, which exacerbated conflicts. The focus on the most obvious manifestations of racism reminded students of color of their anger and confirmed their view that all whites are racist. White students felt guilty and defensive about the historical events. The anger they sensed from students of color confirmed their view that all were militantly antiwhite. The tendency to blend all *others* into homogenous groups made it difficult for students to appreciate the real variations that existed in the class and to consider new information that contradicted or fell outside of the existing dichotomous categories.

Second, difference, conflict, and emotions led to the silencing of important dialogues (Delpit 1988). This silencing developed in three ways. First, students generally were afraid to state their own positions. For white students, feelings of guilt often made them feel tentative and insecure about their own thinking on the issues. They were afraid to ask questions or make statements that might elicit more anger and criticism. Even those white students who brought extensive knowledge about racism to class often hesitated to apply their knowledge to the class. The defensiveness felt by white students led them to adopt a self-protective stance and claim that they are not racist nor responsible for past wrongs. This unfortunately only alienated them from a potentially supportive group and inhibited their willingness to grapple with the implications of American racism.

The second silencing that developed was students inability to critically question or challenge the material and each other was silenced. White students, thinking that students of color were the experts on racial issues, uncritically accepted most of what those students said. They did not inquire about other ways to look at the issue or why people held their positions. Among students of color, the lack of critical questioning manifested itself in a slightly different form. The students of color rarely challenged, disagreed, or questioned each other in front of the white students. There seemed to be a tacit understanding that students of color should not air their dirty laundry for fear of appearing weak or disunified, or for fear of embarrassing their peers in front of whites. In this way, real differences between the politicized and assimilationist students of color or between men and women of color were quieted.

Finally, silencing occurred when people stopped listening respectfully to each other. The either/or analyses often constituted fixed positions that could not be altered by the historical information. The conservative white students, who felt that every student of color was oversensitive to racism, stopped listening when students of color talked about the historical material. No matter what the students of color said, the conservative white student only "heard" tired complaints. Similarly, students of color who believed that all whites are racists and know nothing about racism, could not hear the knowledgeable white students when they offered insights they had learned in other classes.

STRATEGIES TO MEET THE CHALLENGES

Reflecting on the problems that appeared in the previous courses led to a continual rethinking of teaching strategies. Now, I begin the course with a series of classes designed to discuss directly problems that stem from the conflicts around racism and to provide conceptual tools that help students understand how those emotions and conflicts are linked to the way racism has affected all their lives.

For example, on the first day of class of this past semester, I showed the PBS Frontline video entitled *Racism 101*, which documents racial tensions on college campuses. I then asked students to discuss the various dimensions of the racial tensions and to consider the following question: If you were to take the lead in fighting campus racism, what skills and information would you need? The question was formulated with two purposes in mind. First, aware of the potential divisions and conflicts, I wanted to provide students with a common question for the class and to encourage them to consider the possibility of working on the same project. Second, knowing that students start at different points, I did not want to impose a singular agenda for all students to follow. I wanted students to acknowledge their differences and wanted to give them the latitude to decide for themselves what they most needed to learn.

Early in the class, I also took steps to build a collegial, respectful environment to facilitate discussion on difficult issues. In the first weeks, I spent time at the beginning of each class having students introduce themselves. Often this would simply be a quick go-around when people said their names and one good thing that happened to them since the last class. This exercise was both a relaxed, nonjudgmental way for everyone to speak in class and a vehicle for helping students to move beyond a superficial knowledge of one another.

I also asked students to talk explicitly about the kind of classroom environment that would be most conducive to breaking the silence that often accompanies discussions of race. I wanted to talk openly about the emotional and conflictual nature of the issue. This semester, students took the initiative to define a number of "guidelines" for class discussions. To make it safer to talk in class, they asked each other not to "gossip" about people in the class to others outside of the class. They asked that people be aware of how body posture and facial expressions might inhibit discussion. They also asked that people be allowed to complete their thoughts without interruption and that I make an effort to make sure that no one person dominated the discussion.

Another point of conflict related to classroom environment that was confronted early in the term concerned vocabulary. Students wanted to know the acceptable language for designating racial groups: African Americans or blacks, Indians or Native Americans, Orientals or Asians? Some white students did not understand why people were so sensitive about terminology.

To get at this issue, I went around the room and asked people to say any nicknames that they've been called in their lives. Then I asked people what it was like to be called those names. Students said that they often felt embarrassed, humiliated, and angry. I argued, by analogy, that the feelings they had around their nicknames were similar to those experienced by students of color around names for racial groups. Their sensitivity reflected a desire by group members to end the oppressive nature of the ugly so-called nicknames imposed upon them from the outside and to define for themselves what they wanted to be called.

I then challenged students to think about how racism affects the relationships between whites and students of color on campus. Here, I wanted to extend their conception of racism by focusing on the subtle influences of racism on people's lives. To get a sense of the pressures and subtle racism that students of color experience in predominantly white institutions, we read Robert Anson's *Best Intentions—The Education and Killing of Edmund Perry* (1987). Peggy McIntosh's paper entitled "Understanding Correspondences Between White Privilege and Male Privilege Through Women's Studies Work" (1987) did a wonderful job for students of revealing the unacknowledged benefits that are accorded to whites. She argues that whites have an invisible, weightless knapsack of maps, compasses, blank checks and provisions that provide them with advantages and privileges. Because the privileges are often unacknowledged or unrecognized, whites have trouble understanding why people of color feel uncomfortable or oppressed in their presence. Uma Narayan's article "Working Together Across Difference" (1988) offered students an incisive analysis into the problems that arise when different groups try working together. She describes how even well-intended "outsiders" to an oppression cannot fully understand the experiences of those "insiders" who are targets of oppression. Outsiders have to employ "methodological humility" when working with members of another group, to ensure that they be sensitive to the way an oppression enters into relations between groups. All three readings provoked extensive discussion, and they forced students to think critically about their own views and how they shape interactions with members of other racial groups.

The direct discussion of conflicts and differences at the beginning of class, and the efforts to provide analytic tools to understand those conflicts, seemed to be effective in moving students toward a deeper understanding of their experiences. This better prepared them for the historical section. This past semester, white students, in particular, were less defensive and more curious about how the conflicts and divisions may have been developed in educational institutions. Students of color also seemed to be less critical of and more patient with the white students.

From the historical section, we moved to a discussion of contemporary educational issues involving race. Michael Omi and Howard Winant's *Racial Formation in the United States* (1986) provided the theoretical framework for this section. Their review of race relations theory and the concept of racial formation helped to analyze how the broad contours of racial politics since the 1960s shaped educational policies. Their critique of the ethnicity-based paradigm, for example, was used to show how the ideological notions of the meritocracy and the culture of poverty were linked to issues such as compensatory education, Asians as the model minority, and affirmative action. We also looked at the development of Black Power and cultural nationalist positions in the late 1960s, and we traced their relationship to developments in bilingual education, multiculturalism, Afrocentrism, and ethnic studies. At this point, Simonson and Walker's edited collection *Multi-Cultural Literacy* (1988) provided powerful insights into the vision that people of color hold for a better society. Finally, Omi and Winant's (1986) chapter on "Race and Reaction," which discusses the rise of conservative politics, helped to contextualize the contemporary debates on political correctness and affirmative action.

By the end of the class, after struggling with various dimensions of racism for an extended time, many students made considerable progress in their understanding of the issues. At this time, the course confronted one other pedagogical challenge—the paralyzing impact of demoralization and powerlessness. In earlier classes, I learned that my efforts to document the harsh realities and the scope of racism, while successful in sensitizing students to the complexities of the issue, often left them feeling helpless to change something so big and overwhelming. To counteract this potentially debilitating tendency, it was necessary, borrowing a phrase from Henry Giroux (1985), to have students develop a "language of possibility" and a sense of their power to effect change to counteract the paralyzing impact that racism's magnitude can generate.

I therefore asked students to develop a final project that combined two components: an analysis of an issue and a praxis/action component. This was to encourage students to think about how they could apply their knowledge to concrete efforts for change related efforts. Most students simply included in their papers suggestions for reform. But other students took the initiative to actually implement their ideas. For example, one group made a thirty-minute video in which students talked about how racism affected them. They left this video with me to use as a focal point for future discussion. Another group also produced a video, one that sought to educate people about stereotypes that Asian Americans face. Two students carefully went through a fifth-grade social studies text and wrote letters to the editors and publisher detailing their critique of the book's treatment of Native Americans. Two other students developed and conducted an antiracism workshop for white students. One woman of color wrote a powerful autobiographical paper that documented the struggles she experienced at the university.

MAKING A DIFFERENCE?

Did the course make a difference in students' lives? At the close of each semester, students were asked to fill out a course evaluation that includes the questions: What did you get out of this course? How has this course contributed to your intellectual growth or education? Student responses to these questions from the last three Race and Education classes were reviewed. The evaluation form is somewhat limited, since it was not a systematically designed measure of what was learned and only 60% of the students responded. Nevertheless, students' responses to it do provide some insights into the course's impact. The value of the evaluations is that they allowed students to describe, in their own words, what they found important about the class.

For the students filling out evaluations, the overwhelming majority voiced positive opinions. Of the seventy-seven questionnaires, only four students' assessments were negative. One said that s/he did not learn anything "new that I haven't experienced," another wrote "not much" in response to the question, one wrote "no comment," and the fourth left the question blank.

The remaining seventy-three spoke favorably about the course. On one level, the comments of many students indicate that the course successfully provided substantive information about racial issues in the United States and in educational arenas. Seventeen students, for example, wrote that the course greatly increased their knowledge; another twelve said that they gained a better general understanding of issues; another four specifically said they came to understand the complexities and subtleties of how racism operates; and four others said they learned about racism directed at other minority groups.

It also was evident that for a large number of students the significant benefit of the course was that it introduced them to information they had not studied seriously before. Twenty-one students, for instance, said that the course "opened their eyes" and greatly heightened their "awareness" of racial problems. These comments are consistent with the fact that many students come to my course without much prior experience in the area.

In addition to these general comments about the intellectual lessons, a number of students spoke of the deeply meaningful impact the course had on their education and lives. The comments indicate that, for many students, the value of the course lay in both its intellectual and affective impacts. For these students, what was important was not simply that they *learned* a lot, but that the course affected how they *felt* about learning. The following comments reflect the sense of confidence, enthusiasm, and excitement students gained from the course.

> I have never felt as though I've learned as much as I have this semester. The course provided me with personal growth as well as a greater understanding of the problems.

> This course has been a highlight of my semester—and my four years here. I'm thinking about racism in new ways. I'm able to express my feelings outside of class as well.

> This course *greatly* increased my knowledge of myself as well as of others about racism. This course was probably the *most* valuable of all my classes for the info I learned could be used and applied directly toward increasing my awareness as a human being.

> The course as a whole has allowed me to challenge fundamental ways in which I view the world.

I am far more sensitive to the issues of racism than I was before taking Race and Education.

This course went way beyond the classroom in that it has truly affected the way I think and feel about certain issues and has challenged some ideas I used to hold. Moreover, it has made me more aware of myself as a person and as a person of color.

A further reading of student evaluations reveals that elements of how the class was organized and run played a key role in the overall success of the course. Students valued the opportunity to grapple actively with issues through class discussion. They appreciated my acknowledgment of the emotional tensions and fears that sometimes make it difficult to confront issues of race. They welcomed the efforts to create a safe, respectful environment. The following comments suggest that for many students intellectual learning became possible when attention was paid to the affective elements in the classroom.

What was especially great was that in the beginning of the semester, Prof. Osajima made us all introduce ourselves several times so that we would be more familiar with each other. This helped us be more comfortable with the rest of the class and, therefore, more open and willing to talk.

He never pushed anyone to say something they were afraid to say but made the atmosphere of the class a comfortable and understanding one.

I enjoyed the leeway Prof. Osajima gave for class discussion. I would not feel so confident, or organized in my thinking if I had not had the opportunity to talk in class.

Discussions were often intense, which generally means there is some real thought going on. Even frustration has helped me to learn.

The atmosphere of the classroom was relaxed yet the students all held respect for Prof. Osajima. I feel that this type of atmosphere is conducive to learning, not just to earn a grade, but to *really* learn.

Of course, the emphasis on discussion and the classroom atmosphere was not uniformly effective. A few students said they continued to feel intimidated by others and afraid to speak. One student correctly observed that sometimes I tried to make people feel "too comfortable" and did not challenge students to take a hard stand or fully support their positions. Others wanted more organized lectures. Still, the generally positive evaluations of teaching indicate that it is important and worthwhile for educators to devote attention to issues of classroom environment and student interaction as part of their preparations for teaching about racism.

CONCLUDING REMARKS

In the face of campus racial tensions and demographic shifts that promise increases in minority student populations, colleges across the country are recognizing the need to educate students on the nature of racism. As the number of courses in this area grows, it is vital that we continually reflect on, analyze, and write about our efforts. In this way, a body of knowledge and experience can be established to inform our curricular and instructional decisions.

For those developing courses on racism, it is important to pay attention to how societal debates, tensions and conflicts around race affects the configuration of students who take the class and on classroom dynamics. In my experience, students start from different points that raise questions about the content and direction of the course. Students often begin in conflict and see race relations in dichotomous terms. The emotional nature of the issue can silence dialogue.

The presence of difference, conflict, and emotion creates challenging teaching situations. From this past semester, I have learned that it is useful to directly discuss these dynamics and to incorporate materials and instructional strategies to confront their effect. This helps to turn potentially debilitating conflicts and dead ends into avenues that expand the students' analysis of their life experiences in relation to broader social, political and historical conditions.

NOTE

This chapter is a revised and expanded version of an article that originally appeared in *Teaching Education* 4(1), 1991.

REFERENCES

Anson, R. S. 1987. *Best intentions—The education and killing of Edmund Perry*. New York: Vintage Books.

Banks, J. A. 1991. *Teaching strategies for ethnic studies*. 5th ed. Boston: Allyn and Bacon.

Delpit, L. D. 1988. The silenced dialogue: Power and pedagogy in educating other people's children. *Harvard Educational Review* 3:280-98.

Ellsworth, E. 1989. Why doesn't this feel empowering? Working through the repressive myths of critical pedagogy. *Harvard Educational Review* 59:297-324.

Freire, P. 1970. *Pedagogy of the oppressed*. New York: Seabury Press.

———. 1985. *The Politics of education*. South Hadley, MA: Bergin and Garvey.

Giroux, H. A. 1985. Introduction to *The Politics of education*, by P. Freire. South Hadley, MA: Bergin and Garvey.

———, ed. 1991. *Postmodernism, feminism, and cultural politics*. New York: State University of New York Press.

Gollnick, D. and P. Chinn. 1990. *Multicultural education in a pluralistic society*. Columbus: Merrill-McMillan.

Hall, S. 1989. Cultural identity and cinematic representation. *Frameworks* 36:68-81.

Kellner, D. 1992. Popular culture and the construction of postmodern identities. In *Modernity and Identity*. Edited by Scott Lash and Jonathan Friedman, 141-77. Cambridge, USA: Blackwell.

McIntosh, P. 1987. Understanding correspondences between white privilege and male privilege through women's studies work. Paper presented at the National Women's Studies Association, Atlanta, GA.

Narayan, U. 1988. Working together across difference: Some considerations on emotions and political practice. *Hypatia* 2:31-47.

Omi, M. 1991. Shifting the blame: Radical ideology and politics in the post-Civil Rights era. *Critical Sociology* 18:77-98.

Omi, M. and H. Winant. 1986. *Racial formation in the United States*. New York: Routledge and Kegan Paul.

Simonson, R. and S. Walker. 1988. *Multi-cultural literacy*. St. Paul: Graywolf Press.

Suzuki, B. H. 1984. Curriculum transformation for multicultural education. *Education and Urban Society* 3:294-322.

Tatum, B. D. 1992. Talking about race, learning about racism: The application of racial identity development theory in the classroom. *Harvard Educational Review* 62:1-24.

Teaching Education. 1991. Special Issue on Diversity, 4(1).

Umemoto, K. (1989). On strike! San Francisco State College strike 1968-69. The Role of Asian American Students. *Amerasia Journal* 1:3-42.

9

KENT KOPPELMAN AND ROBERT RICHARDSON ⸻⸻⸻⸻

What's in It for Me?:
Persuading Nonminority Teacher Education Students
to Become Advocates for Multicultural Education

We teach a course entitled Understanding Human Differences that has developed a positive reputation among students in the College of Education. Although the course was originally intended to fulfill the human relations mandate for teacher education in the state of Wisconsin, recently it has been redesigned in response to recommendations stemming from the UW system's Design for Diversity initiative and now is being offered as part of the general education program at our university. In this chapter, we will discuss the underlying philosophy of the course and its basic goals, and we describe some of the strategies that we use to meet those goals.

THE NATURE OF THE COURSE

The approach that we take is probably best described as "education that is multicultural and social reconstructionist" (Grant and Sleeter 1985). Since this approach has been fully illuminated in the introduction to this volume, we will note only that courses originally conceived in Wisconsin were created under the state human relations mandate. Teacher education institutions in the state subscribe to the full range of approaches described by Sleeter and Grant (1988) in their book *Making Choices for Multicultural Education: Five Approaches to Race, Class, and Gender.* This course has undergone a series of transformations since its inception in the 1970s and has moved from being a course that merely taught tolerance to one that more directly addresses systemic issues of oppression and inequality in a democratic society.

The course is taught primarily by a faculty of white males, most of whom are full tenured professors. Students enrolled in the course are from small, midwestern communities and are primarily white and middle class. In a weekly general assembly, the course coordinator delivers lectures designed to be both substantive and challenging; other faculty in the Educational Foundations Department share responsibility for facilitating weekly small-group discussion sections. Students are expected to read extensively out of class, to participate maximally in the class, and to experience people(s) of

145

diversified backgrounds. To conclude the semester experience, students prepare a synthesis paper that documents their translation of theory into practice.

INVESTIGATING OUR ASSUMPTIONS

Since we know that values determine how we perceive the world and how we prioritize what is or is not important and valued, we begin the course with a discussion of value systems. Social scientists will admit readily that it is far more difficult to study human beings, especially in complex societies, than to study other forms of life or even the universe itself. As biologists or physicists gather data, they are able to refine their theories and more clearly identify patterns in the data that contribute to new theories. Research on human beings often leads to contradictory findings, creating as many questions as answers, but a few patterns have emerged. One of the most enduring findings among researchers is that people have a tendency to behave in ways that contradict the values they espouse. In other words, there is consistent inconsistency between what people say they value and what they do (Myrdal 1944; Lerner 1957; Raths, Harmin and Simon 1966; Baber and Bay 1987; Stalvey 1989).

We ask students whether or not such hypocrisy is "normal" in our society. In addition, we challenge them to reflect on their lives, on the values they have learned, on how they have arrived at these values, and on how these values influence their behavior. Their responses indicate that students recognize the problem. For example, one student whose parents always advocated honesty remembered a visit to an amusement park where the father claimed his child was younger than she was in order to get a lower ticket price. The student laughed recalling her protest, "I'm not eleven! I'm twelve!" only to be hushed by her exasperated father. We talk about such stories, not in a self-righteous way (students will tell tales on themselves), but in order to analyze and understand the behavior.

Students are given a summary of information from *Values and Teaching* (Raths, Harmin and Simon 1966) about how values have been traditionally taught and their conclusion that these traditional approaches to teaching values were based on the assumption that there is a set of so-called *right values* to which everyone should adhere. One obvious result of this assumption is that those who try to teach values are actually attempting to indoctrinate children or adolescents with these right values. We assert that indoctrination is a powerful tool, because it can also easily be used to get others to say what they are supposed to say, to mouth beliefs and values. It can certainly shape behavior to some degree, but not as effectively as it can shape what people will say (because they know they are expected to say it). Our students are asked to reflect on this as a potential explanation for this issue of inconsistency between expressed values and behaviors, that is, that we may grow up knowing the right words to say but we also learn other messages that more powerfully dictate what we really believe about ourselves and others. And such beliefs are inevitably reflected in our behavior.

The students are given a variety of examples to consider. For many of us who were high-school students during the early 1960s, television news reports of the verbal and physical hostility directed against civil rights activities in the South were distressing. We were suddenly confronted with the reality of white people who claimed to be good people, many of whom claimed to be Christian, who were denying people the right to enter a restaurant or a restroom because of the color of their skin. These so-called good people were fighting to maintain separate water fountains, separate churches, separate schools and separate seating on a bus based on skin color, and it was difficult to determine what values could be used to justify such practices. It did not seem possible that the Ku Klux Klan claimed to be a Christian organization. When we share these memories with our students, they can't understand such behaviors either. One question we ask them to consider is whether or not there might be practices we accept today that twenty years from now college students will consider illogical and immoral. As an example, we provide information about what the culture labels gay bashing and about current Christian perspectives that denounce gay men and lesbians and advocate discrimination against them, and we ask our students to consider how this might look to future generations.

The resolution that usually emerges from these discussions centers on developing a sincere respect for others and a genuine self-respect. No student has wanted to take the point of view that promoting hypocrisy is the way to develop a positive sense of self or self-worth. Students also reject the idea of forcing people to have the same values or to think alike. They say they have much more respect for people who openly express their beliefs, even if they disagree with part or all of those beliefs, than for someone who mouths moral platitudes and then engages in immoral activity for personal advantage. Hypocrisy has been condemned throughout history; this is nothing new. But the students insist they don't want to be hypocrites. They want their values to be consistent with their behaviors. They want to be moral, and they believe that they will benefit from the struggle to be moral human beings, to do what they consider to be the right thing.

Because of the reputation that this course has developed, students enter the experience well aware of the fact that our course stimulates cognitive dissonance; but it does more than that. One of the course objectives is to assist students in the process of moving to some level of commitment; therefore, making commitments becomes a focus of student papers. Professors ask the students to determine personal and professional plans of action. There is no doubt that students experience internal conflict during the course, but the professors openly acknowledge this probability and invite students to visit with them and discuss any of the issues we raise.

In connection with this concern for commitment, students are given a summary of the moral reasoning theory put forth by William Perry (1981). Rather than providing a complete delineation of all nine points on Perry's

Continuum, the major principles of his theory are emphasized. Perry asserts that we all begin as dualistic thinkers, believing that there is good and bad, right and wrong for all moral issues; he asserts that we remain dualistic thinkers until we finally recognize (some never do) that in many areas we simply do not know what is 'right.' What we know is that there are many opinions on these issues, and we need to acknowledge them because one of them may be the right answer. Perry calls this an acceptance of multiple perspectives or "multiplicity." This can develop into a recognition that all opinions are not of equal value, that some opinions have more persuasive reasons for being accepted than others, that people choose to believe an opinion because in their view of the world that particular opinion makes more sense than others, that others choose to believe different opinions because they look at the world differently. Once a person has reached this point, he or she has moved away from dualistic thinking altogether and now is engaged in the process that Perry calls relativistic moral reasoning.

Most students seem uncomfortable with relativism, and they are equally uncomfortable with ambiguity. They want to have a few firm truths in their lives, some certainty. They do not like to think that relativism represents the state of mind most desirable to be a sophisticated moral thinker. Their discomfort is not unusual. Perry has written about the discomfort of many who have tentatively accepted relativism only to become frightened by the prospect of trying to function in such an uncertain moral context. Such people may retreat into dualism, perhaps by affiliating with a political or religious organization that advocates specific ideas about what is right and wrong. Our students feel better about Perry's theory when they are told that it does not stop with relativism but goes on to include what Perry calls "making commitments."

In this final phase of Perry's Continuum, the moral thinker needs some sense of certainty, some truths to which he or she can commit. In trying to determine which beliefs are most compelling, the person never loses sight of the fact that he or she is choosing, that 'truth' is personal, not absolute. In making these commitments, the individual is not denying relativism, but understands and affirms the principle of personal choice as the main factor in determining the meaning of life for each individual. We make our own meaning, and we can advocate that meaning to others, but they have their own choices to make.

Sometimes students perceive a person who is advocating particular choices as a dualistic thinker, so we ask them to look carefully at how the advocacy is presented. If the advocate is willing to acknowledge other points of view, even though disagreeing with them, that is probably a relativistic thinker who has made personal commitments. If the advocate denounces all other viewpoints in an effort to convert the listener(s), that person is likely to be a dualistic thinker. Most students seem to recognize the limitation of dualistic thinking—the danger of forcing people to be with you or against you on moral issues. The logical conclusion students draw from this analysis of

Perry's moral reasoning theory is that an individual benefits from being a sophisticated moral thinker since each of us is confronted with increasingly complex ethical issues in our daily lives.

DEFINING PREJUDICE

The preceding class discussions are intended to establish an appropriate context for our students in preparation for exploring the issue of prejudice. The most important information that students need to have at the beginning of the examination of this topic is that prejudice is a pervasive phenomenon that has existed in all human societies in all eras throughout the world. If they do not already realize this, students often assume that anyone speaking of prejudice is talking only about attitudes of white people. Such an assumption obviously makes white students defensive. To counter this, we use examples from anthropologists and sociologists (Aoyagi and Dore 1964; Bromley 1987; Brown 1966; Castles 1984; Essed 1991), and contemporary events described by journalists (e.g., the problems of Pakistanis in England, the rise of neo-Nazism in Germany, sexual harassment in Japanese corporations, and anti-Semitic activity in France) to illustrate problems of prejudice in societies around the world. After this, we begin to discuss prejudice in the United States.

The first distinction that must be made is between prejudice and bigotry. Most students will deny that they are prejudiced because they confuse prejudice with bigotry. Their confusion is not uncommon. To demonstrate this, students are given a series of definitions taken from a contemporary dictionary that defines prejudice in four different ways, each of which is inaccurate. One of them defines prejudice as hatred which is an inadequate definition of prejudice but an excellent definition of bigotry. A bigot hates. Bigotry is prejudice carried to an extreme, and this confusion between bigotry and prejudice has contributed to the confusion about the nature of prejudice. It is essential that this distinction is understood.

The second distinction that must be made concerns the issue of whether prejudice is learned behavior or an innate personality trait. Students are told about the preponderance of evidence reported by researchers in various disciplines revealing that no one has been able to identify a gene or hormone or chromosome that is the cause of prejudice. Prejudice is learned. We are taught in a variety of ways from a variety of sources to think of women, people of color, people with a disability, people in poverty, and others as inferior, as deficient. The power of the messages and the identity of particular people being demeaned will vary depending upon one's parents, one's neighborhood, and other factors, but the messages are embedded in our language, in our schools, in our media, in our traditions. It is important for students to understand that they did not choose to be prejudiced but were taught to be so. If students accept this assumption, they may accept the proposition that denying that they are prejudiced simply means that they will not be able to find effective ways to diminish the influence of prejudice in their lives.

It was Francis Bacon who asserted that "Knowledge is power." We argue that knowing how one has learned to be prejudiced and being able to identity those prejudices gives an individual the power to control one's prejudices. Our students usually understand this point intellectually. But some of them also begin to perceive the teacher in the pose of an unprejudiced expert and to resent what they also perceive as a holier-than-thou attitude.

To illustrate our point, we use a videotape of a talk show that focused on the topic of prejudice. The host interviews a human relations expert who makes strong statements about the pervasiveness of prejudice and, as a result, he arouses considerable antagonism in the audience. Some questions from the white members of the audience clearly reveal their prejudicial attitudes and provoke confrontational replies from the guest, and even at times from the host. Students are sometimes uncomfortable with the questions and the responses, and after the videotape they seem reluctant to begin discussing it.

To underscore the point that the teacher is not an unprejudiced expert by nature, one of us, Robert, uses the following illustration in his class. Upon his arrival at the residence hall on his first day at college, Robert and his father discovered that Robert's roommate was African American. His father immediately talked to the people in charge to request a room change for his son. The request was denied, so Robert's father took him aside for a serious advisory conversation. The essence of this advice reflected strong negative feelings about black people, coupled with concern for Robert's safety. In that instant, Robert recognized that what he was hearing was consistent with what he had been hearing all of his life, but he had not paid much attention to it until this incident occurred.

Robert explains to his students that he grew up in a home where victims were blamed and where myopic personal experiences were used as rationalizations for prejudice, and that he did not understand this until his father reacted the way he did to the black student who was to be Robert's roommate. This became his wake-up call to the reality of white arrogance and white racism. Robert admits that throughout the videotape they had just watched he could hear echoes of his father, his mother, the people in his neighborhood, and even his teachers. He has struggled with these messages, tried to overcome these rationalizations, and he challenges his students to join him in that struggle. Robert's confession makes it easier for his students to talk about the messages they heard and to connect those messages with the attitudes reflected in the comments on the videotape.

As part of their exploration of the topic of prejudice, students engage in a discussion where they function as if they were a committee for a hospital whose task is to select one individual among a group of nine seriously ill patients to be given a chance for survival. In the past, this had been done whenever new technology couldn't be developed to keep pace with demand. All nine people have a similar need and an excellent chance for survival if selected.

This does not allow students to make their decision based on medical criteria. Within the limited information provided, there is something in each patient that implies a so-called flaw in that person. The activity is designed to stimulate the stereotypes and prejudices that students may have learned and to do so by representing the types of people who are the recipients of such beliefs. As students discuss the patients and attempt to reach a consensus, it is usually evident which individuals in this imaginary group of people are preferred or devalued people. Afterwards, we identify the stereotypes and prejudices that were implicitly or explicitly articulated during the discussion. We challenge the students to recognize these stereotypes and to reflect on what experiences taught them to believe in such stereotypes or prejudices. This activity tends to make students feel particularly vulnerable and defensive.

Kent tells his students about his experience with this same activity and discusses how he eliminated the people he perceived as "inferior." At that time, he claimed not to have "a prejudiced bone in my body," and yet he immediately eliminated one person from the list because the person was labelled mentally retarded. In the discussion following the activity, Kent realized what this choice suggested about his attitudes, and he tried to remember what events might have caused him to learn this particular prejudice.

Several explanations emerged, and one of the first was related to *omission*. There were no mentally retarded children in his neighborhood nor in any class during his school years. They were segregated in separate schools. He never got to know a mentally retarded person. His primary exposure to mentally retarded children, or differently abled children in general, came from the fundraising telethons on television. What were called crippled children would be brought onstage while the host begged for money for the children. It is obvious now that such telethons did not teach viewers to value such children but presented them as pathetic burdens on society whose only value was as recipients of charity, as an opportunity for people donating to a good cause to feel good about themselves.

Another message came from Kent's parents. Kent emphasizes that his parents were loving, caring people who never made derogatory comments about racial or other groups. Their part in this issue stemmed from telephone calls they received when a friend or relative had a child who was born with what the parents perceived as a problem. Kent's parents would express their sorrow on the phone and in discussions with each other afterwards. Clearly they saw a mentally retarded child as a burden on the parents and were expressing their sympathy, but the message that such children were a burden was reinforced by two people with a powerful influence over their son. This is a particularly important example because there is no villain in this scenario, and yet clearly a prejudice was being taught.

The use of such personal anecdotes seems to be quite effective with students. This may be due primarily to the fact that all of the professors teaching

the course are white males. Dismissing such anecdotes seems to be more difficult for students when such comments come from representatives of the dominant group. Our willingness to share personal experiences that contributed to
our individual development opens the doors for students to begin to sort fact
from fiction and to grapple with their own personal and professional identities.

CONVENTIONAL RATIONALIZATIONS FOR PREJUDICIAL BEHAVIOR

Once students understand and accept the pervasiveness of prejudice and the
likelihood that they have learned some prejudices, they can more easily syn-
thesize research conclusions about the causes of prejudice. In addition to discussing the role of competition and the frustration-aggression hypothesis (Levin
1975), we also examine the negative behaviors that stem from prejudices.
These behaviors include not only name-calling and other confrontational behavior, but also avoidance behavior such as choosing to interact only with those
who are "my own kind" or withdrawing one's children from a desegregated
school or moving out of a neighborhood when people of color begin to pur-
chase homes there. When people engaging in these behaviors are asked if they
are prejudiced, most of them deny it, which illustrates the point that prejudice
will control behavior if the person is not in control of the prejudice. Our students begin to recognize that being able to identify their prejudices is to their
advantage because then they can manage those prejudices rather than be managed or manipulated by them.

Recognizing that prejudice is learned is a critical point in the process of
acknowledging one's own prejudice and that prejudices are pervasive in our
society. Some students want to deny the pervasiveness of prejudice, so we
provide them with a wide variety of examples from language, media, literature,
and legislation that reveal prejudicial content. These include expressions heard
from the home, the playground, or the office, such as "I jewed him down" or
"Stop acting like a bunch of wild Indians," "You're a sissy" or "What a retard."
Sometimes students contribute to these examples in class; for example, a married student once asked, "How come when my husband goes out with his
friends he says I'm home taking care of the kids, but when I go out with my
friends he says he is 'babysitting' the kids?"

Students are also introduced to examples of conventional rationalizations
that perpetuate prejudicial attitudes and inaction with regard to discrimination.
The denial rationalization is a denial that prejudice and discrimination exist, or
at least that they are significant problems. Typical denial rationalizations
include arguments for what is often called reverse discrimination or a personal
denial statement such as "I don't have a prejudiced bone in my body." We try
to emphasize in these discussions that the issue isn't about blaming anyone, but
it is about recognizing that the problems of prejudice and discrimination exist.
We challenge students to understand and identify many of the messages
reflected in the culture that teach us to be prejudiced, and we challenge them to

analyze their own attitudes honestly, to ascertain what prejudices they have learned as they have grown up in this culture.

Students often give examples from their own experiences, like the friends who told racist jokes or the football coach who tried what he perceived as inspiring his losing team at halftime by shouting, "You're playing like a bunch of girls!" One student overheard a middle-school teacher in a faculty lounge refer to a child as a welfare recipient by saying, "The only thing we need to teach him is how to fill out the welfare forms." Another student recalled that the special education students in his middle school were kept isolated in Room 2 which caused students and parents to refer to the "Room 2 kids" and for teachers to say, "Perhaps you should be in Room 2," whenever the students judged to be regular misbehaved.

Such comments make it easy for students to understand the victim blaming rationalization (Ryan 1976). We talk about the temptation to see problems as simply a deficiency in the victim, leading to solutions that only require that the victims change. Such statements are actually a version of the denial rationalization because they imply that the problem is not prejudice or discrimination, but that it is a "black problem" or an "Indian problem." Defining the problem as *their* problem means it is not *our* problem. Most students understand and identify statements that blame the victim, but avoidance rationalizations are more difficult.

Avoidance rationalizations are *yes, but* statements. The speaker appears to agree that prejudice and discrimination exist and that they represent a real problem in our society, but then the speaker avoids the issue by saying something that does not address the real issue or represents a false or partial solution. We provide examples of statements such as: "Yes prejudice is a problem, but we'll never have a perfect society" (How about improving the one we've got?); or "I agree sexism is a problem but I think if we stopped paying so much attention to it it would go away" (a transparently false solution); or "At our university we recognize the problem of prejudice, that's why we require our students to take one course in ethnic studies" (a partial, but obviously inadequate, response).

To deepen their understanding of both prejudice and these rationalizations, our students analyze magazine and television advertisements and comic strips and Saturday morning cartoons and situation comedies. One student went to a toy store to analyze the packaging and noted that a chemistry set had pictures of four boys (one was black) but no girls, and also noticed a box for a toy guitar that showed a boy playing the guitar and a girl dancing. One of the most common observations students make after looking at these images is how difficult it is to find images of microcultural racial groups such as Latino Americans or Asian/Pacific Island Americans. Images of Native Americans are easier to find, but students are surprised at how stereotypic these representations often are.

To explore how prejudice can be learned in classrooms, we discuss the concept of the "hidden curriculum" (Giroux and Purpel 1983) and provide students with examples of bias in instructional materials and textbooks. The students analyze these examples to identify the nature of the bias they contain. We explore options for supplementing textbooks to provide more accurate information, and students work in groups to generate strategies to use when they are teaching so their students can learn how to recognize such biases.

Perhaps the most important activity for examining the pervasiveness of prejudice in and out of the classroom is our continuing discussion of the denial, victim blaming, and avoidance rationalizations. Each week we ask the students to identify these rationalizations as they occur in conversation, in textbooks, in literature, in newspapers (especially in the local newspaper's letters to the editor and editorials), and in the students' own papers. Recently a decision was made at our university to change its athletic symbol from "Indians" to "Eagles." The change was not easy because a number of students and alumni did not understand what was wrong with calling our athletic teams the Indians. Debate in formal and informal groups across the campus provided the students in our classes with an excellent opportunity to hear the rationalizations.

For years, the local Winnebago Tribal Council had formally protested the use of Indians for athletic team logos and mascots, and students in the Native American campus organization voted in favor of eliminating the Indian symbol. Despite all this, a large number of white students and alumni denied that anything was wrong with having an Indian logo and mascot for the athletic teams. When they were told the opinions of the Winnebago Tribal Council and the Native American campus organization, they would only say that "these people" should be proud of our use of this symbol, that it was intended to honor them. Of course, they denied that they (or anyone who wanted to maintain this symbol) were being insensitive or racist.

In a letter to the editor of the local paper, an alumnus blamed the Native American campus organization for all the trouble and accused its members of not being "real Indians." There were other letters and comments that blamed Native Americans for "creating a problem where none had existed." There were also many examples of avoidance rationalizations. In one public debate on the issue, a white male student tried to avoid the issue of racism by asking why we couldn't simply abide by the will of the majority on this issue. "If the majority of students want to keep the Indian symbol for our athletic teams, why shouldn't we be able to?" An African American student replied, "If we always went by majority rule I would *still* be sitting in the back of a bus in Alabama."

As a consequence of these debates, our students understood denial, victim blaming, and avoidance rationalizations more clearly that semester than ever before. Since we cannot count on such a learning experience every semester, we collect statements containing rationalizations from various current sources and share them with the students throughout the semester. This not only gives the students opportunities to hear an array of examples, it also reveals how widespread such thinking is. Students will summarize statements made during discussions with family members or friends about issues pertaining to racism, sexism, homophobia, and so forth, and ask others in class to analyze the arguments for rationalizations and to help them develop appropriate responses. These preservice teachers understand that if they are to be effective participants in formal or informal discussions of these issues, they need to become skillful at identifying rationalizations in order to make appropriate responses.

THEORIES OF DISCRIMINATION

Toward the end of the semester, we examine the nature of discrimination in the United States using data from the U.S. Department of Labor, the Census Bureau, and a variety of other sources so that students can understand the extent of discrimination. They are also presented with current theories about discrimination (Feagin and Feagin 1986), emphasizing that prejudice as the sole cause of discrimination is no longer regarded as an adequate explanation. Several theories (e.g., institutionalized discrimination) are based on evidence suggesting that discrimination has been built into traditional institutional practices. If a business hires a white person based on the recommendation of a current employee, it does not necessarily mean that prejudice determined the choice. If most of the employees are white (even if this was a result of past discriminatory practices by the employer), it is probably that most of their friends are white. The word-of-mouth approach simply results in a friend helping another friend to get a job rather than an intentional action to discriminate (Feagin and Feagin 1986). Regardless of the intent, students recognize that the result of such practices still is discrimination against certain groups.

In order to analyze the accusations made about the existence of so-called reverse discrimination, students are provided with data on employment patterns by gender and race. Such data, particularly with regard to high-status jobs, clearly proves that the charge of reverse discrimination is a myth (Andrzejewski 1990). Students are given predictions concerning the workforce of the future based on current demographic data. We ask both males and females how comfortable they would be working for a female boss or being outnumbered by people of color at their worksite. We ask both female and male students to speculate on how they would feel in a marriage where the woman was making more than the man. We talk about the need (and benefits) for men to become more involved in parenting and about the advantages of having child care at the worksite. Students talk about the changes necessary to accommodate the needs they anticipate having in their adult lives, and even more important, the needs their children will have.

In all of these discussions, the common thread connecting the various ideas is the question of what is a just society and what needs to happen in the

United States to make *us* a more just society. This theme permeates their learning experiences in our classes. Reading assignments are from an anthology and include bell hooks, Gordon Allport, Enrique Lopez, Adrienne Rich, Christopher Lasch, Malcolm X, Marilyn French, John Tateishi and others (Colombo, Cullen and Lisle 1989). Our class discussions are student centered and are related to lecture information, reading assignments, and class activities. Student papers are expected to represent a synthesis of new information and personal insight. Many students recognize that it is to their advantage to be aware of these issues as our society experiences the process of change being predicted by the demographers (Book and Freeman 1986). As our students begin to work with their own students, they also recognize the importance of extending their awareness to their students because who will be living most of their adult lives in the next century when the predicted increase in diversity will have become a reality (Posner 1989). Because our preservice teachers care about students, they want to help their students to become competent (or even enthusiastic) participants in this pluralistic society.

IMPACT OF THE COURSE

We know that the course has a positive impact on students. In part, our knowledge is based on the anecdotal evidence of students' written and oral comments to us at the end of each semester. Students have told us that this was the best course they have ever taken. A consistent comment is, "my eyes have really been opened." We have talked to former students who have graduated and now are teaching who say that our course influenced them more as a person and as a teacher than any course they had during their undergraduate years. In addition to such self-reports, we also have the results from an attitude change inventory designed specifically for our course. The inventory includes forty-eight statements on issues of race, gender and class (sixteen for each area). At the beginning of the semester, half of the students are selected randomly to complete this inventory. At the end of the semester, the students who did not previously complete the inventory do so. Comparisons of the group mean scores consistently show a statistically significant change in student attitudes in all three areas (Martin and Koppelman 1991).

"What's in it for me?" has described various arguments presented during the semester to those students who enroll in the Understanding Human Differences course. The chapter title suggests that the primary appeal is to self-interest, and that is accurate but somewhat misleading. The self-interest involved here is not based on materialism or wealth, but on an understanding of the quality of life. Public television recently aired two programs with Bill Moyers entitled "Listening to America" and the "The Good Society." In that second program, Moyers presented people who were working with economically disadvantaged youth to improve their lives, to give them hope for the future. The intent was clearly to show examples of people who were doing their part to create a "good society." At the end of the program Moyers interviewed Robert Bellah, the respected sociologist who recently authored a book called *The Good Society*. After asking Dr. Bellah a variety of questions, Moyers expressed his conclusion that what Bellah was ultimately suggesting was that the people in power were going to have to recognize the changes taking place in the United States and they were going to have to decide to make major changes, to share their power, to share more of the resources of this society with others, especially with those less fortunate. Moyers asked Bellah to explain what would make them do that? What compelling reasons could this highly respected scholar offer? Bellah paused and began apologetically by saying that his answer might sound a little "corny." He looked at Moyers and responded without hesitation, "They will feel better about themselves . . . and they will be at peace with their creator."

It was a shocking statement, shocking for its simplicity. Despite the recent years of greed and graft, of scandal and corruption in government and business, people in the United States have always wanted to believe in a better future, a better life for them and for their children. Bellah was saying that a "better life" could or might now be based more on cooperation than on competition, on our compassion for one another rather than our obsession with self. His words reflected the principles of a Judeo-Christian tradition our politicians fondly invoke but seldom enact. His words reflected a consciousness that combined ethics and pragmatism to create a vision of a future most of us would be pleased to play a part in creating. It would, indeed, be a "good society."

As teacher educators, we accept the responsibility to empower our students so that they can empower their students (Apple 1982; LeCompte and deMarrais 1992). Preservice teachers must gain the skills necessary to analyze discriminatory behavior and to create curricular experiences that do not support or perpetuate victimization (Haberman 1988). If we can successfully challenge nonminority teachers to become committed to progress toward a more just society, all children will be the benefactors, and each of us can be a part of US.

REFERENCES

Andrzejewski, J. 1990. The myth of reverse discrimination. In *Human relations: The study of oppression and human rights*. Edited by J. Andrzejewski. 2d ed. Needham Heights, MA: Ginn Press.

Aoyagi, K. and R. Dore. 1964. The Buraki minority in urban Japan. *Transactions of the Fifth World Congress of Sociology* 3:95-107.

Apple, M. 1982. *Education and power*. London: Routledge and Kegan Paul.

Baber, C. and G. Gay. 1987. Black studies for white students—a critical need. *Momentum* 18:26-28.

Book, C. and D. Freeman. 1986. Differences in entry characteristics of elementary and secondary teacher candidates. *Journal of Teacher Education* 37:45-48.

Bromley, Y. 1987. Anthropology, ethnology and ethnic and racial prejudice. *International Social Science Journal* 39:31-43.

Brown, D. 1966. *Against the world: A study of white South African attitudes.* London: Collins.

Castles, S. 1984. *Here for good: Western Europe's new ethnic minorities.* London: Pluto.

Colombo, G., R. Cullen, and B. Lisle. 1989. *Rereading America: Cultural contexts for critical thinking and writing.* New York: St. Martin's Press.

Essed, P. 1991. *Understanding everyday racism: An interdisciplinary theory.* Newbury Park, CA: Sage Publications.

Feagin, J. and C. Feagin. 1986. *Discrimination American style.* 2d ed. Malabar, FL: Robert Krieger.

Giroux, H. and D. Purpel, eds. 1983. *The hidden curriculum and moral education: Deception or discovery?* Berkeley, CA: McCutchan Publishing Corporation.

Grant, C. and C. Sleeter. 1985. The literature on multicultural education: Review and analysis. *Educational Review* 37:97-118.

Haberman, M. 1988. The nature of multicultural learning in American society (an unpublished manuscript). University of Wisconsin-Milwaukee.

LeCompte, M. and K. deMarrais. 1992. The disempowering of empowerment: Out of the revolution and into the classroom. *Educational Foundations* 6:5-32.

Lerner, M. 1957. *America as a civilization.* New York: Simon and Schuster.

Levin, J. 1975. *The functions of prejudice.* New York: Harper & Row.

Martin, R. and K. Koppelman. 1991. The impact of a human relations/multicultural education course on the attitudes of prospective teachers. *The Journal of Intergroup Relations* 43:16-27.

Moyers, W., H. Weinberg (executive producer), and T. Casciato (producer). 1992. "Listening to America: The good society." Los Angeles: Public Broadcasting Association.

Myrdal, G. 1944. *An American dilemma.* New York: Harper and Row.

Perry, W. G. 1981. Cognitive and ethical growth: The making of meaning. In *The Modern American College.* Edited by A. Chickering. San Francisco: Jossey-Bass.

Posner, G. 1989. *Field Experience: Methods of reflective teaching.* 2d ed. New York: Longman.

Raths, L., M. Harmin, and S. Simon. 1966. *Values and teaching.* Columbus, OH: Charles E. Merrill Publishing Company.

Ryan, W. 1976. *Blaming the victim*. 2d ed. New York: Vintage Books.

Sleeter, C. E. and C. A. Grant. 1988. *Making choices for multicultural education: Five approaches to race, class, and gender*. Columbus: Merrill.

Stalvey, L. 1989. *The education of a WASP*. Madison: The University of Wisconsin Press.

MULTIPLE REALITIES:
MULTIPLE ENACTMENTS

10

WILLIAM D. ARMALINE _____

Reflecting on Cultural Diversity through Early Field Experiences: Pitfalls, Hesitations, and Promise

INTRODUCTION

When I reflect on my own teaching about issues of diversity, about how I confront with my students the existence of institutional oppression in and through schooling, I am struck first by the enormity of the task. How on earth do I even begin to address phenomena that are so complex and that go to the heart of who and what we are? How do I start to understand my own implication and responsibilities, and then move to helping others, in this case preservice teachers, understand how their histories collide with the histories of their students through their pedagogy? More to the point of this chapter, how do I articulate my struggle, how do I illustrate what I think are successes and insights, while at the same time recognize limitations, false starts, and previously unimagined complexities and problematics?

I will not discuss teacher education in general, nor will I even discuss my own coursework in the social foundations of education as a whole. Rather, I will focus on early field experiences used in conjunction with an entry level course involving a critical sociological analysis of schooling in the United States. I base my choice of emphasis on the need to narrow the scope to a manageable portion of the teacher education curriculum. While I recognize that segmenting that curriculum does violence to the overall experience of becoming a teacher, I choose the field component because it brings into bold relief the contrasting and at times conflicting cultural experiences of preservice teachers and the students whom they are being prepared to teach. It gives me an opportunity to discuss an evolving pedagogy designed to interrogate with students our perceptions, expectations, constructions, and ideological positions with respect to how we learn, what is important to know, and how we teach students in our classrooms, given an increasingly diverse population and emerging realizations with respect to institutional oppression and the need for transformative pedagogy.

EARLY FIELD EXPERIENCE

One widespread practice designed to induct preservice teachers into the culture of urban schools is to engage them in field experience. Field experiences provide preservice teachers with opportunities to interact with students and school personnel in the school and community setting. Of particular interest to me here are field experiences designed to occur early in the preservice teacher's preparation, often within the first year of university study.

Webb (1981) found these early field experiences offered by 99% of the 270 institutions studied. At least three claims provide the rationale for these early experiences. First, the immersion into the world of teacher work afforded to students by these experiences lessens the shock when these students assume control of their own classrooms. Second, these experiences help students make career decisions, weeding out those students who are not committed to the teaching profession (Cronin 1983). Third, this experience will help preservice teachers bridge the cultural gap between their own backgrounds and those of their students.

While many hold the view that the best way to improve teacher education (and by extension the education of children) is through preservice teachers working in the field (Becher and Ade 1982), researchers investigating the effects of early field experiences report conflicting results. (See Waxman and Walberg 1986, for a detailed review.) Some researchers report positive effects; others report no effects. Still others (Gibson 1976; Hoy and Reese 1977; Iannaccone 1963; Tabachnick 1980) report that early field experiences seem to promote simplistically utilitarian perspectives on teaching—focusing on the *How?* of teaching to the exclusion of the *Why?* Becher and Ade (1982) found that after their early field experiences, preservice teachers became increasingly authoritarian, rigid, controlling, restrictive, custodial, and impersonal and decreasingly student-centered, accepting, and humanistic. Their studies were corroborated by Waxman and Walberg (1986) who cite studies of first field experiences that document the lowering of preservice teachers' positive attitudes toward teaching and the shifting of orientation from the personal to the institutional, from the need to be humane and nurturing to the need to establish order and control.

As Goodman (1985) pointed out, there has been little research until recently on "what reality confronts preservice teachers once they are directly exposed to the classroom" (42). What is the experience, from the participants' perspective, of being a preservice teacher in an early field experience? How do they make sense of that experience? What do they accept and what do they question? Often, according to Feiman-Nemser and Buchmann (1986), the failure to question the "familiar" in field experiences precludes the preservice teacher from developing warranted assertions with respect to classroom and schooling practice.

CULTURAL CLASH, REFLECTIVE THINKING, AND FIELD EXPERIENCE

One purpose of early field experiences might be to generate the need to question the familiar as a means of reconstructing one's current understanding of school and classroom interactions. This would appear particularly important in situations in which the culture of the school (and most often that of the preservice teacher) and the culture of the student population conflict.

This cultural clash often occurs when white, middle-class preservice teachers enter urban schools. Without the benefit of reflective analysis, the problems are not likely to be recognized as cultural but rather as problems of individual (student) *pathology*, deprived family background, lack of work ethic, and the like. Engaging preservice teachers in the process of reflective thinking (Dewey 1933) in conjunction with their field experience increases the likelihood that they will be more sensitive to problems emanating from the intersection of diverse cultures and more likely to arrive at a decision or action based upon a combination of the relevant knowledge available and the contextual circumstances of the situation. To the extent that preservice teachers are able to engage in reflective thinking (i.e., consciously identifying and defining schooling and classroom problems, generating reasonable *guiding ideas* or hypotheses, and testing them through intelligent action), warranted decisions and actions become more probable.

Although field experiences do not necessarily develop intelligent and ethical practice, it would be inappropriate to conclude that such experiences are necessarily worthless or counterproductive. It is apparent from sparse research that although, as a result of field experiences, many preservice teachers become increasingly bureaucratic, rigid, custodial, conforming, and accepting of existing institutional structures (Beyer 1984; Silvernail and Costello 1983; Zeichner and Teitelbaum 1982), some do not. The critical factor in resisting the negative effects of the teachers' work environment may be the use of reflective sessions in conjunction with field experience (Goodman 1985; Tabachnick and Zeichner 1984; Zeichner and Liston 1987). Research into the process of reflective thinking and the construction of early field experiences that might foster reflective practice is vital to the improvement of early field experience as a central component of preservice teacher education. In what follows, I will explore the problems of developing early field experiences that will engender reflective thinking and will examine the effects of those experiences on preservice teachers and their students. The basis of this exploration is a study of the use of reflective sessions coupled with early field experiences (Farber and Armaline 1992). Following the discussion of the study, I will explore how the experience of conducting the study and examining its results caused me to reflect both on the ways in which students construct meaning and on my own pedagogy.

While the overall goal of the study was to better understand and improve our preparing students to work in urban settings, there were a number of more specific objectives. These included (a) determining whether preservice teachers' abilities to engage in reflective analysis are influenced by programmatic interventions; (b) determining whether reflective thinking (Dewey 1933) influences preservice teachers' abilities to process professional experiences in urban schools, especially as those experiences relate to cultural diversity and cultural clash; and (c) studying further the conceptual and empirical grounding for reflective thinking, and developing a means of coding and assessing reflective thinking in journals.

The study reported on students' abilities to reflect upon and learn from field experience. It examined the effects of restructuring early field experience around planned reflective sessions in which preservice teachers critically examined encounters with teachers, students, and curriculum. We posited that preservice teachers would be more likely to become intellectually engaged and to profit more fully from their field observations and interactions under these conditions. More specifically, the reflective sessions would render preservice teachers would be more likely and better able to examine their own cultural makeup and those of their students as they relate to teaching and learning in urban schools. As a result, they would be less likely to fall victim to the negative outcomes of nonreflective field experiences reported in the literature review.

DESIGN OF THE STUDY

Students placed in urban field sites as a part of the first and second courses in the initial teacher preparation program at the University of Toledo served as subjects. The total sample (N=56) included both males and females, as well as traditional and nontraditional students. A comparison group (N=28) was assigned to a typical early field experience (two-and-a-half hours per week in an urban school), where they worked with regular classroom teachers in whatever way the teacher deemed appropriate. The comparison group was matched as closely as possible to the experimental group over criteria such as age, sex, racial composition, and academic ability. The experimental group (N=28) had an experience designed to develop reflective thinking abilities through reflective sessions following each weekly classroom experience. Each classroom visit lasted 100 minutes, and the reflective session lasted fifty minutes, for a total of two-and-a-half hours. The reflective sessions were designed to develop an awareness of the methods and outcomes of teaching as they are affected by culture and the urban schooling environment. The total time of the experience for comparison and treatment groups was identical. A variety of quantitative measures and qualitative assessments were used before, during, and after the field experience. Initially, all students' ability to think hypothetically and to consider and manipulate multiple variables systematically were assessed by *How Is Your Logic* (Gray 1976). During the field experience, students in both groups kept journals. In addition, discussions engaged in as a part of the treatment were videotaped to document possible changes in reflectivity during the intervention. At the end of the field experience, students in both groups completed a narrative evaluation of their field experience as a final journal entry.

We anticipated that, by comparing treatment and comparison groups over the various measures, this study would begin to shed light on (a) whether preservice teachers' abilities to engage in reflective analysis are influenced by programmatic interventions; and (b) whether reflective thinking influences preservice teachers' abilities to process professional field experiences in urban settings, with particular emphasis on the role of culture in teaching and learning. The study was to aid in the development of prototypic early field experiences for teacher education programs whose goals include laying a foundation for reflective, well-grounded, and ethical practice.

DEWEY AND REFLECTIVE THINKING

The primary conceptual lens used to code the journals is Dewey's (1933) notion of "reflective thinking" (9). For Dewey, "active, persistent, and careful consideration of any belief or supposed form of knowledge in the light of the grounds that support it and further conclusions to which it tends constitutes reflective thought" (9). He saw reflective thinking as the process by which a problematic situation is most likely to be resolved, thereby establishing a sense of coherence and satisfaction.

Dewey (1933) stated that the function of reflective thinking is "to transform a situation in which there is experienced obscurity, doubt, conflict, disturbances of some sort, into a situation that is clear, coherent, settled, harmonious" (101-2). He illustrated and explicated the process of reflective thinking through the use of a series of phases that one employs as one reflects. Those phases are labeled as follows: phase one—suggestion; phase two—intellectualization; phase three—hypothesis generation; phase four—reasoning; and phase five—testing.

Reflective thinking begins when habit or routine action is disrupted and one experiences a feeling of doubt or conflict. One then must pause and consider alternatives to the routine (suggestion phase). These alternatives are examined with respect to the perceived facts of the matter to define the problem more clearly (intellectualization phase). With the problem in better focus, hypotheses or guiding ideas are generated (hypothesis phase) and their ramifications examined (reasoning phase). The culmination of the reflective process is acting on one of the hypotheses in an attempt at verification (testing phase). Should the hypothesis that is tested be verified, the state of perplexity is resolved and coherence reestablished. Action can proceed with new and deeper understanding of one's situation.

Reflective thinking is a reconstructed logic not to be taken as a "recipe." In actuality, it is a dynamic and fluid process. Further, the process of "verification" contained within reflective thinking is not personally removed or objectified, disconnected from the self. Rather, for verification to be meaningful, it must be connected both to the outer world and to one's inner world. Reflectivity begins and ends with one's subJectivity. Reflective thinking is an intentional act of creating meaning, grasping the previously unrecognized relationships between and among elements of problematic situations. One is consciously trying to make sense of a confusing, vague, and/or ambiguous experience.

METHOD

Two readers familiar with Dewey's notion of reflective thinking examined all journals to determine the nature, scope, and quality of entries. Because the overarching concern of the study is the application of reflective thinking to experiences of preservice teachers in the field, readers coded the kinds of problematic situations about which subjects wrote, identified the extent to which they engaged in reflective analysis of those problems, and assessed an additional index for depth of analysis that is determined by the type of concern captured in the problematic itself. In other words, three factors were primary to the analysis.

Factor 1

The first factor is the number and type (category) of problem generated by the students as represented in their journal entries. The categories emerged out of the reading of the journals and were not established prior to their reading. In total, journal entries yielded twelve categories of problems (problematic situations) listed and briefly described below. The categories relate to problems encountered with respect to the preservice teachers, labeled *personal*; problems associated with the cooperating teacher, labeled *teacher*; and problems related to the K-12 students, labeled *student*.

A. Student behavior—any concern that focused on the behavior of the students in the classroom, such as control of students, management, and discipline.
B. Student learning and performance—any concern with the actual performance, abilities, or learning of students in the setting.
C. Student needs—concerns that relate to the physical, emotional, and/or psychological needs of students in the field setting.
D. Personal performance—concerns over the preservice teacher's instructional capabilities and actions.
E. Personal needs—concerns dealing with the preservice teacher's physical, emotional, and/or psychological needs.
F. Personal planning—concerns dealing with the preservice teacher's problems related to planning and time for preparation for instruction.
G. Personal career—concerns related to the preservice teacher's choice of teaching as a career and the responsibilities of being a teacher.
H. Teacher behavior—concerns that focus on the behavior of the cooperating teacher in the field setting dealing with situations that were either disciplinary or noninstructional.

I. Teacher performance—concerns over the cooperating teacher's instructional capabilities and actions.
J. Curriculum—concerns over the choice, preparation, and/or use of curriculum materials by anyone in the instructional setting.
K. Student/student interaction—concerns over encounters between or among K-12 students in the field setting.
L. Teacher/student interaction—concerns over encounters between or among students and anyone in the role of teacher.

Factor 2

The second factor considered in the analysis of journal entries is the degree to which the entry indicates that the writer engaged in the phases of reflective thinking. In brief, each problematic situation that preservice teachers entered in their journals was assessed in terms of the highest phase of reflective thinking indicated. The categories include (A) identification of a problematic situation and no further reflection, (B) identification of a problematic situation followed by the generation of at least one suggestion regarding its resolution, (C) a problematic followed by both suggestion and intellectualization, (D) a problematic reflected upon to the point of generating at least one hypothesis, (E) a problematic reflected upon through the hypothesis phase and including some reasoning about the ramifications of acting upon that hypothesis, and (F) a problematic carried through all the above phases and culminating in some action. In the analysis, entries were coded on the basis of the highest or most advanced phase of reflectivity indicated. When readers differed over the highest phase indicated in the entry, each reexamined the entry until they arrived at a mutually acceptable rating.[1]

Factor 3

The third and final factor in the analysis is another indicator for depth of analysis, represented in the coding system by Levels I, II, or III. Factor 2 assesses the degree to which the journal entry shows reflective thinking in terms of phases. Factor 3 assesses what is called into question and the depth at which the preservice teacher deliberates upon teaching and learning. That is, to deliberate about teaching can be viewed in a number of ways with respect to the scope of activities and factors that make up the act of teaching. Some might restrict deliberation to rather specific teaching and learning acts, in relative isolation from broader social, political, economic, or cultural factors (Berliner 1985; Smith, Cohen, and Pearl 1969, to name two). Others would include these broader issues as vitally important and related to making even the most specific teaching decisions (Aronowitz and Giroux 1985; Beyer 1984; Ginsburg and Newman 1985; Goodman 1985; Zeichner and Teitelbaum 1982).

Approaches to reflecting on field experiences, then, can differ over "levels of reflectivity" (Van Manen 1977; Zeichner and Teitelbaum 1982). The levels used to code journal entries on Factor 3 are Level I—the "technical application of educational knowledge"; Level II—"practical action"; and Level III—"critical reflectivity" (adapted from Zeichner and Teitelbaum 1982, 103-4). The first level of reflectivity involves the application of knowledge gleaned from research on teaching and/or from teaching practice, but it does not involve the questioning of educational ends. "Economy, efficiency, and effectiveness" are the primary concerns at this level of reflectivity.

The second level "is based on a conception of practical action where the problem is one of explicating and clarifying the assumptions and predispositions underlying practical affairs and assessing the educational consequences to which action leads." All educational action is seen as "linked to particular value commitments," with debate focusing on "the worth of competing educational goals" (Zeichner and Teitelbaum 1982, 103).

Concerns at Level II outstrip the instrumentality of Level I. But to debate meaningfully any value position beyond the level of the relationship of a particular practice to its accompanying educational principle, one must move to the third level of reflectivity. Critical reflectivity 'legitimates a notion of inquiry where education students can begin to identify connections between the level of the classroom (e.g., the form and content of curriculum, classroom social relations) and the wider educational, social, economic and political conditions that impinge upon and shape classroom practice" (Zeichner and Teitelbaum 1982, 104). In Level III, questions of justice, equity, and personal fulfillment become issues relevant to education, and teachers must begin to weigh the competing value positions against relevant ethical standards.

For example, the category of "student behavior" could include problems that focus on children who "misbehave" with an emphasis on finding ways that are likely to be effective in "modifying" that behavior. Students might engage in all phases of reflective thinking to resolve the problem and receive a rating on factor 2 indicating such. On factor 3, however, this journal entry would be coded as Level I, exhibiting concerns relating only to management, control, and efficiency.

Another entry dealing with the same category of "student behavior" might exhibit a lesser degree of reflection in terms of phases represented in the entry, but nonetheless be rated on factor 3 as representing a deeper level analysis. A student who expressed a concern over the possible conflict between wanting to teach students to be independent and creative thinkers, while at the same time controlling them through manipulations of rewards and punishments, would be judged as operating at Level II.

A rating of Level III would result if the student not only recognized multiple and potentially conflicting value orientations, but also engaged in critically evaluating each in terms of relevant ethical, cultural, emotional, and/or intellectual criteria and principles. For example, the preservice teacher might discuss the ethical implications of controlling students' behavior in particular ways while at the same time espouse the goal of teaching students to think for themselves. Again, two readers assessed all entries. Where disagreements or questions arose, rereading and discussion between readers resulted in mutually agreeable ratings.

RESULTS

No group differences in logical thinking ability as measured by the "How's Your Logic" instrument were found. Six members of the treatment group and five members of the comparison group scored at the lowest, or concrete, level of logical thinking. Twelve treatment group members and eleven comparison group members were assessed as being in transition from concrete to formal operational thinking. Ten members of the treatment group and twelve members of the comparison group fell into the formal operational category. Given this breakdown, it might be argued that the comparison group showed slightly higher logical reasoning ability than the treatment group members.

Tables 10.1 and 10.2 cross problematic categories found in the journals (Factor 1) with the extent to which preservice teachers engaged in Dewey's notion of reflective thinking (Factor 2), indicated by the highest phase reached for the comparison and the treatment groups, respectively. The cells contain total frequencies summed over all levels of factor 3. In addition, the numbers in parentheses represent Level II frequencies only. No fully developed Level III entries were mutually agreed upon.

Tables 10.1 and 10.2 show that the treatment group outdistanced the comparison group in number of problematic situations addressed. In addition, a comparison of the extent to which the two groups used Dewey's phases of reflective thinking is striking. In the comparison group, there were only thirteen instances of hypotheses being generated (twelve to the hypothesis phase only and one that included reasoning), only one instance of a problematic being reflected upon to the level of reasoning, and none mentioned testing hypotheses. In the case of the experimental group, there were 124 hypotheses generated (seventy-seven to the hypothesis phase only, and forty-seven to the reasoning or testing phase), forty-seven instances of problematics carried at least to the reasoning phase, and twenty-four hypotheses being tested in the field setting.

In looking at the Level II frequencies in parentheses below the total cell frequencies for the comparison and treatment groups, what can be seen is the relative absence of recognition of problematics that go deeper than technical effectiveness in the comparison group (two entries). The treatment group was more likely to identify problematics that reflect a concern over multiple and at times conflicting value orientations and their effects on practice (twenty-eight entries). There are no cell frequencies for Level III of Factor 3 because no entries were found by both readers that clearly employed "critical reflection" in terms of assessing and evaluating completing value claims and orientations.

TABLE 10.1
Problematic Situations Generated by Degree of Reflectivity:
Comparison Group—Total Frequencies

	Phases of Reflectivity					
Problematics	Problem Only	Suggestion	Intellec- tualization	Hypothesis	Reasoning	Testing
A. Student Behavior	26	12	5	1	0	0
B. Student Learning and Performance	12	7	6	3 (1)	1	0
C. Student Needs	1	2	2	0	0	0
D. Personal Performance	6	3	2	2	0	0
E. Personal Needs	6	4	1	1	0	0
F. Personal Planning	0	0	0	0	0	0
G. Personal Career	0	0	1	3	0	0
H. Teacher Behavior	4	2	6	2	0	0
I. Teacher Performance	0	0	4	0	0	0
J. Curriculum	0	0	0	0	0	0
K. Student/Student Interaction	1	2 (1)	2	0	0	0
L. Teacher/Student Interaction	0	0	1	0	0	0

* Numbers in parentheses represent Level II frequencies only. If no Level II frequencies appear, the cell frequency was zero.

DISCUSSION OF RESULTS

The treatment group wrote more, in greater detail and depth, and with more analysis and application of a variety of issues that affect schooling success than did the comparison group. Further, the treatment group, having had the opportunity to reflect systematically and over time, analyzed themselves more deeply in regard to understanding differences between their own culture and those of the students with whom they worked in the field.

TABLE 10.2
Problematic Situations Generated by Degree of Reflectivity:
Treatment Group—Total Frequencies

	Phases of Reflectivity					
Problematics	Problem Only	Suggestion	Intellec- tualization	Hypothesis	Reasoning	Testing
A. Student Behavior	13	7	32	19 (2)	2 (1)	1
B. Student Learning and Performance	9	6	10	15 (2)	2	5 (1)
C. Student Needs	7	6	9	8 (1)	3 (2)	0
D. Personal Performance	10	6	24	17 (1)	5 (2)	12 (5)
E. Personal Needs	8	7	6	11 (3)	2	1
F. Personal Planning	0	0	4 (1)	1	1	0
G. Personal Career	0	0	2	4 (2)	3 (3)	2 (2)
H. Teacher Behavior	0	0	1	0	2 (1)	0
I. Teacher Performance	0	0	2 (1)	0	0	0
J. Curriculum	0	0	1	0	1 (1)	1
K. Student/Student Interaction	0	0	2	0	0	0
L. Teacher/Student Interaction	1	2	4	2	2 (1)	2 (1)

* Numbers in parentheses represent Level II frequencies only. If no Level II frequencies appear, the cell frequency was zero.

This was especially true for racial differences, and to a lesser extent, differences of gender and class. Students in the treatment group (a) engaged more frequently in reflective analysis of their experiences in the field and (b) processed the field experience more fully, especially in terms of the effects of culture on teaching and learning. The following journal entry from a member of the treatment group illustrates her initial reflections on the effect of a student's home environment on school behavior and performance. In the entry, the preservice teacher discussed a visit with a cooperating teacher to the home of an elementary school student who was involved in a fight that day.

> We walked the little girl to her apartment. The building was a disaster. The window on the entrance door was shattered, there were beer cans and liquor bottles lying on the floor and the building, in general, was not kept up at all. I was almost scared to be there. I'm really not too sure what I would have done in that situation. . . . I feel I learned the most from today's class . . . because I learned what type of environment the children actually come from, so I can try to understand a little more what they've grown up with and continue to live with. . . . One thing I really appreciated was the opportunity to learn about a type of background I really knew nothing about. (E.D., 1991, Field Journals)

Although we hoped for even more analysis at deeper levels from the treatment group, it must be emphasized that they were students in introductory course work in teacher education. Many of these students, in fact, were in only their second or third quarter of university study. This student, for instance, recognized poverty as a critical element in the lives of the children she was teaching, but she never reached the point of analyzing how racism, sexism, and the demands of capital affect an individual's life chances. Instead, she and her peers held fast to the belief that hard work and the right attitude on the part of the child's mother were what was needed to change what she "has grown up with and continue(s) to live with."

The most significant insights seemed to occur in the reflective sessions that were held with the treatment group following each of their field experience visits. The students showed a great deal of willingness to engage in discussion of issues of cultural clash in nearly all its forms in an effort to understand and improve their own interaction with the students in their charge. These sessions were the most interesting source of data, perhaps because in conversation comments could be pursued by others in the group and result in greater depth of analysis. In addition, it seemed that students in the reflective sessions developed a sense of connectedness to one another that provided some support when discussions focused on highly personal and sometimes threatening issues and incidents. Further, less experienced and less competent students seemed to benefit from the comments and insights of their more competent peers, and students seemed also to benefit from the comments of the faculty during the reflective sessions. In sum, the reflective sessions following each field visit provided for dialogue, enhancing the social aspect of participants' attempts to construct meaning. Because the reflective sessions were a part of the treatment and hence were experienced only by the experimental group, there is no direct comparison to be made to the other group.

As a final note regarding the study's operation, the system of coding journals developed for this study provides a means for analyzing the degree and the level at which preservice teachers reflect on culture, teaching and learning. As we suggested in the study, there are problems and limitations to using Dewey's notions of reflective thinking (Farber and Armaline 1992). The system nonetheless provides valuable information to the preservice teacher and university professor alike with respect to what is actually being considered problematic, as well as what practical and theoretical/ideological lenses are being used to make sense of the experience.

SUGGESTIONS, PUZZLEMENTS, AND LOOSE ENDS

This study suggests that field experiences in teacher education that include the opportunity to reflect on practice can increase the likelihood that preservice teachers will recognize and attempt to process more of the complexity that marks teaching and learning especially as it unfolds in culturally diverse settings. Given the research on field experiences that documents deleterious effects in terms of preservice teachers' attitudes and orientations toward teaching, the study sheds light on ways that these negative effects might be reversed. The tone of the journals in the treatment group and the reflective sessions that followed each field visit showed almost none of the negativism and loss of idealism cited in the field experience literature.

It appears that if there are opportunities for reflective sessions in conjunction with field experiences, preservice teachers have the capacity to reflect more deeply and in more complex ways than is seen in traditional field experiences, even at very early junctures in their education. In addition, the study begins to address Adler's concern over the paucity of empirical evidence for strategies that "promote critical reflection" (1991, 148). While we found no clearly established and mutually agreed upon pattern of critical reflection in the journals of our students, we did find students in the reflective sessions engaging in analyses of their experience at levels beyond technical rationality and instrumentality. They often thoughtfully examined and questioned curricular and instructional practices in schools, with an eye not merely toward performing their schooling roles more effectively and efficiently, but also toward transforming the goals and purposes of their work.

Yet why is it so difficult for preservice teachers to move to the level of critical reflectivity? Is the expectation unreasonable that entry level students in teacher education begin to consider and understand the multiple ways in which one's identity is constructed in conjunction with social and cultural institutions? Is critical reflectivity beyond the grasp of most entry level students? Assuming for a moment that the answer to these questions is "Maybe not," what resistances might be at work, what barriers to critical reflection might be present in the process of constructing and reconstructing meaning? Clearly we see that the sense that preservice teachers make of their experience is colored by the interpretive lenses or filters through which they view the world (Armaline and Hoover 1989). It is these filters, the ideological constructs out of which we all formulate our world of experience, that are often called into question when we engage in critical reflectivity. And these filters are hard to expose and even harder to critique. At the same time, is my emphasis on critical reflectivity overly prescriptive, directed, and potentially oppressive?

Deborah Britzman discusses her own pedagogical efforts with preservice teachers and found a great deal of resistance to rethinking what I am calling ideological lenses or constructs (1992). She suggests that students' "structures of feeling" are often bases for resistance to what I am referring to as critical reflection. Structures of feeling allude "to the complex array and disarray of the feelings, desires, and commitments toward social life that students already hold. While institutional structures strongly affect thought and feelings, rarely is there space for articulation. This dynamic, between the structures of institutions and the structures of feelings, is both intricately bound and, for the most part, in daily practice, fundamentally experienced as antagonistic" (Britzman 1992, 252).

To illustrate how structures of feeling operate to reinforce dominant cultural and ideological positions, Britzman details a classroom incident with her own students, preservice teachers in a graduate teacher education program in English education. In her illustration, her mostly female class of graduate students read Magda Lewis and Roger Simon's (1986) "A Discourse Not Intended for Her: Learning and Teaching Within Patriarchy." In this piece Lewis and Simon explore power relations between men and women, students and professor, in a graduate seminar, with particular emphasis on whose voice is heard and whose experience is valued. Simon, as the (male) professor in the class, also struggles with how, despite his expressed concern that women be heard, his own pedagogy might "subjugate" his students (Britzman 1992, 255-56).

Britzman believed that experiences of the women in her own class would resonate with the struggles against patriarchy of Lewis and her graduate student colleagues, but their reaction was quite different from her expectations. "I did not anticipate the fact that this article would not be persuasive to my students. I expected that we could simply talk about what was occurring in this other seminar and, in this way, I presupposed . . . the willingness of students to consider texts in relation to their lives" (Britzman 1992, 256). Britzman suggests that her students resisted analyses that emphasized how power relations affect classroom dynamics because such an analysis "directly challenged their unarticulated hopes for a classroom without social conflict" (1992, 256). While both the men and women could recount similar experiences in their own classrooms, they still invoked a belief in the cultural notion of rugged individualism as a way of discounting the struggles of the women in the article as whining and complaining, as simply not credible (Britzman 1992, 256).

If these students, whose experiences in schools paralleled those in the Lewis and Simon article, exhibited resistance to an interrogation of the ideological supports for oppressive social arrangements, indeed if they were resistant even to label the schooling interplay as oppressive, what must be the dynamics of resistance at work in situations where lived experience is vastly different? How powerfully must the structures of feeling of my largely white, middle-class undergraduates mitigate against a critically reflective interpretation of schooling contexts with predominantly African American, low-income children? How difficult must it be for my students to negotiate the realization that as whites, they are privileged and may represent the oppressors? How can they begin to imagine that, despite the best of intentions, their own pedagogy might also subjugate? Are they also deeply invested in maintaining the idea that their classrooms can be conflict free, unmuddled by the complexities of institutional oppression and power relations? And what kinds of subjugation might have been at work in my own teaching? How can I better understand that curriculum does not "speak for itself" and is not the "only authorized experience?" How can I "swallow my astonishment" and begin to "take as credible the kinds of complications (my) students offered" (Britzman 1992, 257)?

Perhaps the notion of structures of feeling helps to reconfigure my perceptions of limitations in students' reflection. Patti Lather reminds us that there is always a danger of assuming a privileged position of "the Grand Theorist" (1991, 137). Rather than assuming false or inadequate consciousness on the part of our students, we might try to enter in conversation with them and take into consideration possible multiple readings of the same situation or text, and not necessarily force a single interpretation or conclusion. The question becomes, "How are students creating meaning?" and not merely "What meaning do they make?"

While this post-structuralist, non-essentialist influence is in many ways compelling to me, I still struggle with the "multiple readings" approach. Clearly, experience varies and no single narrative in and of itself may suffice. But is there not the possibility that, in an effort at recognizing and encouraging many interpretations, we might reinforce interpretations that continue racist, sexist, heterosexist, and class-biased renderings of teaching and learning in schools?

At this point in my pedagogical development, my idea is to inspect possible social and cultural ramifications of adopting the multiple readings that my students and I offer as we proceed through various texts.[2] We need to ask, I think, what it would mean for ourselves, for our students, and for our social and cultural systems were we to act on the various meanings that we construct. In this way, I try to avoid enforcing my own views at the expense of those of my students, while at the same time not falling victim to the critiques of relativism and nihilism leveled against post-structuralist and non-essentialist readings of text. This is not an unproblematic and uncomplicated approach, as the ambiguity of multiple readings engenders a great deal of incoherence and dissonance; and the knowingly foolish, misplaced desire for certainty is ever present and waiting to save me from the messiness of ongoing identity re/construction. Yet hope and possibility lie precisely in that ambiguity and uncertainty.

NOTES

1. There are limitations to using the highest phase found in the entry as an indicator of reflective thinking. It is possible that in Entry A one might be reflecting a great deal by generating a large number of suggestions and matching those suggestions to the objective conditions present in the problematic (intellectualization phase) and never really progress to the "higher" phases of reflective thought. At the same time, in Entry B one might move through the phases without enjoining as many possibilities, thereby securing a higher rating for reflective thinking on factor 2 than is the case with Entry A. In reading the actual entries, this was not a problem that occurred often enough to skew the results, however. A second concern is conceptual, in that this schema runs the risk of presenting reflective thinking as a hyperrational, linear process; and that would be an error. Conceptual distortion is avoided by using factor 3 as an additional indicator for depth of reflective thinking, in conjunction with the realization on the part of the raters that a linear, hyperrational reading of reflective thinking is mistaken.

2. I am indebted to Kathleen S. Farber for her insights into the potentially limiting, oppressing, and subjugating features of critical pedagogy, as well as for her ideas about post-structuralist teaching that is not relativistic.

REFERENCES

Adler, S. 1991. The reflective practitioner and the curriculum of teacher education. *Journal of Education of Teaching* 17(2):139-50.

Armaline, W. D. 1990. Critical theory and the reconceptualization of critical thinking. Paper presented at the annual meeting of the American Educational Research Association, Boston.

Armaline, W. and R. Hoover. 1989. Field experience as a vehicle for transformation: Ideology, education, and reflective practice. *Journal of Teacher Education* 40(2):42-48.

Aronowitz, S. and H. Giroux. 1985. *Education under siege.* South Hadley, MA: Bergin and Garvey.

Association of Teacher Educators. 1988. Images of reflection in teacher education. Reston, VA: Association.

Becher, R. M. and W. E. Ade. 1982. The relationship of field placement characteristics and students' potential field performance abilities to clinical experience performance ratings. *Journal of Teacher Education* 33(2):24-30.

Berliner, D. 1985. Laboratory settings and the study of teacher education. *Journal of Teacher Education* 36(6):2-8.

Beyer, L. 1984. Field experience, ideology, and the development of critical reflectivity. *Journal of Teacher Education* 35(3):36-41.

Borrowman, M. 1956. *The liberal and technical in teacher education.* New York: Teachers College Bureau of Publication, Columbia University.

Britzman, D. 1992. Structures of feeling in curriculum and teaching. *Theory into practice* 31(3):252-58.

Clift, R. T., R. W. Houston, and M. Pugach. 1990. *Encouraging reflective practice in education: an analysis of issues and programs.* New York: Teachers College Press.

Cronin, J. M. 1983. State regulation of teacher preparation. In *Handbook of teaching and policy.* Edited by L. S. Shulman and G. Sykes. New York: Longman.

Dewey, J. 1933. *How we think.* Lexington, MA: Heath.

Farber, K. S. and W. D. Armaline. 1989. Toward a program of critical reflectivity: historical and conceptual explorations. Paper presented at the annual meeting of the American Educational Research Association, San Francisco.

——. 1992. Examining cultural conflict in urban field experiences through the use of reflective thinking. Paper presented at the annual meeting of the American Educational Research Association, San Francisco.

Feiman-Nemser, S. and M. Buchmann. 1986. Pitfalls of experience in teacher preparation. In *Advances in teacher education.* Edited by J. D. Raths and L. G. Katz. Vol. 2, 61-74. Norwood, NJ: Ablex.

Field Journals. 1991. Education in a diverse society: Field experience. The University of Toledo, College of Education and Allied Professions.

Gibson, R. 1976. The effect of school practice: The development of student perspectives. *British Journal of Teacher Education* 2:241-50.

Ginsberg, M. and K. Newman. 1985. Social inequalities, schooling, and teacher education. *Journal of Teacher Education* 36(2):49-54.

Giroux, H. 1991. *Feminism, postmodernism, and cultural politics.* Albany: State University of New York Press.

Goodman, J. 1985. What students learn from early field experiences: A case study and critical analysis. *Journal of Teacher Education* 36(6):42-48.

Gray, W. M. 1976. *How Is Your Logic?* Experimental Edition, Form A. Boulder, CO: Biological Sciences Curriculum Study.

Hoy, W. and R. Reese. 1977. The bureaucratic socialization of teachers. *Journal of Teacher Education* 28:26-28.

Iannaccone, L. 1963. Student teaching: A transitional stage in the making of a teacher. *Theory into Practice* 2:73-81.

Institutional Research Office. 1988. *Resource Consumption Report.* The University of Toledo.

Lather, P. 1991. *Getting smart: Feminist research and pedagogy with/in the postmodern.* New York: Routledge.

Lewis, M. and R. Simon. 1986. A discourse not intended for her: Learning and teaching within patriarchy. *Harvard Educational Review* 56:457-72.

Office of Retention Services. 1988. *Retention in the College of Education 1986-1988.* The University of Toledo.

Silvernail, D. and M. Costello. 1983. The impact of student teaching and internship programs on preservice teachers' pupil control perspectives, anxiety levels, and teaching concerns. *Journal of Teacher Education* 34(4):32-36.

Smith, B., S. Cohen, and A. Pearl. 1969. *Teachers for the real world.* Washington, DC: American Association of Colleges for Teacher Education.

Tabachnick, B. R. 1980. Intern-teacher roles: Illusion, disillusion, and reality. *Journal of Education* 162:122-37.

Tabachnick, B. R., T. S. Popkewitz, and K. M. Zeichner. 1980. Teacher education and the professional perspectives of student teachers. *Interchange* 10:12-29.

Tabachnick, B. R. and K. M. Zeichner. 1984. The impact of the student teaching experience on the development of teacher perspectives. *Journal of Teacher Education* 35(6):28-36.

Van Manen, M. 1977. Linking ways of knowing with ways of being practical. *Curriculum Inquiry* 6:205-28.

Waxman, H. C. and H. J. Walberg. 1986. Effects of early field experiences. In *Advances in teacher education.* Edited by J. D. Raths and L. G. Katz. Vol. 2, 165-84. Norwood, NJ: Ablex.

Webb, C. 1981. Theoretical and empirical bases for early field experiences in teacher education. In *Exploring field experiences in teacher education.* Edited by C. Webb, N. Gehrke, P. Ishler, and A. Mendozza. Provo, UT: Utah State University.

Zeichner, K. M. and D. P. Liston. 1987. Teaching student teachers to reflect. *Harvard Educational Review* 57:23-48.

Zeichner, K. M. and K. Teitelbaum. 1982. Personalized and inquiry-oriented teacher education: An analysis of two approaches to the development of curriculum for field-based experiences. *Journal of Education for Teaching* 8(2):95-117.

11

Elizabeth Quintero and Ana Huerta-Macías _____

To Participate . . . To Speak Out:
A Story from San Elizario, Texas

Introduction

Ms. R. and Ms. N. live in San Elizario, Texas. San Elizario, which four hundred years ago had what may have been the first formal school in Texas, is now one of the ten poorest school districts in Texas. The picture in the district is stark: students there do few science experiments because the district cannot afford the equipment; teachers make their own audiovisual aids at their own expense; student workbooks are recycled from year to year; thirty-five teachers at the elementary school share two television sets and two aging videocassette players; and the heater doesn't always work on cold days (Renteria 1989).

Some school administrators at the state and local levels believe that the underlying causes of all the school's problems are the apathy, low education level, and lack of English skills of the parents of the school children. A descriptive study of parents participating in a three-year family literacy project for limited English-speaking families provided data strongly suggesting that the administration's perceptions of the problems are incorrect.

Our data suggest that two women in our case studies have a passion for critical transformation of their families' educational and community situation. Our data suggest that Mexican women with whom we worked were daily dealing with issues of ethnicity, race, class, and gender. In this process, when provided with even minimal access to information through a critical pedagogy, the women reveal potential to become transformative intellectuals as described by Giroux and McLaren (1986). Yet the complexities of the transformation and pedagogy involved—the social context of the literacy classes, the family situation of each woman, and the community situation in the small border town—can best be understood in the context of Simon's (1988) question regarding human possibility: "A critical pedagogy can only be correctly discussed from within a particular 'point of practice'; from within a specific time and place and within a particular theme. This means doing critical pedagogy is a strategic, practical task not a scientific one. It arises not against a background of psychological, sociological, or anthropological universals as does much educational theory related to pedagogy—but from such questions as: *"how is human possibility being diminished here?"* (1988, 2).

"Stories from San Elizario, Texas" documents a small portion of two women's quests for power in a community where human possibility has been diminished for years. Their personal experience is used as a point of departure to explore some of the most difficult questions regarding critical transformation. The data was collected as part of a qualitative research study. The women were participants in a family literacy project for limited English-speaking families (funded by the Department of Education, Office of Bilingual Education and Language Minority Affairs). Of course, what occurred in the literacy program was only a part of the story. But it was an extremely important part and in many ways was connected with the totality of the dynamics of struggle for transformation in each woman's life. Moreover, the naturalistic documentation methods helped to guard against looking at incidents in isolation and out of context.

Research Methodology

Case studies of Ms. N. and Ms. R. will be discussed in this paper as two concrete and specific examples of the complexity involved in critical transformation of two Mexican women in a border sociocultural context. The case studies are best described through a narrative format and analyzed using a postmodern framework for discussion. Giroux (1990) argues "for a postmodern discourse of resistance as a basis for developing a cultural politics and an anti-racist pedagogy" (6). The framework Giroux (1990) suggests delineates the following categories.

1. a focus on the importance of history as a form of counter-memory (Kaplan 1987),
2. the value of the everyday as a source of agency and empowerment (Grossberg 1988),
3. a renewed understanding of gender as an irreducible historical and social practice constituted in a plurality of self- and social representation (De Lauretis 1987),
4. a rethinking of the borders of one's existence through attention to the contingent, discontinuous and unrepresentable. (Giroux 1990, 14)

First, we will describe the context of the study in terms of the theoretical framework for the family literacy activities implemented in San Elizario. Second, in our discussion of the two case studies we will look at varied events that reflect the categorical articulations of postmodernism as critical resistance. Third, we offer implications for case study research in critically participatory programs to vividly illuminate the urgent need for collaboration of educational research and social policy planning and to create points for pedagogical practice of resistance and social change on a holistic level.

Context of the Study

Project FIEL, Family Initiative for English Literacy, was a family literacy project operating in seven schools in the El Paso, Texas area. Parents attended class with their kindergarten and first-grade children, once a week in their neighborhood school, to participate in the small-group sessions. The groups consisted of five to seven families facilitated by a teacher and assistant. The design of Project FIEL was based on a participatory instructional model that relies heavily on students' prior knowledge and present learning needs and that values cultural and linguistic diversity.

In addition, at the request of parents, critical literacy parent groups were implemented monthly at two schools. The parents met together (the hour prior to the family literacy classes) to interact with each other and with invited community service consultants who led the discussion regarding issues such as parenting, family advocacy, and access to services and information.

Thus, the opportunity for information access, participation and critical analysis was varied in content and scope, but occurred regularly in the community of the participants. The relationship between race and gender surfaced in various ways and the possibility for transformation was complex, but can be seen in the very personal stories of the participants.

Theoretical Framework for Family Literacy Groups

A basic theoretical assumption that affected the original design of Project FIEL and the implementation drama of the day-to-day activity was Freire's (1973) critical pedagogy. The premise of participatory learning based on learners' past experiences and present learning and living needs dictated the design of the project. A brief look at the design helps to shed light on the day-to-day activities.

The design of the literacy groups of Project FIEL had three underlying premises, all of which are solidly grounded on past research in the fields of literacy and language acquisition. The first premise is parent involvement and its positive effect on children's lives (Careaga 1988; Sandoval 1986; Simich-Dudgeon 1987; Snow 1987; Taylor 1983; Taylor and Dorsey-Gaines 1987; Wells 1986). Parents in Project FIEL were actively involved in that they actually participated in class with their children and were encouraged to participate in their children's learning at home and in the community. The second premise is the importance of the holistic approach to learning, which emphasizes that language and literacy be taught naturally as it occurs within any social environment (Auerbach 1990; Bissex 1984; Bruner 1984; Ferreiro and Tebrosky 1985, 1986; Harste, Woodward and Burke 1984; Manning, Manning and Kamii 1988; Smith 1984). The third premise is the acceptance of code-switching (i.e., alternation between two languages in oral or written discourse) as a style of communication that shows bilingual grammatical competence on the part of the speaker (Aguirre 1988; Hakuta 1990; Huerta 1978; Jacobson 1985; Pfaff 1976, 1979; Poplack 1981; Poplack and Sankoff 1980; Turkinoff 1985).

Theoretical Framework for Critical Literacy Parent Groups

The rationale for the participatory parent groups was based upon the transformation process of critical pedagogy (Freire 1970; Giroux 1988; Freire and Macedo 1987; Shor 1987). The methodology is an adaptation of Wallerstein's (1987) problem-posing model. Problem-posing is a group process that uses personal experience to create social cohesiveness and mutual responsibility. Parents identified topics about which they needed information. Speakers from the community were invited to be the dialogue leaders and to speak to the group on a designated topic. The guest provides information to the parents, and with the participation of family literacy staff, led the parents in dialogue regarding their own needs and questions. As the dialogue continued, codes, interpretations of feelings, and possibilities for action were explored. Then action was articulated and planned through written evaluation forms.

Discussion and Analysis

Information for these case studies was obtained through a variety of qualitative methods including interviews, participant and nonparticipant observations, videotaped class segments, and informal conversations with the women. The data was compiled in narrative form and analyzed using a framework of postmodernism as a discourse of resistance. We stress that the literacy classes themselves were not solely responsible for either woman's critical endeavor. Yet the point of practice in time and place gives us as participant-observers a window to view many integrated aspects of transformation. Furthermore, the case studies personalize and dramatize the implications that result from the data analysis.

HISTORY AS A FORM OF COUNTER-MEMORY

"You may wonder," she said, "why I repressed this memory."
(Walker 1989, 363)

Giroux (1990) clarifies that postmodernism "argues for a view of history that is decentered, discontinuous, fragmental, and plural" (15) and "raises central questions about not simply how to rethink the meaning of history and traditions, it also forces us . . . to raise new and different questions" (15). We submit these case studies as examples of both the urgency for this approach of rethinking and requestioning and also to illuminate the manner in which these individual women have begun the process.

History that reflects the complexities of both the general and the specific is a dynamic influence on Ms. N. and Ms. R. The women's stories illustrate discontinuity and the complexities involved in transformation, and the value of postmodern analysis: "Postmodernism not only views the subject as contradictory and multi-layered, it rejects the notion that individual consciousness and reason are the most important determinants in shaping human history. It posits instead a faith in forms of social transformation that understand the historical, structural, and ideological limits that shape the possibility for self-reflection and action" (Giroux 1990, 16).

Both women are daily placed in fragmented, discontinuous situations in the dynamics of changing social, political, and personal boundaries. The historical dynamic as it has related to life and survival for centuries in Mexico is complicated further by other survival issues in San Elizario. San Elizario, Texas is a small community of approximately 3,000 inhabitants, located seven miles east of the city of El Paso on the Rio Grande river which divides the United States and Mexico. The San Elizario area was settled early in the seventeenth century when the Mission of San Elizario was originally constructed as a Spanish fort. San Elizario was designated the first county seat when Texas became a state but was bypassed by the railroads. Thus, San Elizario remained a small rural town when the county seat moved to the City of El Paso.

The U.S. 1980 census showed that the area comprising the San Elizario Independent School District had a total population of 1,987. A survey done in August 1989 indicated that the number of persons in the district had doubled during the previous nine years. Moreover, many (about 60% of adults in the survey) of these new people were Mexican-born and arrived there after 1985. They settled into subdivisions called *colonias* that were affordable but that lacked (and still lack) basic services such as potable water, sewage disposal systems, public transportation and primary medical care. The arrival of immigrants after 1985 into San Elizario created a dichotomous population in the community. Approximately half of the residents are U.S.-born and have been for decades or generations; the remainder are mostly Mexican-born immigrants who settled there within the last decade in search of cheaper housing than what could be found in El Paso. This dichotomy in the population also is reflected in other characteristics. The Mexican-born heads of household have a median of six years of education while those who are U.S.-born have twelve years. The former group are monolingual Spanish- or limited English-proficient while the latter are proficient in English. The Mexican-born heads of households in the survey also earned 28% less than those who were U.S.-born (Brannon 1989). The two women in the case studies, Ms. N. and Ms. R., provide a window of analysis into the Mexican-born part of the population in San Elizario.

Ms. N.

Ms. N. is a Mexican woman in her mid-twenties. She grew up in the state of Chihuahua in northern Mexico. She never went to school and has a sporadic work history of unskilled jobs in Mexico. Her two children, a girl, age six, and a boy, age two, were born in Ciudad Juarez. She came to the United States illegally with the children's father about nine months before she joined the family literacy class. When Ms. N. began the class, the family lived in a two-room shack with no electricity, no water, and no source of heat.

Not much was said by Ms. N. to the literacy staff about the children's father other than she feared that the violence ("Peleamos mucho" [We fight a lot]) and drugs ("Hay muchas drogas en la casa" [There are lots of drugs in the house]) were endangering the children. However, this voicing of her concern and the subsequent asking for advice from the literacy staff showed that she was in fact rethinking the tradition of not discussing family problems with outsiders. One possibility for this rethinking was that she was forced to ask "new and different questions" about her own safety and that of her children for their very survival. As the story unfolds, Ms. N. is seen questioning the authority of the children's father, the authority of social service agencies, and even the immigration service.

Ms. R.

Ms. R. is a Mexican woman in her mid-thirties. She is from Durango, Mexico. She has two children. Her daughter is six years old. Her son is two years old. The family lives in a mobile home with no water, electricity, or sewer services. Ms. R.'s husband works as an unskilled laborer when work is available. Ms. R. is often seen outside the school yard selling various items (perhaps bought and brought from Juarez). She approached members of the literacy staff at various times selling musical greetings cards, blankets, and women's lingerie. She definitely defies the stereotype of the undereducated, passive housewife waiting for things to improve.

Ms. R. did not give the literacy staff very much factual information about her private life, but her actions and opinions voiced during the family literacy classes revealed much about her history and her beliefs about education and life in general. She saw herself as the authority over her child not only in terms of socialization, but also in terms of teaching. She was not intimidated by the school context or the school staff or literacy staff. In fact, she openly (not rudely, but openly) disregarded advice by the instructional staff in many instances before she began to change her interactions with her child during the literacy lessons.

VALUE OF THE EVERYDAY AS A SOURCE OF EMPOWERMENT

". . . They are the only ones who understand me . . . Four skinny trees with skinny necks and pointy elbows like mine . . . Their strength is secret. They send ferocious roots beneath the ground. They grow up and they grow down and grab the earth between their hairy toes and bite the sky with violent teeth and never quit their anger. This is how they keep...When I am too sad and too skinny to keep keeping, when I am a tiny thing against so many bricks, then it is I look at the trees. . . ."

(Cisneros 1989, 74-75)

Giroux (1990) explains that within the postmodern perspective, "All claims to universal reason and impartial competence are rejected in favor of the partiality and specificity and particularity of everyday life, that smooth difference under the banner of universalizing categories are rejected as totalitarian and terroristic" (13).

Again in very different yet specific ways, the two women exhibit how they used every day events in their own quests for empowerment. Given the aforementioned historical dynamics, the context for Ms. N. and Ms. R's interactions in their everyday living situations combines with each woman's individual personality and intellectual development within dynamic social contexts. The variations of critical pedagogical issues addressed in the family literacy classes and the critical parent groups, and the value of the engagement, have been seen in both women's participation. According to Giroux (1990), "At its best . . . as a form of engaged practice, critical pedagogy calls into question forms of subordination that create inequities among different groups as they live out their lives" (16).

Ms. N.

In the family literacy classes, Ms. N. revealed her determination to change her history of no education by her unfailing attendance. Furthermore, Ms. N. showed genuine interest in all topics, and she exhibited confident composure in the classroom context. She participated freely in the oral language activity with the whole class and in the learning activity with her daughter. During the language experience approach activity, which involves varying amounts of writing in either English or Spanish or both, Ms. N. was relatively relaxed about asking for help for her own writing from the teacher or teacher's assistant. She was clearly proud of her six-year-old daughter's developmental writing. Also, she expressed both verbal and nonverbal delight during the group storybook activities. She seldom did home activities, but as more of the everyday hardships of her home life became known, this was understandable.

Moreover, Ms. N.'s illustration of using the everyday as a source of power became most evident during the critical literacy parent groups or *pláticas*. The *pláticas* themes were determined by the parents who attended the family literacy classes. While attendance as a whole in San Elizario was low (as historically characteristic), the parents did not shy away from the most difficult issues. For example, they requested information about child support payments, so the FIEL staff invited two attorneys from the Attorney General's Office in El Paso which deals with enforcement of child support payments. Seven parents attended. (Unofficial rumor reported that most women were afraid to attend because in the small community, word would travel fast regarding who had attended and the women feared retribution from the men.) Ms. N. was one of the women who attended. After the hour-long group session, she stayed behind to ask the attorneys personal questions regarding her situation, one complicated by the fact that she was not legally married or legally a United States citizen. The attorneys made it clear to her that the situation was difficult, but they encouraged her by giving her suggestions of agencies to contact and specific requirements for agency investigation of child abuse.

Four days later, Ms. N. moved out of the home she shared with the children's father. A week after this when the literacy staff learned of her actions, they questioned her as to why she had not contacted any of the agencies with shelters. "I lost the numbers," she said. But when given the numbers again, immediately she telephoned and she found that no agency or shelter would accept her and the children because she was not a legal resident. They advised her to return across the river to Juarez but she responded "No voy a regresar ahí" (I won't go back to Mexico). "Me quedo con una amiga y trabajo como maid y mantengo a los ninos en la escuela" (I'm going to stay with a friend, get a job as a maid and keep the children in school).

Thus, while she did not use any suggestions made by the attorneys at the *plática* because she was not legally able to, she no doubt used the encouragement and intangible transfer of strength to use everyday resources for transformation in the best way she was able. Giroux's (1990) pedagogy asserts that students not only read cultural codes critically, but also learn limits of such codes including a critical view of authority. In her own way Ms. N. exemplified this pedagogy. When she left her home, she had to live in a four feet by six feet shack with no doors or windows for a week with her six-year-old and two-year-old children. Each agency she called about shelter told her to go back across the river to Ciudad Juarez where she would be eligible for Mexican-sponsored shelters. She refused and elaborated her resolve: "Nunca volveré a Mexico donde se tiene que pagar por libros y por uniformes antes de entrar a la escuela. Por esa razón no fuí yo a la escuela. Mis hijos les encanta la escuela de San Elizario, el maestro Mr. Holguin[1] y la maestra Ms. Villa. (Fictitious names have been used throughout this study to protect the privacy of the participants.) La niña esta aprendiendo a leer y escribir. Nunca regresaré." (I will never go back to Mexico where you have to pay for school books and supplies and pay for uniforms before the children are allowed in school. That's why I didn't go to school. My children love the school in San Elizario, Mr. Holguin, Ms. Villa, and the little girl is learning to read and write. I will never go back.) The authorities told her, in essence, that in order to survive, she must return to Mexico. She not only disputed this warning, she did not go.

Another example of Ms. N. using the everyday to transform her situation in her adopted country was when she showed up at the community Christmas fair two hours before it started, stating she had come early to help with whatever she could. Her six-year-old daughter was with her. The fair was held for the purpose of raising matching funds for a Reading is Fundamental program at the elementary school. After helping move some tables, clearing the tables, and moving bags around, she said she was ready for some more tasks. A literacy staff member asked if she could help organize some raffle tickets that first needed to be numbered (the ticket and stub). The staff member had just started numbering when Ms. N. volunteered to do that for her. Ms. N. was given the tickets and pencil. She wrote, then handed the ticket to her daughter to stack. The staff member, having learned earlier of Ms. N's total lack of formal education and total lack of literacy skills. was worried about her ability to actually do the task. Not only was she able to do the task, she was able to actively direct her daughter's assistance. After she finished numbering about two hundred tickets, she asked for another task.

As the booths opened and people came in, Ms. N. and her daughter walked around and watched the entertainment. Ms. N., despite the extreme poverty of her situation, had found temporary work (approximately two weeks in the evenings taking care of an elderly woman) and thus came to the fair with a small amount of money ($5.00). At one point she excitedly showed the literacy staff the picture she had had taken of her daughter with Santa. At another point, she came up to show some earrings she bought from the AVON booth. The N.'s stayed until late in the afternoon. Thus, not only did Ms. N. participate competently in the work, she participated in the fun. The literacy staff saw this ability as empowering as well.

Ms. R.

Ms. R. also considers her daughter's education to be of prime importance and she is ready to do whatever she can to help her with her education. Ms. R. is particularly concerned about her daughter's reading and writing skills. When asked during a pre-program interview what her daughter's greatest accomplishment was, she said "escribir su nombre" (write her name). Ms. R. was also asked if parents should be involved in schools; she answered, "Claro que si" (of course) and added that parents could get involved by going to all meetings and getting information from the school on their children. Ms. R., who has an assertive personality, always made clear to the project staff that she consistently taught her daughter at home on a daily basis and thus played the role of teacher as well as mother. Ms. R., furthermore, had definite ideas about her parent-teacher role, as well as about the way things should be done with her daughter (as will be discussed later) and about the world in general. Ms. R's enthusiasm about helping her daughter with her schooling was evident in her perfect attendance in the FIEL classes during year two of the project.

In the family literacy class, the R. family, particularly Ms. R., did not hesitate to speak out during the discussions. Ms. R. not only asked and answered questions during the initial inquiry, but she also contributed comments that expanded on the inquiry's theme and related it to her family's personal experiences or background. Her daughter tried to do likewise, but often she was cued by Ms. R. to keep quiet either with a "shh," with a stern look, or with a poke in the ribs. However, little by little Ms. R. let her daughter speak up more often in class. The staff consistently emphasized that children's speaking in class was important, positive, and desirable behavior in terms of their literacy development. This speaking out by a child when adults were present was undoubtedly not allowed by generations of authority codes in Ms. R.'s history. Yet in light of the purpose for her child's learning, she tried to change some of her attitudes and behaviors in this classroom context.

During the lessons, Ms. R. guided her daughter so that she would do activities "nicely." Conflict developed as both mother and child asserted themselves. When a single project was assigned to the family teams, however, Ms. R. tended to take over. During a lesson on "Things That Fly, Things that Swim," for example, the parents and children were asked to cut and assemble a spaceship with an astronaut that was attached to the ship with yarn. Her daughter started cutting the pieces, but her mother wanted to cut them. When Marissa started to paste the parts together, Ms. R. said, "Esperate" (wait) that she was still cutting. She then took the pieces and proceeded to paste them. Marissa then loudly said, "Mamá, yo quería pegarlo" (Mom, I wanted to paste it). She then pouted as she watched her mother finish assembling the spaceship and astronaut. The teacher, noticing what was happening, then said, "Yo te regalo uno para que lo hagas en la casa solita" (I will give you one to do at home by yourself). She then handed the materials to Marissa to take home. The teacher did not want to question the parental authority of Ms. R., but she was able to be consistent with the project's literacy goals by stressing everyone's right to participate.

On another occasion, Marissa and her mother were making a drum from a coffee can as part of a lesson on music. Ms. R. essentially decorated the drum by herself, only letting her daughter hold the can for her and letting her glue on a bit of yarn. At one point, Marissa took some strips of construction paper and tried to glue them around the can. Ms. R. pushed her hand away and continued working on the drum. Marissa then sat with her face in hand watching her mother as she took the strips and glued them on herself. Later, Ms. R. did ask Marissa to help her glue the yarn. Marissa held a section of the yarn around the can while her mother was putting the glue around it. The staff believed that Ms. R. felt an urge to take over the project from her daughter because she wanted to ensure that it was done "right." This was evident on another occasion when she turned to see how Marissa was doing and said. "Ay mija, no, no, no, ya me hiciste cochinadas" (Oh, my daughter, no, no, no, you've made a mess) and then proceeded to hold her daughter's hand as she painted with a brush. The staff felt the teacher was wise, therefore, to assign separate art work to parent and child most of the time. This provided a means to let the child do the activity without threatening the mother's authority and thus risking giving her offense or dampening the child's own creativity and desire.

As clearly seen above, Ms. R. had her own definite ideas on how things should be done with her daughter. This was particularly true with regard to teaching Marissa how to write. Despite the information on emergent literacy development that she received from the project staff, Ms. R. insisted on teaching Marissa how to write according to what she thought was the best way.

Thus, she insisted on near perfection in Marissa's writing. She often made comments such as the following while she erased and corrected Marissa's letter shapes and spelling, held her hand, and drew lines on her paper in order to avoid her crooked writing which she insisted should be written in a straight line. For example, she directed in one lesson:

> Así para abajo.¿No me entiende! No tan retirada. Ahora la *-r* . . . Ahí no va la *-e* . . . yo le he ensenado muchas veces. (This way, down. Don't you understand me? Not so far apart! Now the *-r* . . . the *-e* doesn't go there. I've taught you many times.) La *-a* primero, la *a* (The *-a* first, the *-a*; she erases it and rewrites it for Marissa). Haga bonita letra, no fea. (Do the letter nicely, not ugly). Ándale, tu sabes escribir, mira. (Come on, you know how to write, look).

The teacher would often try to encourage Marissa's *free* writing by making comments such as, Va bien, Marissa, va bien, no se preocupe, siga, siga, va muy bien, nos se preocupe." (You're doing fine, Marissa, you're doing fine, keep going, keep going, you're doing real well, don't worry.)

Ms. R. apparently would ignore these comments, however, and keep right on erasing and correcting her daughter's work. Yet, the instructor intentionally never confronted Ms. R. outwardly on her behavior with Marissa, but instead tactfully passed on information about emergent literacy to her. At the same time, the instructor assured Marissa that her writing was fine even though the letters weren't shaped exactly like those on the bulletin board and that it was important for her to keep writing. The teacher commented to the literacy staff often about her frustration with the constant necessity to go through this ordeal and doubted its effect. The staff, however, were encouraged that in spite of this, Ms. R. always returned to the family literacy classes. Later, tangible results were seen.

In fact, Marissa's work folder does show that Marissa wrote seventeen of the twenty-two language experience *stories* collected during the year; she dictated five of these stories to her mother who then wrote them. Four of these dictations, however, were done during the first four lessons they attended. Thus, progress was evident in that Ms. R. let Marissa write herself even though she did consistently correct any writing that did not meet her approval. Ms. R. and Marissa also participated in the interactive reading during each lesson, although to a more limited extent given that there was less time for discussion during that step.

GENDER AS AN IRREDUCIBLE PRACTICE CONSTITUTED IN A PLURALITY OF SELF AND SOCIAL REPRESENTATION

> "No one is more than a functioning or part of the total function . . . We direct ourselves to our own selves through millions of beings-stones-bird creatures-star beings-microbe beings-fountain beings to ourselves."
>
> (Kahlo, cited in Herrera 1983)

Again Giroux (1990) guides the discussion: "What is at stake here is forgoing a notion of power that does not collapse into a form of domination, but is critical and emancipatory, that allows students to both locate themselves in history and to critically, not slavishly appropriate the cultural and political codes of their own and other traditions" (29). The plurality of self and social representation becomes more difficult. Giroux (1990) explains that a postmodern discourse challenges liberal humanism's notion of the subject "as a kind of free, autonomous, universal sensibility, indifferent to any particular or moral contents" (21).

From the historical perspective of gender, the historical, structural, and ideological limits concerning women in Mexico are well known. Illich (1982) elaborates regarding rural Mexico where both Ms. N. and Ms. R. are from: "From afar, the native can tell whether women or men are at work, even if he cannot distinguish their figures. The time of year and day, the crop, and the tools reveal to him who they are . . . to belong means to know what benefit and kind of woman, or kind of man. . . . Gender is in every step, in every gesture, not just between the legs" (8).

The gender issues relate to history and to work. The complexity further involves the subjugation of women in the process of political action originally (or supposedly) designed to assist immigrants, including women. As Giroux (1990) warns: "A pedagogical issue here is the need to articulate difference as part of the construction of a new type of subject, one which would be both multiple and democratic" (25). Mouffe (1988) says: "In order that the defense of workers' interests is not pursued at the cost of the rights of women, immigrants or consumers, it is necessary to establish an equivalence between these different struggles. It is only under these circumstances [authoritarian] power becomes truly democratic" (42).

Ms. N.

This need for equivalence relates directly to a pervasive problem in the San Elizario community regarding United States citizenship and Ms. N. particularly. Many men have, one way or another, achieved residency status which brings with it the potential for eventual U.S. citizenship. Typically, many of these men form liaisons with Mexican women who are in the United States illegally. The men promise to marry the women, which would give the women the same potential for citizenship through residency status. What often happens is that many men in fact never marry the women, but in the words of a social worker (who asked to remain anonymous) in the community, "they hold the promise over the women, like a threat, and virtually use the women as slaves."

Ms. N. is in this situation with her children's father. Ms. N. and her children's father had been together six or seven years. They lived in Juarez, Mexico, where the two children were born, until several months ago, yet because the father has U.S. residency status the family came to live in San

Elizario. However, unless there is a legal marriage and her "husband" applies for her residency status on the basis of his, Ms. N. has no mechanism for obtaining citizenship on her own. She worries about the effect of her relationship with Mr. N. on her children because "Peleamos mucho" (We fight a lot). She also worries she confided in the interview because her "husband" often insists on taking the six-year-old daughter with him to the topless bars at night with his friends. "Digame que puedo hacer" (Tell me what I can do). She vocalized and questioned how to break the tradition of accepting everything the father says and does. With her daughter's safety at stake, she sought advice and tried various resistance approaches.

Ms. R.

Ms. R. has been much more private about her personal history than Ms. N. When invited to return to family literacy classes, when year three classes began in September, Ms. R. agreed at first and came to the first class with her daughter. However, her husband, accompanied by a male companion, furiously screamed at her from the car in the school parking lot demanding to know why she was there. He remained in the school parking lot throughout the whole class. Ms. R. was clearly distracted and upset. She did not return to the classes and gave the excuse that she and her husband had too much work to do. However, almost ironically, when asked what was most useful to her from the literacy class, she repeated, "Tener la oportunidad de participar la nina. Tiene la libertad para hablar" (That the little girl has the opportunity to participate, the freedom to speak up). Ms. R.'s history of speaking up against her husband's wishes was at best questionable. Her difficulty was apparent again a few weeks after the parking lot incident, when Ms. R. was urged to stay in the school hallway with her daughter as she and the literacy staff were talking. She said she would like to, but "No avisó" (I didn't tell him ahead of time). The encouraging intergenerational dynamic, however, was that she saw value in her daughters opportunity to speak up, to participate, and in her own developing ability as a parent to encourage this. It is possible that this situation shows "people placed self-consciously in their histories by making them aware of the memories constituted in difference, struggle, and hope" (Giroux 1990, 15). Another example in a family literacy class involved this inconsistency in gender dynamics illustrated by the situation of Ms. R. and her daughter.

> *Teacher:* ¿Que cosas hacemos con los amigos? (What things do we do with friends?)
> *Other Child:* Jugar, platicar. (Play, talk.)
> *Marissa:* Una niña no debe de pelear con sus amigas. (A girl should not fight with her friends.)
> *Teacher:* Los amigos se deben de perdonar si se pelean. (Friends should forgive each other if they fight.)
> *Marissa:* Se deben de decir "I'm sorry." (They should say "I'm sorry" to each other.)

Teacher: ¿Que juegos juegan con ios amigos? (What games do you play with friends?)
Other Child: a las muñecas (dolls)
Other Child: a la pelota (ball)
Marissa: . . . mi amiga es mas grande que yo . . . me prima esta alta . . . (my friend is bigger than I . . . my cousin is taller . . .)
Teacher: ¿Su mamá puede ser su amiga? (Can your mother be your friend?)
Marissa: . . . mi papá . . . (my father)
Ms. R.: Es que los regaño y el no . . . a el no le dan motivo, a mi es la que me dan motivo, por eso dice que es su amigo. . . . (It's because I scold them and he doesn't . . . they don't give him a reason to, I'm the one they give reason to [scold] that's why she says he's her friend.)

Not only is Ms. R. verbalizing the inconsistency in gender roles regarding family discipline, but also the child on her level is probing differences in gender socialization.

REDEFINING ONE'S PLACE IN THE WORLD

"Helped are those who love the entire cosmos rather than their own tiny country, city, or farm for to them will be shown the unbroken web of life and the meaning of infinity."
A. Walker, "The Gospel According to Shug" (1989, 288)

The fourth point of discussion in the postmodern framework regards the inclusion of the "contingent, the discontinuous, and the unrepresentable as coordinates for remapping and rethinking the borders that define one's existence and place in the world" (Giroux 1990, 14).

Ms. N.

Ms. N., despite her courage of taking risks to transform her situation, was aware of some of the basic dichotomies of her situation. In the family literacy class when a lesson theme was "Parenting on the Frontera," she listed the positive aspects of living in El Paso (or San Elizario, in her case) and the negative aspects.

Positivas: Me gusta porque se facilita mas que allá en las estampillas y que la nina aprenda el Ingles. Porque hay oportunidades de buscar trabajo tambien allá pero se gana muy poco. Tambien me gustaría aprender el Ingles. Ahorita el maestro Nuñez me esta dando clases. (I like it because it's easier here with [food] stamps and for the girl to learn English. Because there's job search opportunities over there also, but one earns very little. I'd also like to learn English. Mr. Nuñez is giving me classes now).
Negativas: No hay nada negativas. Solo los charcos. No hay pr donde caminar. (There's nothing negative. Only the puddles. There's no way to walk).

Likewise, she listed the positive aspects of living in Mexico and the negative aspects.

Positivas: La gente en la tarde sale para afuera. En el kiosko toca el conjunto y toda la gente coopera para pagarles. (People go out in the evenings. The band plays in the gazebo and everybody chips in to pay them.)

Negativas: Cobran en la escuela y cada rato piden dinero y piden uniforme. Y si no hay dinero no se pueden registrar. Y piden dinero para los utiles. En las escuelas grandes piden uniformes y maquinas de escribir. Y están mas caros los cuademos. Hay mas cholos. (They charge tuition and they're always asking for money and a uniform is required. And if there's no money you can't register. And they ask for money for supplies. In the big schools they ask for uniforms and typewriters. And the notebooks are more expensive. There are more "cholos" [social rebels].)

Despite Ms. N's acknowledgement of the discontinuous—mostly in the area of schooling—she did not focus on the incredible hardships she endures in San Elizario in order to survive. Clearly, her choice to stay and endure relates to the importance of her children and their education.

Ms. R.

Likewise, Ms. R. both in her parent interviews and in informal conversations reported that her most important struggle in life was securing education for her children. In her parent interviews, for example, she answered many questions in this way.

Q: What is your greatest desire for your child?

Ms. R.: "el estudio" (education) "que sigan estudiando" (that they continue their education)

Q: What do you envision her to be doing in the future?

Ms. R.: "maestra" (teacher)

Q: What is her greatest accomplishment?

Ms. R.: "escribir su nombre" (to write her name) "leer y escribir" (to read and write).

Q: What is your greatest accomplishment as a parent?

Ms. R.: "venir aqui a la escuela" (to come here to the school).

Yet evidence subtly evolved of Ms. R.'s developing ability to redefine her place as parent in her daughter's world and to contemplate the value of past experience as it relates to the present and the future both for herself and her daughter. Ms. R. gradually not only began to let Marissa speak up in class; she herself also began to pick up on Marissa's comments and to expand on them by sharing her personal experiences. She was using her everyday experiences to empower both her daughter and herself. As time elapsed, Ms. R. evidently was gaining more and more self-confidence with regard to her oral participation. The second-to-the-last lesson for the year, for example, was about cotton—something that Ms. R., it turns out, was very knowledgeable about. During that lesson, she not only taught the group about the different stages in the growth of the cotton plant, but at one point she also corrected the teacher.

Teacher: Sale una flor amarilla . . . despues se seca la flor. (A yellow flower blooms . . . then it dries.)
Ms. R.: No, se hace verde. (No, it turns green.)
Teacher: ¿Se hace verde? (It turns green?)
Ms. R.: Sí, sí . . . se va abriendo y luego se seca. (Yes, yes . . . it blossoms, then, then it dries).

During this same lesson, Ms. R. expanded on the subject by talking about the difference between river versus well water for growing cotton and fruits, thus again showing her expertise in this area. Ms. R., furthermore, exemplified growth in the Freirian sense of literacy as liberation, as she made apparent by her comment during a post-project interview. When asked what she most liked and what had been most useful to her from the project she replied, "tener oportunidad de participar . . . tener la libertad para hablar" (having the opportunity to be involved . . . having the freedom to speak up). During this same interview, in addition, she was asked for suggestions for future lessons. She responded, "mas oportunidad para leer y escribir" (more time for reading and writing), thus indicating that she was now very comfortable with these types of activities and with their potential for helping her children succeed in school. She also stated that she was not worried about helping her children with school. This is another step forward considering that in the pre-interview she indicated that one of her needs was "como educar a los ninos" (information on how to educate her children). Ms. R. not only obtained some of this information through the classes, but also she developed confidence in reading, writing, and oral language activities as powerful tools to help her children's literacy growth.

Implications

Giroux maintains that it is necessary to illuminate "how power works in this society within the schools to secure and conceal various forms of racism and subjugation" (29). Thus, the schools are a place to begin providing students the opportunities to engage critically with the strengths and limitations of their lives. A postmodern perspective demands that school issues be addressed when discussing "dropouts" of minorities and women. In many discussions the "dropouts" are considered only as victims of their own poor choice (Stitch and McDonald 1989). Yet data reveals from extensive work done on the family attitudes and responses to schooling in racial minority immigrant families (Delgado-Gaitan 1987; Diaz, Mehan and Moll 1986; Goldenberg 1984; Trueba 1989), that first generation immigrants—large numbers of whom have less than three years of schooling in their countries—encourage their children to stay in school. The idea of "a better life" resulting from a "good education" seems to keep the immigrants' children in school. Yet by third generation, the children of minorities have learned that due to discrimination and other social inequities school completion does not necessarily mean a better life.

After much investigation of high-school students in urban settings, Fine (1990) maintains:

> We can and must improve public schools to retain and critically educate a greater percentage of students, particularly low-income students. But at the same time, the degree must have exchange value across class, race, and gender lines; the economy must be rich for all; housing, childcare, health care; and social services must be designed to accommodate *all* . . . Far more fundamentally, it keeps us from being broadly, radically, and structurally creative about transforming schools and social conditions for today's and tomorrow's youths. (65)

Without these changes, we must ask, "But is it fair to say that today all children inside the U.S.—even those of 'undocumented workers'—have legal access to a public education?" (Fine 1990, 61-62).

Ms. N.'s children and Ms. R's children are receiving education due to the incredible tenacity and dedication of these mothers. In no way is the children's access to education equal. From the standpoint of educational funding, a child in San Elizario school is allocated much less than a child from a community with a strong tax base. Furthermore, the community conditions that impede a child even getting to school (acres of ankle-deep mud to cross on foot to reach the paved road to meet the school bus) and health conditions that put great risk on each child's ability to stay in school (regular outbreaks of hepatitis due to no running water or sewer services in many neighborhoods) cry out the inequities of societal conditions that directly affect children's schooling.

West (cited in Winkler 1990) says that research on race, class, and gender have led to "a vast balkanization and fragmentation" of scholarship. He advocates analysis of the problems of women and minorities in the world outside of academia, and he says we must "Provide a synthesis that would look for the common concerns and issues that affect women and members of minority groups. Put social theory at the center. We must analyze the structure and institutions that have impact on culture" (A9).

Likewise, Christine Sleeter (1990) acknowledges that while schools can be made more hospitable to children through attitudinal changes of teachers and administrators, more must be done: "But if ultimately multicultural education aims toward redistribution of power and other social resources, then more effort should go into developing strategies for social and institutional change, rather than dwelling on attitudinal change" (23).

Thus, the implications embedded in these case studies demand restructuring schools, redefining curricular issues, and rethinking development programs for teachers so that the strengths of women as Ms. N. and Ms. R. can be both used and served by transformative critical learning situations. However, the most dramatic implication from this view of two women's lives is the desperate need for holistic change—on a societal level—of the factors that diminish possibilities in the lives of oppressed groups. It is almost trite to point out that classes and school are only a small part of these women's lives and that even the most radical changes in education cannot affect them positively if other aspects of their lives are not addressed.

Finally, we offer the case study format as a method of data collection that captures the passion and subjectivity of people's lives. Educational researchers cannot allow piecemeal attempts at change to ignore these qualities. Case studies such as these give momentum to integrated problem solving on a global scale.

> Time is short.
> Where do we live?
> Inside this morning.
> How long have we been here?
> Only the lakes remember
> our arrival. Go there at dawn
> when reeds ride the slow wash.
> An answer will come
> from the small world of crayfish.
> What do we do?
> Balance our shadows
> like oaks in bright sunlight,
> stretch and tumble
> as much as we're able,
> eat up the light
> and struggle with blindness.
>
> Roberta Hill Whiteman
> (1988, p. 34)

NOTE

1. Fictitious names have been used throughout this study to protect the privacy of the participants.

REFERENCES

Aguirre, A. 1988. Code-switching intuitive knowledge and the bilingual 8-23 classroom. In *Ethnolinguistic issues in education.* Edited by H. S. Garcia and R. C. Chavez. Lubbock, TX: College of Education, Texas Tech University.

Auerbach, E. 1990. *Making meaning, making change: A guide to participatory curriculum development for adult ESL and family literacy.* Boston, MA: University of Massachusetts.

Bissex, G. L. 1984. The child as teacher. In *Awakening to literacy.* Edited by H. Goelman, A. Oberg and F. Smith, 87-102. Portsmouth, NH: Heinemann.

Brannon, J. 1989. Narrative and preliminary results of 1989 San Elizario household survey. Unpublished raw data.

Bruner, J. 1984. Language, mind and reading. In *Awakening to literacy*. Edited by H. Goelman, A. Oberg and F. Smith, 195-201. Portsmouth, NH: Heinemann.

Careaga, R. 1988. *Keeping LEP students in school: Strategies for dropout prevention*. Program Information Guide, series no. 7. Rosslyn, VA: National Clearinghouse on Bilingual Education.

Cisneros, S. 1989. *The house on Mango Street*. New York: Random House.

De Lauretis, T. 1987. *Technologies of gender*. Bloomington: Indiana University Press.

Delgado-Gaitan, C. 1987. Mexican adult literacy: New directions for immigrants. In *Becoming literate in English as a second language*. Edited by S. R. Goldman and K. Trueba. Norwood, NJ: Alex.

Diaz, L., Moll, L., and H. Mehan. 1986. Sociocultural resources in instruction. A context-specific approach. In *Beyond language: Social and cultural factors in schooling language minority children*. Los Angeles: California State Department of Education and California State University.

Ferreiro, E. and A. Teberosky. 1985. *Literacy before schooling*. Portsmouth, NH: Heinemann.

Fine, M. 1990. Making controversy: Who's "at risk"? *Journal of Cultural Studies* 1(1):55-68.

Freire, P. 1970. *Pedagogy of the oppressed*. New York: Continuum.

——— . 1973. *Education for critical consciousness*. New York: Seabury Press.

——— . 1985. *The politics of education*. South Hadley, MA: Bergin & Garvey.

Freire, P. and D. Macedo. 1987. *Literacy: Reading the word and the world*. South Hadley, MA: Bergin & Garvey.

Giroux, H. A. 1988. *Teachers as intellectuals: Toward a critical pedagogy of learning*. South Hadley, MA: Bergin & Garvey.

——— . 1990. The politics of postmodernism. *Journal of Urban and Cultural Studies* 1(1):5-38.

Giroux, H. A. and P. McLaren. 1986. Teacher education and the politics of engagement: The case for democratic schooling. *Harvard Educational Review* 56(3):213-37.

Goldenberg, C. N. 1984. Low-income parents contributions to the reading achievement of their first-grade children. Paper presented at the meeting of Evaluation Network/Evaluation Research Society, 10-13 October, San Francisco.

Grossberg, L. 1988. Putting the pop back into postmodernism. In *Universal abandon? The politics of postmodernism*. Edited by A. Ross, 167-90. Minneapolis: University of Minnesota Press.

Hakuta, K. 1990, Spring. *Bilingualism and bilingual education: A research perspective*. Focus, November 1. Washington, DC: NCBE.

Harste, J. C., V. A. Woodward, and C. L. Burke. 1984. *Language stories and literacy lessons*. Portsmouth, NH: Heinemann.

Herrera, H. 1983. *Frida: A biography of Frida Kahlo*. New York: Harper Row Publishers.

Huerta, A. G. 1978. Code-switching among Spanish-English bilinguals: A sociolinguistic perspective. Ph.D. diss., University of Texas, Austin, TX.

Illich, I. 1982. *Gender*. New York: Pantheon.

Jacobson, R. 1985, March. *Title VII demonstration projects program in bilingual instructional methodology*. Final report submitted to OBEMLA, Grant No. G008102506. San Antonio: VTSA and Southwest Independent School District.

Kaplan, C. 1987. Deterritorializations: The rewriting of home and exile in western feminist discourse. *Cultural Critique* 6:187-98.

Manning, M., G. Manning, and C. Kamii. 1988, November. Early phonics instruction: Its effects on literacy development. *Young Children* 44(1):4-8.

Mouffe, C. 1988. *Radical democracy: Modern or postmodern?* In *Universal abandon? The politics of postmodernism*. Edited by A. Ross. Minneapolis: University of Minnesota Press.

Pfaff, C. W. 1979. Constraints on language mixing. *Language* 55:291-318.

———. 1976. *Syntactic constraints on code-switching: A quantitative study of Spanish-English code-switching*. Papers in Sociolinguistics. Austin, TX: Southwest Educational Development Lab.

Poplack, S. 1981. Syntactic structure and social function of code-switching. In *Latino language and communicative behavior*. Edited b y R. P. Duran. Norwood, NJ: Ablex Publishing Corp.

Renteria, R. 1989, March 31. Separate and unequal: The story of Kelli, Veronica and school finance. *El Paso Times*, p. 6A.

Sandoval, M. 1986. Parents as tutors. In *Issues of parent involvement and literacy: Proceedings of the symposium*, 89-90. Washington, DC: Trinity College.

Shor, I. 1987. *Freire for the classroom: A sourcebook of liberatory teaching*. Portsmouth, NH: Heinemann.

Simich-Dudgeon, C. 1987. Involving LEP parents as tutors in their children's education. *Eric/CLL News Bulletin* 10(2):3-4.

Simon, R. 1988. February. For a pedagogy of possibility. *Critical Pedagogy Networker* 1:14.

Smith, F. 1984. The creative achievement of literacy. In *Awakening to literacy*. Edited by H. Goelman, A. Oberg, and F. Smith, 135-42. Portsmouth, NH: Heinemann.

Snow, C. 1987. Factors influencing vocabulary and reading achievement in low income children. In *Togepaste Toalwetenschap in Artikelen, Special 2.* Edited by R. Apple. Amsterdam: ANELA.

Sticht, T. G. and B. A. McDonald. 1989, January. *Making the nation smarter: The intergenerational transfer of cognitive ability.* Executive Summary. San Diego, CA: Applied Behavioral and Cognitive Sciences.

Taylor, D. 1983. *Family literacy: Young children learning to read and write.* Portsmouth, NH: Heinemann.

Taylor, D. and C. Dorsey-Gaines. 1987. *Growing up literate: Learning from inner-city families.* Portsmouth, NH: Heinemann.

Trueba, H., G. Spinler, and L. Spindler, eds. 1989. *What do anthropologists say about dropouts?* New York: Falmer Press.

Trueba, H. and C. Delgado-Gaitan, eds. 1988. *School and society culture: Teaching content through culture.* New York: Praeger.

Tukinoff, W. J. 1985. *Applying significant bilingual instructional features in the classroom.* Rosslyn, VA: InterAmerica Research Assoc.

Walker, A. 1989. *The temple of my familiar.* New York: Hardcourt Brace & Jovanovich.

Wallerstein, N. 1987. Problem-posing education: Freire's method for transformation. In *Freire for the classroom: A sourcebook for liberatory teaching.* Edited by I. Shor, 33-44. Portsmouth, NH: Heinemann.

Wells, G. 1986. *The meaning makers.* Portsmouth, NH: Heinemann.

Whiteman, R. H. 1984. *Star quilt.* Minneapolis, MN: Holy Cow Press.

Winkler, K. J. 1990, November 28. Proponents of multicultural humanities research call for a critical look at its achievements. *The Chronicle of Higher Education,* A7, A8, A9, A13.

12

Lourdes Diaz Soto and Tina Richardson ─────────

Theoretical Perspectives and Multicultural Applications

> O Let America be America again
> The land that never has been yet-
> And yet must be.
> Vincent Harding

As noted in the introduction to this volume, the socialization and education of teachers, service providers, and school administrators who are predominantly monolingual/monocultural continues to challenge colleges of education because the cultural and linguistic diversity of school populations continues to increase (Soto 1991a). As student demographics in educational settings change, statistics show that the incidence of hate crimes has risen (Klanwatch Intelligence Report 1991). Although only the most blatant incidents are reported, surveys indicate that one in five college minority students attending predominately white campuses has been victimized (Mabry 1991). Based on these figures, it is clear that monocultural adults in educational settings will need to gain multicultural knowledge in both the cognitive and affective domains.[1]

The learning process seems to require self-reflection, awareness of societal and educational progress relating to issues of race, class, and gender; and awareness of the basic roles of oppressors and oppressed. In addition, the ability to redesign, reconstruct, and enhance learning environments provides the context for a possibilities-oriented paradigm. The idea is to chart new directions capable of meeting the educational needs of children growing up in an increasingly complex society.

The purpose of this chapter is to relay two interactive and reflective methodological approaches and the accompanying learning experiences of the facilitator and participants. My colleague and I are both newly arrived female faculty of color in a small private nonsectarian institution of higher education. We have both taught the recently required multicultural course to graduate students in our college for a year and a half, and we have felt a real need to share our experiences. Colleagues have relayed that faculty in similar situations have experienced feelings of isolation, frustration, and in our own terms, "complete burnout."

This teaching experience is unlike previous ones because of the complete emotional investment it requires from both the facilitator, the participants, and the institution. The college realized the importance of providing an experience of this nature prior to our arrival. As Andrzejewski has noted in her chapter, the state of Minnesota mandated human relations training for teachers in the early seventies; even though we teach at a nonsectarian, private institution, the college in which we teach has felt the impact of that legislation. Conservative factions at the college and/or department levels continue to express concern about content and process. At both the college and university levels, insights from research on changing demographic trends has spurred activities and discussions about the racial, ethnic, and gender distributions of students and faculty.

Historically, this institution was all male so that the inclusion of female students and faculty has challenged the more seasoned veterans among faculty and staff. Support and resistance to these changes is evident at both the faculty and student levels. Kranz's (1972) description of racial confrontation groups is still relevant: "historically, Whites have exhorted non-Whites to make changes so that they would be acceptable as full fledged Americans. However, events in the U.S. have shown the dishonesty and tragedy of this emphasis" (70). We also realize the tragedy of the latter approaches to diversity, and we endeavor to provide progressive alternative strategies for promoting multiculturalism. Our roles as facilitators of multicultural education have extended beyond the classroom walls, so that an impact is being felt within the college, the institution, and larger community. For many of our colleagues this is encouraging, but for the more conservative it is alarming and threatening.

The differing theoretical perspectives we chose emanated from our differing educational fields; the first author is interested in teacher education and the second in counseling psychology. The similarities between our educational philosophies stem from a desire to see in our lifetimes educational equity, social justice, and the democratic schooling of American children.

Teacher Education Application

The teacher education multicultural course is comprised of interactive and reflective methodological approaches with the ultimate goal of pursuing education that is both multicultural and social reconstructionist (Sleeter and Grant 1989). Since an explanation and discussion of this theoretical position occurs earlier in the book, we will not elaborate on the nature of multicultural social reconstructionist education except to note that students learn to analyze the circumstances of their own lives, practice democracy, develop social action skills, and form coalitions across race, class, and gender lines.[2] In our courses, students are expected to engage in reading activities, journal writing, class activities, discussion sessions, and practical applications relating primarily to issues of educational inequity. The amount of time devoted to a particular area depends on group needs and individual interests. The not so hidden agenda is to have an impact on graduate students' capacity for self-reflection about cultural ideologies and daily experiences. One anticipated outcome is the development of an application project capable of influencing existing local issues of inequity.

Counseling Psychology Application

Traditionally, the counseling profession has emphasized the importance of self-understanding as a major component in the development of effective counselors and therapists. However, historically, white mental health professionals have ignored or minimized the importance of the cultural/ethnic differences that exist between themselves and persons of Asian, African, Native, and Latino American origins (Atkinson, Morten, and Sue 1979; Marsella and Pedersen 1981; Richardson 1988; Vontress 1971). Neglecting these important issues has resulted in culturally encapsulated counselors who use treatment strategies and/or who develop outcome goals that may be inconsistent with the behavioral norms and values of persons who do not share their cultural assumptions. One of the primary objectives of the course on counseling multicultural issues is to engage majority group students in a self-examination experience related to culture, class, race, and ethnicity that helps them develop a multicultural personal and professional identity.

The methodological approach to teaching multicultural issues in counseling used by the second author is based on an integration of key concepts identified in the cross-cultural counseling literature. Counselor education programs have begun to acknowledge the significant roles of and manners in which the trainee's or practitioner's own race and/or ethnicity, cultural biases, and prejudices may influence the delivery of psychological services. As a result of this heightened awareness, one of the objectives of many training programs is to train counselors who are culturally competent.

Multicultural development is theorized to occur in a three stage process of awareness, knowledge, and skills (Pedersen 1988). For the purpose of the course, each stage is defined in the following way. *Awareness* refers to the process of examining the accuracy and appropriateness of attitudes, opinions, and assumptions about one's own culture as well as the culture of others. *Knowledge* refers to the process of acquiring and comprehending accurate facts and information about one's own culture and the culture of others. *Skills* refer to the ability to utilize one's awareness and knowledge to interact effectively with individuals or groups from diverse cultures.

In the awareness component of the course, students are engaged in an educational experience that examines their awareness of the social, political, and cultural impact of the counseling and mental health profession. In addition, the importance of self-understanding as it relates to their own cultural identity and racial consciousness is stressed. Racial consciousness as used here refers to awareness of one's own racial group membership, ethnic identity, and underlying cultural values, and to an understanding of the sociopolitical implications resulting from membership in a particular racial group. Students are exposed to various cultural value systems (Katz 1985) and various racial consciousness models (e.g., white racial identity). White racial identity development is theorized to progress via six stages during which a person struggles to abandon racism and develop a nonracist white identity (Helms 1990; Richardson 1992).

During this component of the course, students become acutely aware of (a) how ethnographic, demographic, socioeconomic status (SES), and other affiliation variables systematically influence them (Pedersen 1988); and (b) more aware of what is required to further develop a multicultural personal and professional identity. To a large extent, the knowledge component of the course develops simultaneously with the awareness component. Influencing the accuracy of the students' knowledge requires two major endeavors: (a) clarifying key concepts and (b) exposing students to new information.

With respect to the first endeavor, an essential collective experience for students is defining and/or redefining words such as *multiculturalism, culture, diversity, racism, sexism, classism, affirmative action, reverse discrimination,* and *stereotyping*. Consistently, students indicate a limited grasp of these terms coupled with a strong negative reaction to discussing them. As students increase their understanding of these concepts, the second endeavor is to provide accurate information about historical and present-day experiences (related to social issues and utilization of counseling services) of various cultural groups (i.e., American racial/ethnic groups, gender groups, SES groups). Learning takes place through lectures, reading assignments written from the perspective of members of the groups being studied, media presentations, class discussions, and group presentations by class participants. Students begin a continuous process of bridging gaps in their knowledge and information base about various cultural groups in order to progress toward a multicultural professional identity.

The next step in developing a multicultural identity is the translation of awareness and knowledge into actions, behavior, and skills. First, it is worth noting that active participation in a course of this nature most likely will translate into some type of behavior change. For many students, the course provides at least fourteen weeks of multicultural interaction in which they have the opportunity to acquire new behaviors in a relatively safe environment. Many students inevitably share with the class their attempts to make behavioral changes within predominantly monocultural environments. However, at the same time, students indicate that one course is not enough to reinforce the most committed desire to develop a multicultural identity that includes the acquisition of effective multicultural skills. While this course may provide the critical incidents necessary for trainees to initiate developing multicultural skills, very little can be stated about the duration of their motivation to acquire skills. Nevertheless, by the end of the course many students recognize a need for more mulicultural educational experiences that are effectively integrated into their entire graduate curriculum.

Some of the salient features of this course for the students seem to be the intense affective reactions to the course content in each of the three previously described components and the stimulus that a female faculty of color apparently provides. Managing affective responses and confronting conflict seem to be necessary criteria for any faculty member who commits to teaching a multicultural course. Therefore, I have found it necessary to provide students most of whom are white with a model of racial consciousness development (Ponterotto 1988) that helps them to understand their cognitive, behavioral. and affective reactions to the multicultural educational experience. Others in this volume have noted that many students enter the class having given little thought to multicultural issues or to being a white person in a racist and oppressive society. As a result, some students have an initial shock response to the material presented and/or experience denial regarding the reality of racism, sexism, classism and other forms of societal oppression. As exposure to multicultural issues increases, students typically develop intense emotional reactions to the class and/or the instructor in the form of frustration, anxiety, anger, guilt, and/or hostility. This is a critical point in the course because students need assistance managing these reactions. At the same time that the validity of their reactions, particularly the affective responses, are being acknowledged, students are simultaneously challenged by additional course material. Unfortunately, progress for some students toward developing a multicultural identity may become stalled due to intense defensive reactions that may result in retreating from multicultural issues altogether. On the other hand, many students utilize the class to confront their affective reactions and integrate their newly acquired knowledge to facilitate the development of multicultural counseling skills.

Challenges and Opportunities

The multicultural experiences present both challenges and rewards to the participants and the facilitator. The level of affective engagement for participants and facilitator, regardless of method or theoretical perspective, is quite high when compared to other courses we have taught. Existing theoretical bases and empirical data provide only limited guidance to prepare and present experiences that address students' level of readiness to receive messages and process information. In fact, there are times when students respond to the racial, gender, and cultural characteristics of the professor instead of to the curricular and societal context. Classroom dynamics may suggest that our ability to be effective educators is as related to our ability to process and manage students' projections as is our ability to manage the content and process.

The teaching challenges have included the inherent multiple roles of faculty as facilitator, role model, and member of an oppressed group. Sharing both knowledge and power in the educational process appears to be a novel experience for many of the participants. Course evaluations indicate that both the topics and methods are interesting, valuable, and a lifelong challenge for the students. The numbers of learners in these process-oriented models have ranged from thirty to sixty students who major in reading, counseling psychology, school psychology, special education, elementary education, foundations of education, educational administration, science education, and bilingual education. Small group discussions and community-based activities have been facilitated by graduate student assistants convinced of the importance of addressing issues of inequity in our current educational system.

The following accounts afford voice to the participants and help to depict the experience/process of the teacher education multicultural course. With the voluntary consent of several students, excerpts from classes are shared below with the reader.

SELECTED REFLECTIONS ON RACISM

Many students enter class giving very little thought to the existence of racism and being naive and/or oblivious to the presence of it in their day-to-day lives. As the course progresses, they begin to recognize blatant and subtle forms of racism and to realize their negative impact. Many class participants expressed dismay at the local situation and the recency of racist activities.

> Excerpt #1:
> As a native to the area who moved away . . . to live in the South and return to the area . . . I was shocked at the degree of racism and prejudice in the area as compared to the South. At times I have seen White Southerners act somewhat patronizing to Blacks in rural areas . . . but *never* the unfounded hate and resentment between middle-class Blacks and Whites that I have observed in the Lehigh Valley and the Delaware Valley. Recent incidents in public schools (e.g., the neo-Nazis movement) have long passed in Atlanta, yet in Pennsylvania, the incidence of such racism appears to be on the rise. . . . I believe the line between racism and prejudice and discrimination is artificial—that is, I'm not sure we can truly discern between them. At some level prejudice yields discrimination and racism is the result.

> Excerpt #2:
> Over the weekend I was surprised to read in the paper about several accounts of KKK in the Nazareth area. I am amazed that this type of activity is still going on. . . . It makes me angry to see this type of ignorance still continuing in society.

> Excerpt #3:
> Racism has the potential to kill dreams.

Selected Reflections on Gender

Participants reflect the complexities of the oppressive nature of sexism. Issues of gender equity were viewed differently based upon the learner's own gender and race.

Excerpt #4:
My parents are equal partners and fairly liberal minded. Thus I absorbed these traits; equality of sexes is not a conscious thought for me because it has become a given . . . it is a natural aspect of life and therefore does not bum upon my soul as other issues do. (white male)

Excerpt #5:
Women are not treated equally and anyone who thinks they are needs to take a much closer look at society. . . . Women are not paid the same salary. . . . Yes, rape and sexual harassment have been recognized as crimes but unless the rape is by a total stranger at gun point . . . many Americans still entertain the 'she asked for it' belief . . . in spite of the obvious fact that no one asks to be raped. (white female).

Excerpt #6:
I also have the opportunity to interact with many young adults. . . . I worked hard to raise my children so they would view people as individuals and value but not stereotype diversity. My daughter can sink a fence post with a trac-tor . . . and my son did just recently shorten the skirt of a female friend. (white female)

Excerpt #7:
Each day as a . . . principal, I experience sexual harassment, and I can attest to the fact that it is *degrading, humiliating, frustrating*. One feels helpless in such a situation. (white female)

Excerpt #8:
Personally, I have been the victim of sexual discrimination in some way, shape or form. . . . I have listened to tasteless jokes, poor comments and sex-ist remarks. . . . I work twice as hard for less acknowledgments or credibility than my male counterparts. (white female)

Excerpt #9:
For a black female in America gender issues are one of the many problems that I endure. I don't think white America especially White women realize just how difficult it is to be a young and educated black woman. Whenever there are discussions about women, people tend to think about white middle-class women. I really hate that. . . . When people discuss race they tend to talk about only the black male. Too often black women have to choose between their race and sex. I feel as though I am caught. (black female)

Excerpt #10:
. . . riding high on the hide of black women, who not only supported black men, white women and white men: What a hell of a burden! . . . Family as important as it is . . . has maintained that the woman's place is beside her man or behind him . . . it's about money and power and not about people. . . . America and South Africa are being built from the same imperialist blood that beats at the heart of Europe, and Columbus . . . as we now see this influence. How could this happen to such a proud, powerful people? (black female)

Selected Reflections on Social Class

The majority of the participants could not relay social class distinctions in their childhood histories so they reflected and reasoned on social class distinctions. Examples of participants distal reactions to social class concerns are evident in the following quotes. One of the objectives of the course was to assist students in gaining an intrinsic understanding of the intricacies of socioeconomic status issues. These reflections are examples of how superficial social class issues were initially understood.

Excerpt #11:
People are often oblivious to their surroundings and take for granted all that they have until someone or something raises their awareness or until what they take for granted is somehow threatened. Unfortunately, I think our society teaches that unless its a personal problem, its not a problem at all . . . If you're not a part of the solution, then you're part of the problem.

Excerpt #12:
They (east-enders) were the lower class kids with strange clothes and strange parents. We didn't have a name for it then, but we recognized that they looked different, fought more, used more curse words. . . . We also knew that there were more of them than there were of us. . . . Furthermore, I remember that the teachers expected less from the east-enders. . . . The west-enders and the teachers knew that we would succeed because we were 'better'.

Excerpt #13:
In college . . . class didn't make a difference to me at all. . . . There was a certain nobility to their poverty.

Selected Reflections on Power

The participants perceive themselves as power brokers; yet when reflecting upon social action strategies they viewed themselves as an oppressed group.

Excerpt #14:
In my opinion, power in education is being able to get your children to learn . . . power is getting a child to want to learn more and to ask questions.

Excerpt #15:
Power is the ability to motivate students to want to learn.

Excerpt #16:
Educators have the power to help form, guide and shape our future by educating our children—our future.

Excerpt #17:
The people wielding power in education determine what is learned and how it is going to be learned.

Selected Reflections on Ageism

Participants described intergenerational bonds as sources of motivating strength and kindness.

Excerpt #18:
[M]y grandfather passed away. I was going to give my B.S. diploma from— to him but he passed away before I could finish high school. From there on out everything was dedicated towards him; an All-American swim season, better jobs, and to help other students through teaching. From both grandparents I learned courage, respect, moral values, love, determination, and foresight.

Excerpt #19:
Ever since I was a young child I have been very close to my grandmother . . . her home has been a second home to me and she has been a second mother . . . she has spent her life giving and doing for other people—especially her family.

Excerpt #20:
. . . most influence on my life was my maternal grandfather . . . he died sixteen years ago of a heart attack . . . he was and continues to be the most important adult whom I could talk to, be close to, and respect . . . a hero . . . to this date I am still struggling to find such a person.

Excerpt #21:
Nana has always been the epitome of self-reliance (widowed at 27) . . . she bought a house, she put two children through parochial schools and gave them each a higher education, she cooked, sewed, budgeted, carpentered, painted, and gardened. . . . I learned to be independent and self-reliant (although, I still let men kill the bugs) . . . she receives just $200 a month from social security.

Selected Reflections on Social Action Strategies

This group of educators expanded their knowledge of how various forms of oppression function within this society. Some of the preceding excerpts were indicative of a lack of awareness regarding multicultural issues while others indicated progress toward heightened awareness. For many students their heightened awareness was evident as they began to identify personal strategies for social reconstructionist multicultural education concerns. Many students offered detailed plans (which almost reflect a personal oath) for action.

Excerpt #22:
It is tragic that one must fight to reclaim a city, fight to get distributors to obey laws [WE CAN project in New York City], fight to feed hungry people with food that is in abundance (Second Harvest Food Bank) and fight to shelter people. We have grown to be a materialistic society. What matters is what 'I' have . . . not what 'we' need.

Excerpt #23:

I have stopped referring to this as my 'doom and gloom' class ... now that I have seen programs which are actively combating the problems we've been learning about.

Excerpt #24:

The ... leaders of service to humanity made me feel less powerless ... encouraged me to deny fear, rejection, and timidity and become bolder, more self-confident in my approach to social issues ... there are successes that make service worthwhile. I would like to share a quote that inspires me: 'Practice random kindness and senseless acts of beauty'.

Excerpt #25:

Being in an educational environment makes it quite conducive for me, as an individual, to make a decided impact on some of our country's concerns. I have an interest in diversity issues specifically racism and sexism, and I hope to use the monetary resources available to me to better educate myself on these issues ... so that I can work on developing programs ... for students at my institution. ... My thoughts for next year include establishing a multicultural issues committee to be comprised of faculty, staff, students and administrators to grapple with pertinent issues and to provide cultural programming on campus ... something we lack at this point.

Excerpt #26:

I guess what I am trying to say is that one step I feel compelled to take now is to point out biased attitudes in a nonthreatening way. I am not a threatening person, so perhaps I can be successful and make a small dent. Miracles, I don't expect, but I can no longer not say anything.

Excerpt #27:

I plan to integrate multicultural education on a daily basis. One of my most influential areas is supervision of teacher instruction ... a revision of our supervising guidelines to include teachers' accountability for the consideration and implementation of multicultural topics. ... Survey the staff ... to develop an ongoing staff development ... provide inservice. ... Each year the students will be involved in a community service project to help them better understand the needs of the population. ... Textbook selection committees will be trained in the sensitivity to multicultural issues. ... Handbook revisions ... I will do my best to scrutinize teacher referrals and student's input. I will also make decisions based upon knowledge gained from this course.

Excerpt #28:

I ... will not shy away from potentially controversial subjects and issues. I will encourage class discussions and journal writing about personal fears, feelings and biases. Furthermore, I will not ignore disputes that seem to stem from prejudice and stereotypes. I will encourage victimized students to be assertive without being insulting. ... I want to guide them so they can see how the system works and see how they can make a difference in the world. [Plans to] Include works from diverse cultures and present multiple viewpoints of historical events . . . use stories that address issues of poverty in various contexts . . . contributions of women and restrictions of women throughout time . . . works which portray women as strong and competent; read works where homosexuality is treated with dignity . . . we will discuss the variety of languages present in the world . . . how language differences have affected history . . . how a culture views the elderly is often critical to understand basic (cultural) values . . . the presence of exceptional people in history is enormous . . . this provides a great area for discussion.

Excerpt #29:
[P]erhaps the greatest impact is to my personal disposition. I now realize, more than ever, that I must serve as a model for tolerance and equity for the adults and children I work with. I must model the desired behaviors, advocate for children and individuals and raise these issues to educators' consciousness. One of our very first classes ended with Dr. Soto saying, 'It is a long walk from home to school for our children'. . . . I suppose it is a long walk for each one of us.

Our range of personal and professional experiences addressing multicultural issue has lead each of us to take different approaches to arrive at the same goal, empowering individuals in order to have a positive impact on society. The primary differences lie in the frameworks we use to process information about the inequitable stratification of people in this society on the basis of race, social class, culture, gender, and disability. Both teaching applications assist students in their understanding of the nature of oppression in modern society. Students learn the importance of forming coalitions across race, class, and gender lines. They also learn that resources must be distributed much more equally than they are now.

A major component of both models (teacher education and counselor education) is to engage students in self-examination of their own roles in a society that is multicultural. The rationale behind this process is to afford participants an opportunity to redesign, reconstruct and enhance learning environments within the context of a possibilities-oriented paradigm. Students develop skills in articulating their understanding of oppression, envisioning goals for eliminating it, recognizing their power to effect change, and working collaboratively and constructively toward multiculturalism. Students begin to realize that they can affect educational settings and meet the multicultural needs of the their community.

The learning that has taken place for the participants and the facilitators has been collaborative, formative, challenging, and exciting. We envision possibilities and continue to reconstruct, redesign, and learn from each other. Our ability to influence the learning process within the setting and within the community has depended upon collaborative and formative experiences. The sharing and learning that take place among the facilitators and the participants often appears personally painful but ultimately valuable and rewarding.

Based upon what we have learned, we venture to make the following recommendations.

1. Patty Lather's (1986) research as praxis model serves as initial inspiration for a call to researchers viewing examples of existing praxis. Researchers may need to view the practitioners' experiences (in the trenches) in order to gain insight into future needed research directions for multicultural education. The idea of viewing praxis first implies the need for qualitative and ethnographic methodology coupled with experimentation.

2. Multicultural issues need to be *effectively integrated* into *all* aspects of the institution's curriculum. A vision of redesign and reconstruction, and a possibilities-oriented paradigm, can help to guide this endeavor.

3. Institutions should not relegate the teaching of multicultural courses to junior faculty and/or faculty of color. Role modeling and a collaborative commitment to multicultural professional development may prove useful for all faculty.

4. Multicultural issues should be made personally relevant. Self examination regarding issues of race, class, gender, culture, disabilities, religious affiliation, and so forth has proven valuable to participants within the context described in this paper.

5. Participants need to engage in constructive and critical evaluations of the cultural assumptions of their professions and of the social and political impact such assumptions may have upon learners and clients.

6. Participants need support and validation for the range of reactions they may experience as a result of the course content and process.

7. Participants need to acquire a broad knowledge base and strategies for collaborative social action capable of affecting the university and the community.

The demographics of learner and clients in academic settings are changing to include a broader range of people. The success of professions in these settings will depend, in part, on the ability of colleges and universities to prepare educators who have the appropriate awareness, knowledge, and skills to work effectively within such a multicultural context. These professionals need to be agents for social change, who have the ability to form coalitions and utilize resources so that effective services are provided to all learners and clients regardless of race, class, gender, culture, religious affiliation, or disability. It may be that if institutions responsible for training programs initiate self-evaluation of the current status of its respective professions and develop strategies for improving the delivery of services, then perhaps *some* educational equity, *some* social justice, and *some* democratic education of all people will be achieved in our lifetimes.

Hoping that our experiences may help others who teach at predominantly white universities we have shared our efforts. Although our disciplines and theoretical frameworks are different, our recommendations regarding the key issues that need to be addressed by instructors, administrators and researchers are consistent.

NOTES

Gratitude is expressed to our teaching assistants: Marcia Barone, Roberta Stern, Judy Crane, Lisa Bradford, Leon Caldwell, Jody Rose; and to the graduate students who so willingly shared their personal reflections.

1. Nationwide, culturally diverse enrollment in public elementary and secondary schools is expected to be approximately 30% of the total school enrollment (Feistritzer 1985). By the year 2010, approximately 40% of all school-age children are expected to be culturally diverse (Hodgkinson 1985). Since the 1970s, public primary and secondary student enrollment has only increased approximately 12% for whites, but enrollment has increased approximately 25% for African Americans and approximately 150% for American Latino, Asian and Native groups combined (Feistritzer 1985). However, the demographics of teachers in these settings have remained predominately white. Approximately 90% of all public school teachers are white with the next largest ethnic group being African American (an estimated 8.6%) followed by Hispanics (an estimated 1.8%). Asian American and Native American teachers combined represent less than 1% (Feistritzer 1985).

2. This possibilities-oriented paradigm deals with oppression and inequality from the vantage point of interrelated theories (i.e., conflict theory, cognitive development theory, and theory of culture) with grounding in daily lived experiences. The multicultural and social reconstructionist model can be characterized by Freire's (1985) process of "conscientization" and Shaw's (1921) quote: "You see things; and you say, 'Why?' But I dream of things that never were; and say, 'Why not?'" Both suggest that through education students should learn to question society, unlearn oppression, and become empowered to envision, define, and work toward a more humane society. The model reflects the ideals of democracy by affording learners the opportunity to articulate, debate, organize, work collectively, and develop strategies for social action.

Using the multicultural and social reconstructionist model as the theoretical basis for the course, the areas of knowledge emphasized include issues of race, class, gender, special needs, religious diversity, linguistic diversity, and ageism. Students learn to analyze the circumstances of their own life, practice democracy, develop social action skills, and form coalitions across race, class, and gender lines.

3. Excerpt #22: "In giving possession such as a house (Habitat for Humanity)—something I would value—I can't help but feel a little bit envious. That's possession I would value after four years of college and two years of graduate school, after two years of volunteer service (Peace Corps), and fourteen years of teaching . . ."

REFERENCES

Atkinson, D. R., G. Morton, and D. W. Sue. 1979. *Counseling American minorities: A cross-cultural perspective*. Dubuque, IA: Brown.

Feistritzer, C. E. 1985. The condition of teaching: A state by state analysis. Princeton, NJ: Carnegie Foundation for the Advancement of Teaching.

Freire, P. 1985. *The politics of education: Culture, power, and liberation.* Trans. by D. Macedo. South Hadley, MA: Bergin & Garvey.

Helms, J. E. 1990. *Racial identity: Theory, research, and practice.* New York: Greenwood Press.

Hodgkinson, H. L. 1985. The same client: The demographics of education. Washington, DC: Institute for Educational Leadership.

Katz, J. H. 1978. *White awareness: Handbook for anti-racism training.* Norman, OK: University of Oklahoma Press.

———. 1985. The sociopolitical nature of counseling. *The Counseling Psychologist* 13(4):615-24.

Kranz, P. L. 1972. Racial confrontation group implemented within a junior college. *Negro Education Review* 23:70-80.

Lather, P. 1986. Research as praxis. *Harvard Educational Review* 56:257-77.

Mabry, M. 1991, Sep/Oct. Confronting campus racism: What you can do to fight a growing menace. *The Black Collegian*, 78.

Marsella, A. J. and P. B. Pederson. 1981. *Cross-cultural counseling and psychotherapy.* New York: Pergamon Press.

Pederson, P. 1988. *Handbook for developing multicultural awareness.* Washington, DC: American Association for Counseling and Development.

Ponterotto, J. 1988. Racial consciousness development among white counselor trainees: A stage model. *Journal of multicultural counseling and development* 16(4):146-56.

Richardson, T. Q. 1988. White racial consciousness and the counseling profession. Unpublished manuscript.

———. 1992. Using White racial identity categories to predict intergroup relations. Unpublished manuscript.

Shaw, G. B. 1921. Back to Methusela, Pt. I, Act I. First edition. New York: Brentanos.

Sleeter, C. and C. Grant. 1989. *Making choices for multicultural education.* New York: Merrill.

Soto, L. D. 1991a. Teacher preparation and the linguistically diverse young child. *Education* 30(10):1-4.

———. 1991b. Understanding bilingual/bicultural young children. *Young Children*, 46(2):30-36.

————. 1992. Success stories. In *Research directions for multicultural education.* Edited by C. Grant. London: Falmer Press.

Southern Poverty Law Center. 1992, June. American's schools confront racial and ethnic intolerance. *Klanwatch Intelligence Report,* 7-9.

Vontress, C. E. 1971. Racial differences: Impediments to rapport. *Journal of Counseling Psychology* 18:7-13.

13

ROBYN S. LOCK _____

Beyond Bats and Balls:
Teaching about Knowledge, Culture, Power, and Ideology in Physical Education

INTRODUCTION

Probably one of the most marginalized and least understood content areas in public schools and institutions of higher education is physical education. Since physical education occupies such a marginal place, it typically has been overlooked by the educational establishment as a site of cultural reproduction. In addition, its power as a traditional socializing agent has been underestimated. The notion abounds in higher education as well as public schools that physical education teachers do nothing but throw out a ball and let the children play. After all, how difficult can it be to play? Yet the process of play, what we play, how we play, and how we come to understand what it means to play are forms of ideological struggle grounded in the dominant paradigms of knowledge, power, and culture. Further, who defines what will be presented as physical education is an essential component in the construction of power relationships.

Since physical education is socially, politically, and culturally situated, it is by its very nature part of the larger sphere of oppression and it reproduces dominant cultural values and norms. Despite the attempts of teacher educators to infuse new methods and materials into the traditional physical education curriculum, it has remained essentially unchanged in the last twenty years (Lock 1992). Unless intervention occurs, preservice teachers in physical education will, in all probability, replicate the same pedagogical strategies and curriculum that they experienced as public school students prior to entering a college or university. Since the population of students who will occupy our nation's schools is becoming increasingly diverse, equipping preservice physical education teachers with the knowledge and capacities to critically reflect on their own experience and biographies is a critical issue for teacher educators in physical education.

My own marginalization as a female in physical education and as a female athlete has led me to try to begin to understand how the forces of culture, ideology, knowledge, and power play themselves out in very specific ways. As a child, I was a relatively talented athlete in a very traditional, white, middle-class male way. My interests and behaviors were tolerated by my family. I tried to ignore what other students in elementary school used to say about me. Being ostracized was a price I was willing to pay because playing with the boys was always so much more gratifying to me than any conversation I could possibly have had with girl friends. As a matter of fact, it was in those conversations with other girls that I felt the most alienated because I lacked the cultural capital necessary that would have helped me to connect with the topics of conversation in which they were routinely engaged.

I use this personal but brief biographical sketch to underscore how these experiences have helped to shape how I *feel* about the concepts of knowledge, culture, power, and ideology. Lacking the cultural capital which would have allowed me to connect to the traditional female world, I entered the male domain of sports, but only as a visitor for a brief stay. My sex marginalized me in that context as well. And so I learned very early about how the concepts of ideology and power serve either to legitimate one's experience or to negate it.

It is a moral imperative for me to understand (and to help my students understand) how the process of education serves to marginalize whole groups of people who, for one reason or another, lack the power to access the very system that, in theory, is there to empower them. If physical educators hope to achieve success in the twenty-first century, it is imperative that we begin to redefine and restructure pedagogical approaches to better meet the needs of a diverse range of students (Martin and Lock 1991).

The purpose of this chapter is to, explain how I, as a teacher educator, attempt to infuse a critical theoretical feminist analysis of the structure and culture of the gymnasium into teacher education and to explore the impact dominant ideology has on the process of preparing teachers in physical education. It will include a brief analysis of the historical influences that have contributed to the conservative nature of physical education, which in turn have contributed to a technocratic ideology that has ultimately limited physical educators' abilities to deal effectively with issues of diversity.

TECHNOCRACY AND THE TRAINING MODEL

Historical Context

Historically, the field of physical education has suffered from a lack of respectability. Physical educators have tried to gain credibility by adopting rigorous empirical positions concerning the nature and content of physical education. In that endeavor physical educators have been seduced by science, disassociating the *play* element of their teaching to become more closely aligned with *work*. It is no accident that within the field of physical education the respected subdisciplines are the hard sciences such as exercise physiology or biomechanics. Unfortunately this only serves to reproduce the dominant ideological forms of knowledge.

Teacher education within physical education has suffered a similar identity crisis. In an attempt to overcome the *bleacher teacher* concept or the idea that teaching *gym* involves nothing more than throwing out a ball, teacher educators have developed a technocratic approach to the study of teaching and professional preparation. Positivistic, behavioristic research positions hold that effective teaching can be defined and developed in physical education, just as they have been described in the mainstream of education.

Teaching and learning in physical education are grounded in the assumption that these concepts are technological processes that can be developed and controlled. This approach supposedly provides preservice teachers with a systematic, objective way of looking at the teaching process that in turn improves student learning since teaching behaviors have been controlled and analyzed. ALT-PE (Seidentop, Birdwell, and Metzler 1979) and MOST-PE (Metzler 1981) are evaluation instruments based on this concept and are designed to measure teacher on-task behavior and effectiveness while at the same time increasing teacher productivity and accountability (McKay, Gore, and Kirk 1990). Preservice students in physical education learn how to manage equipment, manage student behavior, keep students on task, write behavioral objectives, analyze and give performance feedback without regard, for the most part, to the implications of their teaching. Through undergraduate preparation newly graduated teachers see their mission as the production of performance because they are seldom, if ever, introduced to the ethical and political questions surrounding the social context of their profession (Lock and Martin 1991). It is the ethical and political questions that are ignored which are important.

Some in the profession view as progress these recent technocratic developments. But this approach to teacher development does not engender a critical examination of key aspects of physical education: the impact of the teaching process; the nature of physical education's and students' understanding of whose interests are served in the promotion of this approach to teacher education.

The technocratic rationality defines the teacher as technician and the nature of physical education's content as easily quantified and measured. Students graduate from teacher education programs in physical education with specific and selective definitions of teaching, learning, sport, performance, and research that reflect technocracy and largely ignore the cultural context of the experience. The nature of the content of physical education and whose interests are served in the promotion of this approach to teacher education remains largely unexplored.

Teaching cannot be objective in the sense that our own personal values do not make a difference in the outcome. As Kaelin (1979) has stated, education is not a science at all, but rather an art form that imparts values. Within physical education, the technocratic assumptions concerning the process of teaching and learning have reinforced dominant ideology and have served to marginalize and disenfranchise women and minorities. The technocratic approach leads to false assumptions about reality and the personal meanings generated in the social context of the gymnasium. This approach also ignores the fact that schools and classrooms, including gymnasiums, are sites of power struggles between groups.

Even though a significant amount of research in the last twenty years (Lock 1992) has pointed to inequitable teaching practices (sexist, racist, homophobic, classist), research also indicates (McKay, Gore and Kirk 1990) that for the most part these practices still pervade the gymnasium. Physical education programs, especially at the secondary level, remain mostly oriented toward competitive team sports or individual sports, a practice presupposing that all students who enter the gymnasium find these activities inherently valuable and interesting. They also presuppose that all students can be and want to be successful in these activities.

The Culture of Teaching in the Gymnasium

Woods (1983) has stated that people develop cultures when they come together for specific purposes (intentionally or not). What emerges from the interactions between the members of the group is a consensus, often illusive and undefined, concerning how members of the group will operate within the cultural context.

By the process of socialization or induction, preservice teachers come to understand what it means to be a physical educator. The culture of teacher education provides a set of values that form the link between culture and individual action (Sparkes 1989). Even though preservice teachers actively define and use the gymnasium culture (Sparkes 1989), they still take the messages about what is a good teacher or a bad teacher from the dominant technocratic approach.

Sparkes (1989) maintains that the ability of the teacher to interpret the formal structure of the individual school determines the competent teacher. These competent teachers share patterns of understandings that form the basis of the *work culture*. Teacher cultures then are embodied in the work-related beliefs and knowledge shared among them and they provide the basis for making their individual teachers' behavior meaningful.

The technocratic approach to teacher development provides a view of the culture of teaching and learning that is thus very limiting. Without exploring the nature of culture itself, whose cultures are valued and why, preservice teachers emerge from teacher education programs with limited perspectives on the critical issues of race, class, and gender. They also emerge with virtually no understanding of how these variables get played out or of how such variables affect students' lives in the gymnasium.

Ideology and the Apprenticeship of Observation

Lortie (1975) has maintained that the preservice teacher is inducted into the culture of teaching through an "apprenticeship of observation" that involves the experiences within both the teacher preparation program and the individual school housing that program. The teacher ideology that emerges from the prolonged process of observation includes assumptions about the nature of knowledge, human nature, the role and function of education, the specific skills and techniques of teaching, and criteria for assessing adequate pupil performance (Sharp and Green 1975). These beliefs and values are shared not only at the individual level but also within the group of teachers as well, thus serving to support some groups within schools at the expense of others (Sparkes 1989). These beliefs, assumptions, and values are so held in common that they provide the foundation of what is accepted as common sense practice for successful teachers. As Sparkes (1989) has noted, "The operation on this consciousness in schools is seen to perpetuate particular forms of curriculum and pedagogy which support the interest of certain powerful groups, in society by leaving the status quo unchallenged" (322).

Content and Control

Research has shown that physical education teachers have a positive bias towards students who are conforming, cooperative, high-achieving, and orderly (Martinek 1983). This bias toward order and control gets reinforced through the observation model and within teacher education programs and is fundamental to the ideology within the gymnasium. Students who question the physical education program or refuse to participate are viewed as the problem. The curricular content itself is rarely, if ever, questioned as the reason for the rebellion.

Within the teacher preparation program, preservice teachers are infrequently encouraged to question the content of their own programs much less the content of what they will teach as future educators. The lack of questioning serves to reinforce the status quo by implying that the content and pedagogy are universally beneficial to all students. The ideology and culture of the gymnasium remain largely unchanged as a result. Teachers who can manage well, that is, who insure the smooth operations of the gymnasium while promoting student compliance, are valued and viewed as "good."

The technocratic rationality contributes to a cultural view that promotes the skilled, competitive, and strong student while marginalizing the unskilled, uncompetitive, weak, and sensitive student (Dewar 1989). Teaching becomes a mechanistic task based on an input/output model with little room for examining the meaning or impact of the teaching process.

THE INTERSECTING VARIABLES

It is beyond the scope of this chapter to explore the cultural and social foundations of physical education using an in-depth critical theoretical feminist critique. However, the variables that have an impact on the students' perceptions of the education they receive in the university setting must be explored and explained in relation to one another if the problems in physical education are to be understood.

The students who come to a university aspiring to be physical education teachers bring with them a biography that shapes their perceptions of themselves and the world around them. As students, they encounter professors who also have biographies that set the stage for interaction with students and the dissemination of information in very particular ways. In addition, students encounter a curriculum that may or may not connect to their biographies and past experiences. How these variables interact becomes an important part of the professional preparation process and influences how issues of diversity are perceived and handled in the classroom.

The Students

Students who enter the teaching profession in content areas other than physical education tend to be white females (Bennett and LeCompte 1990). They are women who tend to come from middle- to upper-middle class families and are comfortable in their gender role identification. The women who enter the teaching force tend not to be politically active and to make slightly less money than their male counterparts.

In contrast to the traditional academic content areas, the students who enter the professional preparation program in physical education tend to be white and male (Hultstrand 1990). Students (both female and male) who choose physical education as a career generally are students who have had extensive past experience in sport and have been successful in that experience (Dewar 1989). But the students who choose physical education tend to come from backgrounds that reflect homogeneity rather than a multiplicity of experiences or multicultural backgrounds. In addition, these students tend to have experiences in their secondary years that reinforce the notion of sex-appropriate physical activities for males and females as well as the idea that certain ethnic minorities are better suited for some activities rather than for others (Lock 1991).

The evidence suggests that students aspiring to be physical education teachers tend to hold more conservative political views than other college students (Bain 1989). In addition, the preservice physical education teachers tend to demonstrate lesser traditional academic achievements, that is they have poorer grade point averages than other students (Dewar 1989).

Students who are attracted to physical education as a career generally believe that teaching physical education is primarily skill oriented, and that it involves learning how to play games and transmitting games and sports to others (Dewar 1984). According to Dewar (1989), students also viewed teaching physical education as an avenue to coaching while affording one the opportunity to maintain high levels of personal participation in sport. Dewar (1989) also stated that students who were attracted to teaching physical education believed that the roles of the teacher and the coach were nearly identical.

Partly because of the view of teaching held by students who enter teacher education in physical education, both male and female preservice students generally see physical education as a transitory career; that is, they see themselves moving on to other positions. Females see themselves eventually becoming wives and mothers. Males see themselves becoming coaches or administrators (Lock 1991). In fact, many students consider the physical education major course of study as prerequisite to a career peripheral to teaching (Dewar 1989).

The students who enter the professional education sequence also have expectations of the program that reflect their personal biographies and experiences as students in elementary and secondary physical education. All entering students expect to receive ample time in what they called "real teaching" (Graber 1989). However, some of these students want only prescriptions for teaching or a cook book approach. They see training in specific skills as essential for success. In contrast, other students want to be educated about some of the more critical issues confronting the teachers of today (Graber 1989). These very different perceptions and expectations among groups of students within the same program can lead to personal and professional conflicts that may remain unresolved unless planned intervention occurs. Without intervention the notion that teaching is a technocratic process may also remain the dominant perception of the teaching and learning process.

Dewar (1989) suggested that a career in physical education attracts individuals who do not question the dominant ideology or want to change past teaching practices. In fact, she stated that the recruitment and retention process in typical physical education programs, through a system of rewards, reinforces dominant ideology by rewarding and keeping individuals who benefit from such a system. It is no surprise that the individuals who select physical education as a career are the individuals who have thrived and been successful within the system.

The apprenticeship of the observation model directs the preservice teacher to understand the teaching process in physical education as one of management (Schempp 1989). The fundamental priority of the "good" teacher is management, both of student behaviors and teacher behaviors. The ability to establish and maintain order is considered a critical dimension of good teaching, that is, the teacher is effective as long as the teacher keeps the students busy and time is not being wasted. If students are not encouraged to critically examine their own biographies and ideological positions within the gymnasium, little change will ever occur in the process of developing teachers in physical education.

The Professional Educators

Most faculties in physical education departments in institutions of higher education remain essentially white and male. The lack of diversity among faculties as well as the dichotomy of who is responsible for teaching particular courses reinforces traditional cultural ideologies that defines roles for men and women. In many institutions, responsibility for the undergraduate teacher preparation is the domain of the few female faculty members in physical education while the hard sciences, such as exercise physiology or biomechanics, remain the domain of the male faculty members.

This gendered dichotomy reflects general perceptions of the nature and purpose of undergraduate education. Faculty members engaged in traditional empirical research within physical education generally have little time or interest in a critical theoretical approach that would foster a more complete examination of the impact of ideology. The dichotomy also gives the impression to undergraduates that teacher education is so-called "women's work."

Another problem emerges directly from this gendered dichotomy. Often the minorities and few women on the faculty inherit the burden of dealing with issues of race, class, and gender. In all probability, this occurs because sexism is viewed as a problem that belongs to women, since women are the ones oppressed, and racism is viewed as a problem that belongs to people of color since they are the ones oppressed.

Two problems emerge from the process of locating ideological issues with women and minority faculty members. First, the real issues of cultural reproduction and hegemony are ghettoized in the department, thus marginalizing race, class, and gender as peripheral issues. As a result, women and minority faculty members tend to be responsible for teaching about these issues. Second, by ghettoizing the issues, the white male purveyors of the hidden and written curriculum maintain a position that contributes to the idea that racism, sexism, and classism are not their problems; therefore, they do not have to change the content of their courses or method of teaching. In addition, many in higher education tend to think that gender as an issue in educational policy and practice has been dealt with and therefore needs no more attention (Bennett and LeCompte 1990).

The Knowledge Base

The knowledge base itself is problematic. Most of what is taught in physical education curricula is competitive and sport oriented. Most also reflect interscholastic, intercollegiate and professional men's sport, both in the time of year when the activity is presented to the students and by the language used to present the activity. What gets defined and what counts within physical education as the "real thing" is an ideological tool that reproduces dominant/subordinate power relationships within the gymnasium. As Susan Birrell (1992) has noted this ideological structure justifies the treatment of people within that context and thus reproduces inequality. What is taught or passes as knowledge is as important as what is omitted as knowledge.

Consider the relationship between this problematic knowledge base and the concept gender. Undergraduate students tend to view useful knowledge as coming from the biological/physiological courses they take. What these courses teach and how they are taught direct students to view gender as a variable in performance, where women are assumed to be deficient and men the norm.

In addition, undergraduates generally believe that the issue of gender was an issue of equal access now improved and no longer needing attention. Although some males believe they are committed to fair treatment of girls and women, they tend to believe that inequality is a way of life and consequently consider issues of equity relatively unimportant (Lock 1991). As Dewar (1987) has noted, the dominant view of gender as an issue of sex difference traits residing in individuals tends to reinforce and legitimate patriarchal ideology.

In a recent study, I had the occasion to discuss the issue of inequality with sixteen female, undergraduate students. I asked them about their feelings concerning the inequitable treatment of women in physical education. With one exception, all of the women felt that inequality was "natural" and "a way of life for women." Perhaps their feelings could best be summarized in the words of one student. She said, "I think if a woman doesn't have an opportunity, a lot of it's her own fault. If she won't take the initiative, it's her fault. You have to realize that you will always come up against things, you will always be the minority no matter what you do. You have to learn to get past that yourself . Individuals can do it—but as a whole—to go against the odds—it won't happen" (Lock 1991, 14).

Accompanying such views of gender inequality as natural in physical education is an appalling lack of a feminist voice or perspective. A recent review of the literature in five prominent journals in physical education found that only eighty of over 6,000 published articles since the passage of Title IX in 1972 included a feminist perspective or feminist analysis (Lock 1992). Although feminist writing does now voice a new perspective within physical education, the feminist position remains marginal. A few "maverick physical educators" are aware of implications of critical feminist pedagogy for physical education (McKay, Gore and Kirk 1990). Even so, Bain (1990) has noted that it is difficult to assess the impact of a feminist critique given its relatively recent appearance. She continued, ". . . one might conjecture that its radical feminist roots will be perceived as threatening by many in the mainstream of physical education, especially given the conservatism of physical educators" (11).

Other issues of diversity are marginalized as well. A review of the multicultural education literature in physical education (Lock and Martin 1991) revealed a significant lack of published articles relative to the issues of race or class. There appeared to be few models for effective infusion of multicultural education in the physical education classroom. Physical educators seemed unfamiliar with the terminology associated with multicultural education and were therefore inclined to infuse it in a peripheral fashion. Most of the published articles demonstrated a lack of clarity about the purposes and goals of multicultural education. They also perpetuated abstract concepts of equity that tended to reproduce the dominant cultural values and norms without assessing the inherent structural inequities in schools. It also was interesting to note that the term *multicultural education* did not exist as a descriptor in the *Physical Education Index*.

A CLASSROOM EXPERIMENT

Professional preparation programs clearly need to be grounded in preservice students' existing knowledge and experience. Seidentop (1986) has stated that university preservice teacher education programs do not provide prospective teachers with a concept of quality physical education programs nor with the teaching skills needed to implement the program. However, how *quality* gets defined remains problematic. It would seem that not only do preservice teachers need a solid foundation in the technology of teaching and learning that would contribute to a definition of *quality*. They also need to reflect critically upon their own experience as students and as student teachers in order to deconstruct the forces that have shaped their notions of ideology and culture, what is accepted as truth, knowledge, and reality.

There exists a clear need to ground the professional preparation program in the knowledge and experience the preservice students already hold. Students need to understand the link between their experiences in school as students and the notions of ideology and culture that emerge during the preservice experience. To bridge the gap and help students make the connections between ideology, culture, power and educational practice, I have attempted to ground the secondary methods course (one of four in the pedagogical sequence) in a critical theoretical position that would aid in the process of merging theory and practice.

Students in our physical education professional preparation program are well grounded in the technology of teaching. As a prerequisite to admission into the program, all students must take the Introduction to Teaching Physical Education course. During that course, as well as the elementary methods block, they learn to identify and manage their teacher behaviors through the Physical Education Teaching Assessment Instrument (PETAI). The PETAI focuses on specific teaching behaviors such as performance feedback, motivational feedback, organizational time as well as planned presentation. The purpose is to ground the preservice students in the technology so that they are able to code their own teaching behaviors through the use of a computer program. This position theoretically enables the preservice teachers to control the teaching process, thereby enhancing the learning by students in the classes.

However, as practical and useful as the PETAI is as a tool for evaluation, it still limits any discussion of the impact of the teaching process on students. For example, not included in the categories for observation are any racist, sexist, classist, or homophobic practices in which the preservice teachers might engage. The limitations of the technological tool become apparent quickly. A good teacher does not engage in any practice that marginalizes any member of a class, but such practices cannot be identified much less measured by this instrument.

A critical analysis of teaching behaviors beyond the technical realm is necessary. At some point preservice teachers need to reflect critically on their own perceptions. To encourage this I thought it appropriate to redesign the secondary physical education methods course to better deal with the issues of race, class, and gender in the context of physical education.

The course is constructed so that I meet with the students every day. The first five weeks of the quarter we meet in the classroom. The next four weeks the students are placed in a secondary setting for a field experience. Twice during the field experience we meet as a class to discuss specific issues and assignments. The last week of the quarter we meet again in the classroom to bring closure to their experience both in the classroom and in the field.

In part, the course serves to prepare them for the requirements of the student teaching experience; consequently, some of the assignments mirror the expectations of student teaching. The students are required to prepare a notebook that includes lesson plans, unit plans, the observation instruments (which I will describe) as well as a daily log that they write during the field experience.

The course begins with a discussion of the purpose of education and specifically how physical education contributes to the educational process. The approach I use in the course is grounded in critical feminist theory. The initial phase includes a critique of current practices at the secondary level by examining their personal experiences in their secondary physical education classes. The purpose is to help them begin to recognize how similar programs are in content, method, and evaluation procedures.

During this time we also examine the racial, ethnic, class, and gender composition of the secondary classes by looking at the language used to describe various groups of students who are successful in the gymnasium. Important questions asked are: what is success, who is successful, why are they successful, who is not successful, and why are they not successful? The purpose is to get the preservice students to begin to recognize the cultural and ideological forces that have shaped their concept of physical education.

The students also are given a model of reflectivity developed by Farber, whose chapter in this book fully discusses its components and applications. By teaching and using this model, the students can begin to address in a more neutral space some of their biases and prejudices. I have found the model extremely useful because it enables the students to reflect on their own experiences as students, reflect on how dominant ideology has contributed to their own oppression as well as that of others, and examine how the gymnasium is a site of constant struggle between groups.

The next phase of the course includes the critical examination of the issues of race, class, and gender. I use Bennett and LeCompte's book, *The Way*

Schools Work, to deal with these issues. Using a specific problem and the model of reflectivity, we explore the issues of race, class, and gender. For example, when dealing with the issue of sexism, I ask the students to reflect on what the atmosphere of the gymnasium would be like if feminine behaviors were valued instead of masculine behaviors. The students are placed in groups and asked to use the model of reflectivity to examine the problem. They are able then to disclose beliefs and values without the embarrassment of having to own those beliefs and values. It is important to create an atmosphere in which the students feel free to express even the most unacceptable positions. Only then can the real issues emerge and honest discussion begin.

Nine observation instruments were developed to help the preservice students observe the components of gymnasium, teaching, content, school, and community in their field experience from a critical theoretical position. The first three instruments focus on the students in the school. The preservice students observe the public school students in a variety of settings (cafeteria, halls, libraries, learning centers). The instruments serve to guide their observations by using the information we have generated and discussed in the classroom. The purpose is to help the preservice students examine the dynamics of power and power relationships from a critical theoretical perspective.

The next two instruments deal specifically with the process of teaching. The preservice students are asked to examine the lesson plan of the cooperating teacher (if there is one) using the criteria generated in class. The next instrument helps the preservice student evaluate the degree to which a nonsexist environment has been developed by the cooperating teacher.

Three of the instruments help the preservice student to evaluate the atmosphere of the school. Each student is asked to make an appointment with the principal to discuss discipline policies, curriculum development, and the style of leadership preferred by the principal. In addition, preservice students are asked to walk around the school to get a feel for the school through the physical appearance of the halls and building itself. Any field experience would be incomplete without a trip to the faculty room, so one of the instruments deals specifically with their reactions to the interactions among the faculty in that context.

The last observation instrument is designed to help preservice students examine the school's environment in relation to its community. Included as items for observation are the businesses in the community, the homes surrounding the school, as well as the political atmosphere within the community.

During the time of the field experience, the students are required to return to the classroom two separate times for discussion of the observation instruments. Each discussion critically examines the issues embedded in each of the instruments. The instruments are designed to help the preservice students examine the day-to-day occurrences in the school through a different lens. For example, one instrument helps to critically examine the nature of success in the gymnasium. Typically, white able-bodied male students emerge as the dominant force in the physical education classroom. This occurs usually because of the content being taught as well as the way the content is taught. Preservice students are asked to observe the students who are not successful.

The classroom discussion becomes a place for the analysis of these types of situations through the instruments. At this time, I challenge preservice students to critically examine the culture that fosters an environment such as the one just described. The issue of success, of how success gets defined and by whom, is discussed in terms of power, dominance, knowledge, and the culture of the gymnasium. I attempt to critically compare and contrast their experiences as students in physical education classes to the experiences of the students they see in their field experiences.

All preservice students also are required to complete a daily log in which they critically reflect upon their experiences using the reflective model. They can choose an incident or a problem that they encountered during the day. The purpose is to use the model to positively resolve the conflict or problem. The daily log becomes a written dialogue between the individual student and me. I ask all preservice students to submit the log weekly so that I can read and respond; I am then able to help them in their analysis as well as intervene if any problems exist.

In addition to using the observation instruments and developing the daily log, the preservice teachers are expected to complete tasks that more closely resemble real teaching. The preservice teachers also are required to write lesson plans and unit plans as well as team teach during the five weeks in the public schools. It is at this time that I incorporate the technology in which they have been well grounded. Their teaching behaviors are analyzed using the PETAI. We discuss how they might manage their time, equipment, and organizational patterns in a more efficient manner, one that would contribute to an effective classroom. These discussions are important and are tied to the concept of what it means to be a good teacher.

Indeed, this all might seem overwhelming. But when we return to our classroom for the final week of the quarter, I try to help the preservice students bring all this information together. The purpose of the class is to encourage preservice students to reflect on their own biographies and experiences and the impact these variables have on their perceptions of the educational process.

CONCLUSIONS

Teacher education programs critically need to research, design, and address issues of race, class, and gender in physical education. The work of Martin and Lock (1991) suggests that today's physical education graduates are no better prepared to address the issues of diversity than were their predecessors. The teacher educator as courier of the curriculum is the critical link between the letter and the spirit of the law. Teacher education institutions must initiate programs that foster changes in prospective teachers' consciousness. The secondary methods course previously described evolved out of a concern for equipping preservice teachers with the knowledge and skills to reflect critically on their own experiences and biographies, reflection that will influence them as teachers and their future students.

I cannot speak to the success of this experimental approach. Frequently students will share their confusion, sometimes anger, over the cognitive dissonance created as a result of the conflict between their critical theoretical experience in the classroom and the reality of their experiences as students and their field experience in the public schools. In part, the intent of the course is to create cognitive dissonance to the point where so-called common sense notions of teaching and learning are questioned. Occasionally, students share their relief and gratitude because someone has finally been honest in describing the oppression that they experienced as a student in the public schools.

This process can be and is very frustrating. Perhaps it is unreasonable to expect preservice teachers to deconstruct the influence of the dominant ideology in their own lives in a brief ten-week period. What I can do is raise preservice students' consciousnesses about these issues and give them the knowledge and skills to deal effectively with these issues at a personal level. Hopefully, then, they can continue that work at a professional level.

REFERENCES

Bain, L. L. 1989. Implicit values in physical education. In *Socialization into physical education: Learning to teach.* Edited by T. J. Templin and P. G. Schempp. Indianapolis, IN: Benchmark Press.

———. 1990, April. The impact and implications of research on teaching and teacher education in physical education. Paper presented at the annual meeting of the American Educational Research Association, Boston.

Bennett, K. P. and M. D. LeCompte. 1990. *The way schools work: A sociological analysis of education.* New York: Longman Press.

Birrell, S. 1992. Woman athlete: Fact or fiction. Paper presented at the National Girls and Women's Sport Symposium in Slippery Rock, PA.

Dewar, A. M. 1984. High school students subjective warrants for physical education. Paper presented at the Olympic Scientific Congress, Eugene, OR.

———. 1987. The social construction of gender in physical education. *Women's Studies International Forum* 10(4):453-65.

———. 1989. Recruitment in physical education teaching: Toward a critical approach. In *Socialization into physical education: Learning to teach.* Edited by T. J. Templin and P. G. Schempp. Indianapolis, IN: Benchmark Press.

Farber, K. 1987. *Thought and knowledge: A neurophysiological view.* Ph.D. diss., Ohio State University, Columbus, OH.

Graber, K. C. 1989. Teaching tomorrow's teachers: Professional preparation as an agent of socialization. In *Socialization into physical education: Learning to teach.* Edited by T. J. Templin and P. G. Schempp. Indianapolis, IN: Benchmark Press.

Hultstrand, B. J. 1990, November-December. Women in high school physical education teaching positions—Diminishing in number. *Journal of Physical Education, Recreation, and Dance* 61(9):19-21.

Kaelin, E. 1979. Being in the body. In *Sport and the body: A philosophical symposium.* Edited by E. Gerber and W. Morgan. Philadelphia: Lea and Febiser.

Lock, R. S. 1991, November. Young women in physical education: Constructing meaning through diverse experience. Paper presented at the annual meeting of Research on Women and Education, a Special Interest Group of the American Educational Research Association, San Jose, CA.

————. 1993. Women in sport and physical education: A review of the literature on selected journals. *Women in Sport and Physical Activity Journal* 2(2):21-49.

Lock, R. S. and R. J. Martin. 1991. Multicultural education: A pedagogy of equity in physical education. Paper presented at the annual meeting of the American Alliance of Health, Physical Education, Recreation and Dance in San Francisco, CA.

Lortie, D. C. 1975. *Schoolteacher: A sociological study.* Chicago: University of Chicago Press.

Martin, R. J. and R. S. Lock. 1991. Cultural realities: Cultural reproduction in physical education. An analysis of nonsexist behaviors of student teachers. *Teacher Education Quarterly* 18(2):45-55.

Martinek, T. J. 1983. Creating Golem and Galatea effects during physical education instruction: A social psychological perspective. In *Teaching in physical education.* Edited by T. J. Templin and J. K. Olsen. Champaign, IL: Human Kinetics Publishers.

McKay, J., J. M. Gore, and D. Kirk. 1990. Beyond the limits of technocratic physical education. *Quest* 42(1):52-76.

Metzler, M. 1981. A multi-observational system for supervising student teachers in physical education. *The Physical Educator* 38(3):152-59.

Schempp, P. G. 1989. Apprenticeship-of-observation and the development of physical education teachers. In *Socialization into physical education: Learning to teach.* Edited by T. J. Templin and P. G. Schempp. Indianapolis, IN: Benchmark Press.

Seidentop, D. 1986. The modification of teacher behavior. In *Sport pedagogy.* Edited by M. Pieron and G. Graham. Champaign, IL: Human Kinetics Publishers.

Seidentop, D., P. Birdwell, and M. Metzler. 1979. A process approach to measuring teaching effectiveness in physical education. Paper presented at the annual meeting of the American Alliance of Health, Physical Education, Recreation and Dance, New Orleans.

Sharp, R. and A. Green. 1975. *Education and social control*. London: Routledge and Kegan Paul.

Sparkes, A. C. 1989. Culture and ideology in physical education. In *Socialization into physical education: Learning to teach*. Edited by T. J. Templin and P. G. Schempp. Indianapolis, IN: Benchmark Press.

Woods, P. 1983. *Sociology and the school*. London: Routledge and Kegan Paul.

14

Evelyn McCain-Reid _____

Seeds of Change:
A Pilot Study of Senior Preservice Teachers'
Responses to Issues of Human Diversity
in One University Course

Introduction

This paper describes a pilot study undertaken to determine the impact that two models of instruction, the Societal Curriculum/School Curriculum Model (scscm) and a Multicultural Education Infusion Method (meim), had on students' learning when they were incorporated into one preservice teacher education course. The Societal Curriculum/School Curriculum Model (Cortes 1976) was used to assess pre-service teachers' knowledge and sensitivity to human diversity. The scscm model also was used to make teachers aware that individuals and groups in our society are constantly and intimately engaged in a *hegemonic* learning process, where messages about human diversity are subtly absorbed both from society and schools and often go unquestioned. Although this knowledge may support our understanding of who we are and our connection to others, this information may also serve to miseducate. The Multicultural Education Infusion Method (Sims 1983) draws upon the Cortes model by incorporating interdisciplinary concepts (formal classroom curriculum knowledge) with controversial issues from society (societal curriculum knowledge). The two models were combined to encourage understanding and sensitivity to group struggles and a positive attitude toward diversity (Bennett, Niggle, and Stage 1990).

The study was conducted at a small, predominantly white, state institution in Ohio. Twenty senior secondary preservice teachers in the process of completing the last course in their educational sequence participated. The study involved sixteen white females and four white males, and an African American female professor who served as the principal investigator. Though the study sample is small and the absence of minority preservice student teachers is apparent, the situation is fairly typical of predominantly white institutions. Therefore, the study promises to shed light on the issues and challenges encountered by educators when they focus on issues of human diversity in their education curriculum.

235

As has been noted by numerous other authors in this volume, a multicultural approach to education and issues surrounding human diversity promises to be among the most challenging educational issues of the twenty-first century. We know from American history and housing patterns that white Americans for the most part have not consistently and intimately lived in and interacted within minority communities. Thus, their knowledge of minority children is limited. It appears, then, that if we expect our future teachers who are mostly white, female, and middle class, to effectively educate minority students (i.e., develop an awareness and sensitivity to the issues and concerns that affect minority students' daily lives), we as teacher educators must challenge our students to critically analyze commonly held views concerning American minority groups. According to recent research (Banks and Banks 1989; Grant and Sleeter 1984, 1985; Sleeter and Grant 1987; Gollnick and Chinn 1986), we must also encourage them to become sensitive to the natural differences that occur as a result of different ethnic backgrounds, religions, socioeconomic levels, native languages, mental abilities, and so forth, and we must help them design curricula that responsibly address and connect issues of race, class, gender, and disability.

THEORETICAL FRAMEWORK

Multicultural education researchers have greatly contributed to our knowledge and understanding of human diversity in American society, and of how messages about human diversity are communicated through policies, practices, and procedures that connect American society and schools. Mainstream America historically has dominated and controlled information about human diversity in society and schools. Therefore, knowledge about diverse groups that is brought into the classroom by teachers and students is often limited, narrow, and by necessity misrepresented.

Multicultural education research explores why some groups (i.e., white, middle class, male) have historically dominated resources in a capitalist democratic society such as ours. Based on this inequity, questions arise such as: what messages are communicated to preservice teachers about youth from different ethnic, racial, social class, and disability groups, and how do those messages bias their conceptions of youth? Because our teaching pool is primarily white, female and middle class, knowledge by its members about human diversity has been shaped by limited, narrow, and often negative messages from mainstream society. Teachers must develop curriculum and teaching methods that benefit a diverse group of students. These methods also must enhance the quality of knowledge about diverse groups by eliminating negative messages brought to the classroom and by enhancing positive ones. Multicultural theory cautions that we all lose when these social prejudices filter into schools through institutional policies and practices.

According to Cortes (1976), our ideas about diversity are influenced by the messages we receive from society: family and friends, the community, organizations, mass media, records and videos, and personal interactions with others. Social messages influence individuals on local, national, and worldwide levels, and they affect one's self-image and understanding or misunderstanding about others—even one's vision about the nation and the world, and hopes for the future. Such messages can become a part of the school curriculum when they are brought to and communicated in the classroom through the practices of administrators, teachers, and students. For instance, teachers may be guided by their social biases as they choose educational materials to use with diverse groups of students.

Teachers must, therefore, provide classroom activities that expand students' knowledge about others. One way to help students understand others is to encourage them to develop relationships with persons different from themselves, maintain ongoing friendships with persons different from themselves, and to interact with diverse groups in different settings. This will enable students to observe how issues may affect people's lives differently in various situations.

The Societal Curriculum/School Curriculum Model (SCSCM) creates this cultural sensitivity in teachers by challenging their views about human diversity. Following this model, students keep an ongoing journal about diversity around campus and in the community, then teach a lesson based on what they observed.

The classroom may serve as a place where teachers can provide more opportunities for students to develop their understanding of diversity. The Multicultural Education Infusion Method (MEIM) introduces controversial issues from society into the curriculum by asking students to write position papers comparing their philosophy of teaching to their ideas about diversity. As students reflect on their views about diversity, they critically analyze their teaching method, challenging themselves to consider where their values come from, and consider how they fit in the classroom.

The MEIM Model extends the SCSCM Model by incorporating information about diversity from society into the curriculum and classroom activities in order to challenge students' knowledge about diversity. Students learn to approach educational topics from the perspectives of diverse groups.

The course incorporated these two models and challenged students to examine their ideas about diversity in society and schools. Classroom activities constantly challenged students to explain their views about human diversity and to justify their teaching approach. Furthermore, students were asked to share their experiences as they learned to teach more effectively to a diversity of students.

REVIEW OF LITERATURE

A limited number of research studies exist on Multicultural Education and preservice training (Baker 1973, 1977; Bennett 1979; Grant 1981; Hennington

1981; Mahan 1982), with information focusing mainly on statistical methods and data. However, a small number of articles and books exist on the issue of human diversity and the growing need to incorporate multicultural issues as a central focus in the classroom. A particularly useful source is Grant and Sleeter's *Making Choices for Multicultural Education: Five Approaches to Race, Class, and Gender*.

The Bicentennial Commission on Education for the Profession of Teaching of the American Association of Colleges for Teacher Education offers possible reasons for teacher educators' neglect of human rights and minority group issues at the core of curriculum:

> Unfortunately, teacher educators have not always been conscious exemplars of human rights. Few actively advocate the rights of minority groups or promote cultural pluralism. Today, leaders ask the education profession to develop in students those attitudes and beliefs which support cultural pluralism as a positive social force. Thus, the education of teacher educators must be substantive enough to develop a respect for the culture, lifestyles, and contributions of non-mainstream cultures. Teacher educators also need a commitment to universal human values in order to promote harmonious coexistence. (108-9)

Grant and Koskela (1986) argue that the call for incorporation of ideas about human diversity into university coursework has gone largely unanswered. Dawson (1981) echoes Grant and Koskela, comparing the attitudes of teacher education faculty at Historically Black Colleges and Universities (HBCU) and at predominantly white universities. According to Dawson, numerous teacher educators at HBCUs believe that their commitment to minorities (as evidenced by working at these schools) is sufficient proof of their involvement in multicultural education. Likewise, many teacher educators at traditionally white universities believe that their work in monocultural and monosocial geographical regions exempt them from any obligation to commit time to multicultural education. Dawson views these attitudes as "erroneous and as typifying the exemption syndrome" (5), with university curricula reflecting business-as-usual education. This implicit acceptance of segregated American education and/or education excludes the lifestyles, values, and customs of minority groups.

As noted earlier in this volume, in the mid-1970s such accrediting agencies as the National Council for Accreditation of Teacher Education (NCATE) joined the multicultural education reform movement, attempting to make teacher educators and program designers more responsive to human diversity by integrating multicultural goals at all levels of the teacher education institution. Like the NCATE framers, Sims (1983) also discourages programs that incorporate multicultural education by adding additional hours to teacher certification programs or by offering multicultural elective courses. Instead, the writer challenged university administrators and teacher educators to incorporate the Multicultural

Education Infusion Method (MEIM) which incorporates issues of diversity at the core of curricula and challenges preservice teachers' commonly held views. According to Sims, MEIM produces effective teachers competent in all traditional skills and more—*more* being a knowledge and understanding of the traditions, attitudes, and customs that shape the behaviors of culturally diverse people. To Sims, the MEIM approach establishes a curriculum fabric with "strands of multicultural education interwoven so closely that they are a part of the whole, and also a component of each separate part" (1983, 43).

THE STUDY

As the preceding review of literature suggests, much has been written on the need for incorporating issues of human diversity in the classroom, but little research has been done on the actual incorporation of Multicultural Education as a central focus of study or on the implications arising from its implementation. Also, the research that has been undertaken relies mostly on statistical methods and data, and as a result, does not provide a qualitative portrait of how students actually think about diversity. Therefore, this pilot study was undertaken with the following goals: 1) to determine the prevailing attitudes of preservice teacher educators toward multicultural issues; 2) to elicit their subjective responses to information about issues of race, class, gender, and disability; and 3) to establish how this information influenced their attitudes toward teaching.

Method

The study was undertaken in a ten-week senior-level social cultural foundations course, titled Teacher, School and Society, in which twenty students were enrolled. The students were initially introduced to the ideas of human diversity through Grant and Sleeter's (1988) five approaches, and the course was conducted in a lecture/discussion format, focusing on assigned readings that would challenge and inform students on issues of race, class, gender, and disability as they relate to educational issues. The readings were chosen for their potential to introduce controversial topics and to raise such questions as the following. Which groups were barred from the polls in the South during the post-Reconstruction period due to literacy test laws and why? What impact did these laws have upon the lives of blacks, Mexicans, Puerto Ricans, and Native Americans? How did *Brown v. Board of Education* affect the lives of secondary education teachers and students? What was the impact of *Lau v. Nichols* on secondary teachers and students in the San Francisco school system?

After working together to establish a definition of multicultural education as "educational policies and practices that recognize, appreciate, and affirm diversity in regard to ethnicity, gender, social class, and disability," students were asked to consider the five approaches introduced, along with the conventional business-as-usual approach. They were then told to complete six assignments that required them to establish their ideal future teaching situation (i.e., community, school staff, classroom comprising different race, class, gender, and disability, grade level K-12, subject matter) while they examined various multicultural issues in relation to that teaching situation. All assignments were designed to elicit from students their knowledge and understanding of human diversity. Moreover, many of the assignments also incorporated the aspect of assessment or evaluation. Miller (1979, 1988, 1990) maintains that student evaluations of teaching materials and procedures, professors' content, and themselves as students is critically important to the learning process in a university setting. As he states, "though more than one mode of assessment should be used, the single most important form of evaluation in university classrooms is that of students" (1979, 64).

The first assignment, the Teacher Education Journal, required that students respond in writing to issues of diversity as they arose out of daily experiences (e.g., observations from other courses, residence hall living, television, newspapers, previous public school experience, home, baseline criteria for the course) from the first day of the course through the last regular day of class. The second, the Philosophy of Teaching Paper, required students to analyze critically their views of teaching as a profession (e.g., where did their ideas and values come from and how do they fit into the the classroom?). This analysis also involved historical information that helped to shape teaching philosophies (e.g., such legal and social issues as desegregation and status group interest). The third, the Professional Journal Critique, required students to present a brief summary of a professional article, followed by a critique that incorporated baseline criteria and discussed implications for educators and/or teacher educators. The fourth, an Interview with the Professor, involved a thirty to forty-minute audiotaped interview that required students to respond to a combination of ten open-ended, probe, attribute, and contrast questions designed to challenge their currently held views and assumptions, their approach to teaching, and their daily interactions with groups different from themselves. The fifth, a Microteaching Demonstration, required students to submit a written plan—including a belief statement—outlining a specific lesson focusing on human diversity and to teach the lesson using a multicultural education or education that is multicultural perspective. They were then asked to conduct the lesson with the professor and other class members using a role-play method teaching to their hypothetical future class where diversity is present. And finally the sixth, the Evaluation of the Microteaching Demonstration, required each student to submit a written evaluation immediately following each student's demonstration.

These six assignments served as tools for developing critical thinking skills for the students and also served as the sources of information for the study. Though the information itself was subjective, as were the methods used to obtain it, the procedures approximate the actual classroom experience much more closely than do statistical methods and information, and as a result, offer a valid, but often overlooked, source of information for teacher educators.

RESULTS

Results of the study are reported according to the six assignments that gave direction to the study.

Teacher Education Journals

All twenty group members responded to issues of race, class, gender, and disability in the teacher education journals. Several participants reported that they felt comfortable interacting with different racial groups and had long-standing and genuine relationships with minorities. However, others stated that they felt uncomfortable when interacting with different racial groups and that they strongly opposed T-shirt slogans that expressed racial messages (such as "It's A Black Thang, You Wouldn't Understand"); some went so far as to suggest that racial messages on T-shirts should be banned or outlawed.

Many participants strongly opposed interracial dating and marriages as inappropriate behavior. Some respondents in this group reported that they came from small towns where their parents and community members (i.e., ministers, friends, community leaders) taught them that they should never interact closely with blacks, Jews, and internationals; thus, interracial dating and marriage were out of the question to them. For example, one white male student first apologized to the professor who is African American, and then stated that he had never considered African American women as possible dates, he did not find them attractive, and therefore could not possibly consider dating or marrying an African American. Several group members responded that their parents taught them to interact only with their own kind, which was "God's word," while others stated that they were "uncomfortable" and "frustrated" discussing issues raised in the course regarding race, class, gender, and disability. A white female student expressed that she respects African Americans, Jews, and internationals as long as they live in "their" communities and did not attempt to live and interact in "her" neighborhood. She stated that she felt unsafe in the company of African American males and that she strongly believed that African American males were prone to crime, which contributed to her discomfort.

However, as the course progressed, some of the sample members began to question friends who made racial jokes and who labeled different ethnic groups in a negative way. Several participants reported that in the past they had participated in racial jokes and found it "fun," but because of issues raised in this course, they began to take racial jokes more seriously. One member of this group reported addressing the issue of labeling and putting down people due to ethnic difference quite strongly with her roommate, who made the statement "Boy, Jews sure have a lot of money, don't they?" This respondent also reported overhearing a group of white males talking in the library who stated in a loud condescending voice within earshot of some Chinese students, "Boy this place looks like Chinatown on the weekend."

Some sample members also reported on social class differences in their journals. Many student responses demonstrated their lack of sensitivity toward human diversity and their lack of understanding about systemic economic oppression in a capitalistic society. Although many of them had begun to challenge biased statements made about minority groups in society, they failed to place these societal messages within institutional structures, particularly schools. One female described a telephone conversation with her brother-in-law in which he stated that he was tired of his taxes going to pay for lazy minority and low-income people who depend on social programs; when she pointed out to him that she was white and on social assistance, he offered no response. She expressed that she was unable to see how persons in our society who hold negative views of minorities would have an impact on learning in the classroom. She further expressed that the Society Curriculum/School Curriculum and the Multicultural Infusion Model had little impact on her thinking. She wanted to see society function as it did in earlier periods in our history (i.e., prior to laws that allowed groups to mix and confuse everyone), when groups in society were segregated and attended segregated schools, and when multicultural education (i.e., diverse groups of people interacting together and sharing similar views) was not of concern in schools.

Several respondents also reported that, in the past, they believed that street people and low-income people on social programs were in those positions because they refused to work or because they wanted that quality of life, but recently they realized that their thinking about low-income individuals, derived mainly from print and electronic media, was unfounded. A number of students cited a change in their opinions, coming to recognize that many street people have loving and caring families and money, and that other reasons may be responsible for their situations.

Several participants reported on issues of gender in their journals. Some of the males felt that women tended to contradict themselves on women's issues, as when some women expect males to open doors for them and others are absolutely insulted by the act. Some males commented on women who competed with them in the athletic weight lifting program; they asked the women, "Don't you know that the focus of men's strength is at the upper portion of their body and women's strength is at the lower portion of their bodies?" and the women replied, "So, what is your point?" Several females reported being opposed to affirmative action policies for women because these policies sometimes appeared to hurt men. They noted that while working in summer jobs they observed women who worked alongside men and were paid equally due to affirmative action policies, but often they noticed the male workers assisting women in lifting heavy objects. Other females reported that women around campus were ignorant of activities in support of women. They reported that when they participated in the "Take Back the Night" project, many of their roommates and friends who are senior teacher education majors asked, "What is this "Take Back the Night' thing?"

One sample member reported that he uncovered biases toward the disabled or differently abled. He described opposing his peers who made fun of a friend's *little person* girlfriend. According to him, he learned from her that the preferred language of this group is *little people* rather than *dwarfs*. He also reported learning that, in her view, the university imposes extreme limitations on little people and other differently able groups by not having elevators and access ramps installed in buildings, by not installing telephones and other utilities within easy reach, and by having a complicated process for reporting and defending problems of lack of access.

Philosophy of Teaching Papers

As stated previously, this assignment asked students to offer an analysis of their hypothetical classroom and to describe their philosophy of teaching. They were challenged to read prior to beginning this assignment professional works such as Giroux' *Teachers as Transformative Intellectuals* and Kanes' *The First Year of Teaching*; Grant and Sleeter's *After the School Bell Rings*; and Grant and Koskela's "The Relationship Between Preservice and Campus Learning Experiences." Respondents Teaching Philosophy responses fell into the following categories: those who saw teachers as: 1) facilitators of knowledge (the teacher should present only the course material as represented in the textbooks); 2) initiators of knowledge (the teacher should present ideas to students who would act on the knowledge based upon their background experiences); 3) motivators of knowledge (the teacher should motivate students to become independent learners); and 4) leaders of knowledge (the teacher should guide students to gain knowledge).

A number of sample members saw themselves as facilitators of knowledge and reported that they had not given much thought to their philosophy of teaching (some had completed their student teaching and others were involved in student teaching at the time of the course). They described a facilitator of teaching as one who leads the discussion and takes it in a direction where the leader feels it important to refine students' thinking on an issue. They saw themselves as facilitators of discussions in the classroom regardless of students' backgrounds.

Several participants viewed themselves as initiators of knowledge where the teacher uses the inquiry method to ask questions that trigger students to think about a topic in a different way. They reported that they had accumulated knowledge throughout the years that had empowered them; they were now aware of the power of knowledge and of the classroom as being a place where teachers are to transfer this knowledge or power to students regardless of race, class, gender, or disability status. However, they saw no differences in students' backgrounds or how these differences might affect students' abilities to learn.

Several participants reported that they were motivators of knowledge whose role was to creatively and actively engage students in classroom discussions of human diversity regardless of views of race, class, gender, and disability status and to engage them in a critique of modern society from these different group perspectives. However, they wanted to encourage students to resolve group differences and to understand others by recognizing laws that govern society and institutions.

And finally, some respondents reported that they were leaders in the classroom who saw their responsibility to students and society as being one of "taking up where parents left off," by teaching children to respect group differences. Their hope was to resolve conflict in a positive way by teaching an "acceptance of and respect for differences," bringing about a "group unity" that would eliminate group conflicts.

Professional Journal Critiques

In response to this assignment, students summarized an article of their choosing from a professional journal of their choosing and critiqued that article by discussing implications for educators and/or teacher educators. The group as a whole cited the need for professionals to show more sensitivity to issues of diversity in their writing. A number of students noted insensitivity to multicultural issues especially in English journals, noting that the majority of the articles were written by majority group members about majority and minority group students and therefore expressed an American white, middle-class, assimilationist attitude. They reported that when majority writers wrote about minorities, they failed to address cultural traditions or how teachers could address cultural differences in the classroom. One respondent compared two articles written about Hmong students, one written by a white and the other written by an Asian. According to the respondent, the white author showed no sensitivity to Asian culture, but instead expected Asian students to adapt to the white culture. In contrast, the Asian writer talked specifically about the need for greater sensitivity on the part of teachers and a greater awareness about cultural differences. The writer then went on to explain the common practice in the Hmong culture of socializing children not to look directly at adults' faces and how this behavior could be misinterpreted by a teacher not familiar with the culture.

Another participant reported on an article where African American and Hispanic students were viewed as discipline problems in the classroom. But no attempt was made to understand their behavior in terms of African American or Hispanic traditions and culture, nor was any distinction made between Hispanics and other ethnic groups such as Mexican, Puerto Rican, or Cuban students.

Respondents reported that social class issues were unclear to them in professional writings. Some participants acknowledged reading articles that briefly described social class differences as an economic concern. One participant discussed an article where the author emphasized the economic pressures placed on low-income families by their children's desire to dress like other students. The article then went on to say that school districts were attempting to remedy these financial pressures and deter gang activity in schools by implementing a uniform dress code for all students in their districts, but there was no discussion of how low-, middle-, and upper-income parents responded to this policy.

Several participants reported reading articles about the "vanishing white male movement" and the "black male endangered species movement" that impressed them as both sexist and racist. According to respondents, both types of articles seemed to establish males as a separate group in need of "protection" and both argued against the other. According to white males, too much attention was being given by the schools to minorities, and according to black males, schools were overwhelmingly at fault for failing to educate black males.

Some students who were special education majors directly addressed issues of the disabled. They saw a need for regular education teachers to take more special education courses in order to understand and meet the needs of special education students in the classroom. They wanted to see these changes for teachers who work in mainstream settings with the disabled.

Interviews with the Researcher

The interviews with students were constructed around four basic types of questions designed to elicit information on students' views of race, class, gender, and disability. Grand tour or general questions were used around a topic to elicit general information, that is, "Tell me what you think about children who are poor?" Probe questions were used to elicit components of a conceptual category, that is, "You have described two categories of poor students. Are there others?" Attribute questions were used to elicit descriptions about a specific category, that is, "What constitutes a wealthy student, a poor student7" And lastly, contrast questions were used to search for differences among related categories, that is, "What differences do you see between a wealthy student and a poor student?"

All of the respondents talked about race, class, gender, and disability in their interviews. Several students reported that they felt very comfortable interacting with groups who are racially different, but that they had problems interacting with differently able groups. Some students reported that they had no friends outside of their racial group and that they were uncomfortable interacting with racially different groups whether invited or uninvited by a member or members of the group. A number of students reported that they grew up in communities where they were taught in the home and in the community to interact with their own kind.

Several respondents reported that they felt uncomfortable interacting with low-income people who had "dirty clothes," "oily hair," or "body odors."

Many students also reported that they felt extremely uncomfortable discussing the concerns of homosexuals and lesbians because they shared their families' and churches' disapproval of these groups, and they asked that discussions of the gay community be discontinued. Some respondents expressed the opinion that individuals with disabilities were unclean and should not be responsible for preparing or serving food in restaurants. One participant talked about going to a restaurant where a disabled person was uncontrollably salivating while serving food, and another talked about a person working in a restaurant who was spilling the food he was attempting to serve.

Microteaching Demonstrations

In response to being asked to demonstrate their understanding and commitment to multicultural education approaches (or business as usual approaches) by teaching a K-12 lesson, sample members designed and taught a thirty to forty-minute lesson to their hypothetical class that incorporated information about race, class, gender, and disability. Students reviewed Sleeter and Grant's (1988) five approaches to human diversity and were encouraged to use any one of the approaches in their demonstration.

Fifteen out of twenty participants demonstrated human relations strategies and how these strategies could be incorporated in their classrooms to raise the level of awareness of and appreciation for race, class, gender, and disability. For example, one teacher passed around photos depicting males and females of different races, religions, and political orientations, as well as individuals with disabilities, and asked students to tell how they were similar to and different from persons in the photos. The teacher then summarized the lesson and explained that although we are alike and different from others, we must learn to appreciate and tolerate the differences.

Some respondents demonstrating human relations strategies focused on how group conflicts arise from group differences, stating that group conflict should be approached from a positive perspective in the competitive classroom setting. For example, one teacher offered written scenarios of situations in South Africa. Students were given scripts that placed them in particular roles (e.g., President Botha and other players in the South African government, Afrikans, and South African whites) that created conflict. The teacher then summarized the exercise by questioning the students about the group differences and explained that although our external trappings are often different, inside we are the same and must live together in harmony.

A few respondents, since they viewed many veteran teachers as consciously and/or unconsciously encouraging negative messages and stereotypes about different groups, demonstrated multicultural education and education that is multicultural and social reconstructionist approaches to their microteaching demonstration. They wanted to engage their students in activities that recognized sensitivity to cultural pluralism and in projects that would bring about change in the American educational system. One student expressed the need for Americans to become sensitive to multicultural issues in the United States and to take that mind-set into other countries as well. This participant argued that her lesson on America's need for cultural sensitivity in international marketing was education that is multicultural and social resconstructionist since it focused first on the need for cultural sensitivity at home in the United States prior to approaching global markets. For example, this teacher argued that this lesson called for sensitivity to human diversity in the United States prior to entering international markets; otherwise, problems would occur in those markets in the translation of culture and language. The teacher explained that the Coca Cola company experienced difficulties marketing its product in China because Coca Cola in Chinese means "to bite the waxed tadpole." Likewise, Chevrolet experienced problems marketing the Nova in Spanish-speaking countries because Nova in Spanish means "it won't go." And finally, the Sunbeam mist stick curling iron was difficult to market in Germany because, translated into the German language, the name means "manure wand." This teacher then summarized the lesson by emphasizing the need for Americans to show cultural and language sensitivity on a global level.

Evaluations of Microteaching

All students were asked to evaluate one another's microteaching demonstrations and were encouraged to offer their opinions, views, and assessments regarding the multicultural issues raised by the demonstrations. Criteria for microteaching demonstrations were as follows: students' lessons were to teach to human diversity with their hypothetical diverse classroom setting in mind; they were to demonstrate their understanding and commitment to a teaching approach of either multicultural education or education that is multicultural and social reconstructionist approach to teaching; they were to consider the diversity in the classroom and explain how the lesson considered the diversity present. On the first day of class, the professor and students defined multicultural education and agreed that it was necessary in order to teach effectively in a diverse classroom setting.

Students' evaluations of the microteaching demonstrations fell into several general categories best expressed by the following statements: "were given a different view of the classroom," "were not so helpful," "helpful," "somewhat helpful," and "very helpful and challenging." Several respondents evaluated the lessons as offering them a different view of how issues of race, class, gender, and disability can be incorporated into lessons in the classroom, and they reported that their thinking had been challenged about a host of issues that might arise from presenting issues of diversity in a "mixed" classroom setting. They also learned about ways that they might deal with possible intense situations.

A number of respondents evaluated the lessons as "not so helpful." They stated that they had not been made aware of issues of human diversity in other classes in the teacher education program, but that they were now aware of this information and were comfortable with it.

Some participants evaluated the lessons as "helpful" in showing them how to incorporate issues of diversity in the classroom and in familiarizing them with issues that had been unclear or unfamiliar to them at the beginning of the course.

One student evaluated the lessons as "somewhat helpful" in regard to thinking about how to include information about cultural and social differences and similarities in the classroom; she would now show more sensitivity to different student learning styles.

And finally, several students reported that, after completing the assignments, they had found the lessons "very helpful and challenging." But the most important thing to them was that they could better understand various teaching strategies that incorporated issues of diversity into the curriculum.

DISCUSSION OF FINDINGS

Based upon the previous data, the study's findings in regard to students' prevailing attitudes about multicultural issues, and in regard to their responses to information about those issues and their responses to potential influence on their teaching, indicate three significant areas of concern: 1) the relatively low level of sophistication and experience that students possessed and demonstrated regarding issues of human diversity; 2) the students' consistent reliance on business as usual and human relations approaches when incorporating the ideas of multiculturalism into their own philosophies of teaching; and 3) the lack of previous classroom preparation—noted by the students themselves—designed to educate them on the relevance of human diversity and multicultural issues.

Level of Sophistication

Much of the data collected reflected a relatively low level of awareness on the part of the respondents about the issues of human diversity. Though several respondents reported personal friendships with minorities and others spoke of mutual tolerance, a majority of the sample initially demonstrated relatively unsophisticated and uninformed views concerning human diversity and multicultural issues. These were illustrated clearly in the journals and interviews, where several students expressed opposition to interracial dating and marriage, affirmative action policies that appeared to hurt males, the presence of differently able individuals in the workplace, and homosexuality as an acceptable lifestyle worthy of discussion.

This information might need to be appreciated for what it implies. A number of studies have found that beliefs of youth and young adults are closely aligned to those of their parents (for example, Hollingshead 1949; Kandel and Lesser 1972). In the case of many majority parents, those beliefs may range from full acceptance of racial mixing, to a refusal to allow a minority into the house (Grant and Sleeter 1986). This data might also reflect the influence of students' community leaders, teachers, and professors whose responses to and presentations of information about minority groups were often omitted, neglected, or casually approached and presented in a negative or stereotypic light within conversations and discussions in the home and the classroom.

Particularly, public school and higher education curricula developed mostly by majority group members with limited and stereotypic notions of minority groups have in the past omitted or neglected minority concerns. When those concerns were made part of classroom discussions, they were offered as alternatives subordinate to mainstream curricula ideas, rather than occupying an equally central position in the curriculum.

Respondents who felt uncomfortable discussing minority and differently able groups in open forums also reported that they came from rural isolated areas where no minorities lived. Their only information about minority groups had come from television and hearsay. Others had been socialized in suburban communities with extremely limited interactions with minorities. This data, then, might reflect that students' initial resistance to, or discomfort with, issues of human diversity arises partially out of their lack of exposure to ethnically or culturally different populations (for instance, many of them had not, in their past, had a minority teacher or professor).

However, even more interesting to those involved in teacher education and teacher training was the data from the Philosophy of Teaching Papers, the Microteaching Demonstrations, and the Evaluations of Microteaching, which indicated that a majority of the students believed in using human relations and/or business as usual approaches in planning and conducting classes. The implications of this data are discussed in the next section.

Reliance on Business as Usual or Human Relations Approaches

The group of respondents in this study initially expressed a desire to affirm human diversity and agreed to make these issues central to their curriculum and thinking. Many strongly advocated multicultural education. However, the data revealed that at times they felt uncomfortable discussing the concerns of some groups (i.e., gays and lesbians), and that they failed to affirm human differences and to show how they would incorporate curricula content that seriously engaged their students in the change process. For instance, they reported that they would recognize and plan for issues of race, class, gender, and disability groups in all assignments by using multicultural education strategies; but the philosophy of teaching data showed that 100% of the sample reported that they viewed all students the same in the classroom (i.e., this data offered no recognition of human diversity). And fifteen of the twenty respondents, instead of adopting a multicultural approach in their microteaching demonstrations, demonstrated human relations strategies for teaching diverse groups of students.

As the investigation progressed then, though the group understood the concept of Multicultural Education, its members apparently experienced difficulty incorporating its themes into their assignment. This might account for the significant number who used human relations strategies. However, we must bear in mind Wesley's (1949) admonition that, even though human relations strategies may help to develop attitudes of tolerance, these strategies in the classroom do not address needed policy changes in regard to race, class, gender, and differently able groups in schools and in the broader social arena. Rather, human relations teaches people to "get along" with each other or to "create harmony between groups," as the students put it, suggesting that this approach to teaching ignores the need to confront the causes of conflict.

Lack of Previous Educational Background

It is relevant to acknowledge here that, prior to conducting this study, the principal investigator made some assumptions in regard to the participating respondents. They were students who, as seniors, had already completed an urban education component of the teacher education program, as well as a series of four human relations minicourses attached to an introductory teaching course. This was to be their final course in teacher preparation. It was assumed they would be drawing on both personal experience of minorities and knowledge gained about minorities in their previous classes. It was assumed that they had developed the conceptual sophistication to refocus and manipulate their prior knowledge and to integrate multicultural education ideas into their current strategies. However, it became apparent that many of these students were unaccustomed, not only to this first substantial introduction to multicultural issues, but also to a participatory class format—they were used to being "told" what to do. They also were being challenged—many of them for the first time—to take ownership for their beliefs about volatile issues that their parents, American society, and institutional representatives have in the past ignored or stereotyped.

Many students themselves were concerned that multicultural education concepts had not been introduced much earlier in their education, and they pointed to a lack of consistent training regarding multicultural issues throughout their teacher education program. Though the program incorporates an urban education component (i.e., one course with an urban field experience) during the students' sophomore year and incorporates eight hours of human relations training to satisfy the NCATE multicultural mandate, these students failed to link the content of the Urban Education course with human relations sessions.

Those students who were interested in multicultural education expressed concern mainly about the amount of research that would be required of them as first-year teachers if they were to accept the challenge of teaching about the lifestyles, contributions, and accomplishments of culturally diverse and differently able populations. However, the data collected also reflected several positive aspects in regard to the teaching and incorporation of multicultural education. Though several respondents initially seemed to resist ideas presented in the class, their ideas began to change as they were presented with more information. Several journal entries reported a move from acceptance of the status quo (tolerating racial jokes or slurs based on ethnicity or social class) to a questioning of these behaviors and even the courage to confront peers on their attitudes and behavior.

Respondents also displayed a growing sensitivity and awareness in their Professional Journal Critiques, where they demonstrated remarkable critical skills in identifying the authors' different levels of multicultural awareness. Several respondents expressed the desire for additional information about various groups, especially on social class differences.

Though it's true that several group members were experiencing the "storming" process and communicated an unwillingness to accept multicultural education concepts, several others were beginning to work through their previously held biases about groups different from themselves and were seeking ways to include this information in their curricula.

RECOMMENDATIONS

Though the sample from this pilot study is small and care must be taken not to generalize too much about its findings, several recommendations can be tentatively drawn from the data presented. The students' level of sophistication and their own frustrations over the lack of exposure to multicultural issues in previous teaching courses suggest a definite need for the incorporation of a multicultural education approach in all teacher education curricula, beginning with introductory courses. As Grant (1981) has argued, one course of intensive instruction in multicultural education is sufficient to make a lasting impact on preservice teachers' views of classroom teaching. Therefore, issues of diversity must be centrally placed in all teacher education coursework in ways that challenge preservice teachers' views of minorities throughout their teacher education program. At the same time, current teacher education courses should be carefully assessed for overlap so that the inclusion of multicultural education courses does not increase teacher certification hours unless necessary (more does not necessarily mean better).

The multicultural theoretical perspective that articulated the models used in this study and the resulting data obtained from a group of senior preservice teachers might also imply that those of us who assume responsibility for preparing future teachers to work in diverse classroom settings can no longer allow students' thinking about majority and minority groups to go unchallenged in our classrooms. Student responses to the professor's African Americaness and gender also indicate a need to challenge students' thinking about human diversity in our society. Because these assignments were ungraded, many participants felt comfortable to make biased statements about African Americans in the presence of an African American authority figure, their teacher. Students' knowledge of human diversity and their negative opinions about African Americans is of concern to this researcher since in less than one year these teachers will teach African American youth. Their knowledge and opinions may well indicate a need for teacher educators to assess our own knowledge about and sensitivity to minorities—a need to get involved in development workshops to assess our commitment to, and understanding of, multicultural education—for we who serve as role models for future teachers cannot fail in our attempts to accurately cultivate their thinking from a diverse group perspective.

And lastly, given the demographic changes in both teacher and student populations and the number of states that are now beginning to mandate preservice coursework in multicultural education, educators need more research on the impact of multicultural education and need additional recommendations made for strengthening such coursework. Martin's (1991) research suggests that some legislators and educators share similar concerns for multicultural education and that some are working toward those concerns. But substantial progress requires more research, particularly in policy and multicultural education.

Which group concerns are centrally placed in the curricula is much more than a concern for fairness. Preservice curricula should challenge students' knowledge and understanding of human diversity in society. Those curricula should also challenge how that knowledge is brought into the classroom via institutionalized policies, practices, and procedures, and via knowledge that teachers and students hold about themselves and others. The theoretical perspective used in this study and the two models incorporated in this course challenged students' views of human diversity and the knowledge exchanged in the classroom. Preservice curricula should present the lifestyles, contributions, concerns, and accomplishments of all groups in order to challenge preservice teachers' views and understanding of what it means to live in a diverse society. As Anyon (1983) states: "The conceptual legitimacy conferred by school knowledge on powerful social groups is metabolized into power that is real when members of society in their everyday decisions support—or fail to challenge—prevailing hierarchies. The idea that certain groups have legitimate social power leads to the belief that these groups deserve our support and that contending ones do not" (51).

We as teachers and teacher educators must make it a part of our professional standards to make sure that those contending groups receive our support, and through that support, the chance for a more meaningful education.

References

Anyon, J. 1983. Workers, labor, and economic history, and textbook content. In *Ideology and Practice in Schooling*. Edited by M. W. Apple and L. Weis, 37-60. Philadelphia, PA: Temple University Press.

Baker, G. 1973. Multicultural training for student teachers. *Journal of Teacher Education* 24:306-7.

———. 1977. Two preservice training approaches. *Journal of Teacher Education* 28:31-33.

Banks, J. 1987. *Teaching strategies for ethnic studies*. Boston, MA: Allyn and Bacon.

Banks, J. and C. Banks, eds. 1989. *Multicultural education: Issues and perspectives*. Needham Heights, MA: Simon and Schuster.

Bennett, C. T. 1979. The preparation of preservice secondary social studies teachers in multiethnic education. *Hight School Journal* 62:232-37.

Corcoran, E. 1982. Classroom contexts as settings for learning to teach: A new direction for research in teacher education. *Action in Teacher Education* 6:52-55.

Cortes, C. E. 1976. Need for geo-cultural perspective in the bi-centennial. *Educational Leadership* 33:290-92.

Coser, L. 1956. *The functions of social conflict*. New York, NY: The Free Press.

Dawson, M. 1981. A matter of linkage: Multicultural education and educational equity. In *Educational Equity*. Edited by M. E. Dawson et al., 1-14. Washington, DC: ERIC Clearinghouse on Teacher education.

Doyle, W. and G. Ponder. 1975. Classroom ecology: Some concerns about a neglected dimension of research on teaching. *Contemporary Education* 46:183-88.

Gay, G. 1975. Organizing and designing culturally pluralistic curriculum. *Educational Leadership* 33:176-83.

Giroux, H. and A. Penna. 1979. Social education in the classroom: The dynamics of the hidden curriculum. *Theory and Research in Social Education* 7(1):21-42.

Gollnick, D. and P. Chinn. 1986. *Multicultural education in a pluralistic society*. Columbus, OH: Merrill Publishing.

Grant, C. 1981. Education that is multicultural and teacher preparation: An examination from the perspectives of preservice students. *Journal of Educational Research* 75:2.

Grant, C. and R. Koskela. 1986. Education that is multicultural and the relationship between preservice campus learning and field experiences. *Journal of Educational Research* 79:4.

Grant, C. and C. Sleeter. 1985. The literature on multicultural education: Review and analysis. *Educational Review* 37(2):97-118.

———. 1986. *After the school bell rings*. Philadelphia, PA: Falmer Press.

Hennington, M. 1981. Effect of intensive multicultural, non-sexist instruction on secondary student teachers. *Educational Research Quarterly* 6:65-75.

Hollingshead, A. 1949. Elmtown's youth, the impact of social class on adolescents. New York: J. Wiley.

Howsam, R. B. et al. 1976. Educating a profession. Reprint with postscript, 1985. Report of the Bicentennial Commission on Education for the Profession of Teaching of the American Association of Colleges for Teacher Education. Washington, DC: American Association of Colleges for Teacher Education.

Howsam, R. B., D. C. Corrigan et al. 1976. *Educating a professor*, 108-9. Washington, DC: American Association of Colleges for Teacher Education.

Kandel, D. and G. Lesser. 1972. *Youth in two worlds*. San Francisco, CA: Jossey-Bass.

Mahan, J. M. 1982. Native Americans as teacher trainers: Anatomy and outcomes of a cultural immersion project. *Journal of Educational Equity and Leadership* 2:100, 110.

Martin, R. 1991. Power to empower: Multicultural education for student teachers. In *Empowerment through multicultural education*. Edited by C. Sleeter. Albany, NY: State University of New York Press.

Martin, R., G. Wood, and E. Stevens. 1988. *An introduction to teaching: A quest of commitment*. Boston, MA: Allyn and Bacon.

Miller, R. 1979. *The assessment of college performance*. San Francisco, CA: Jossey-Bass.

Miller, R. I. 1988. *Evaluating major components of two-year colleges*. Washington, DC: College and University Personnel Association.

———. 1990. *Major American higher education issues and challenges in the 1990s*. London: Jessica Kingsley Publishers.

Sims, W. E. 1983. Preparing teachers for multicultural classrooms. *Momentum* 14(1):42-44.

Sleeter, C. and C. Grant. 1987. An analysis of multicultural education in the United States. *Harvard Educational Review* 57(4):421-44.

———. 1988. Making choices for multicultural education: Five approaches to race, class, and gender. Columbus, OH: Merrill Publishing Company.

Standard for the Accreditation of Teacher Education. 1976. Washington, DC: National Council for Accreditation of Teacher Education.

Wesley, C. H. 1949. Education and Democracy. In *Improving Human Relations*. Edited by H. H. Cummings, 27-31. Washington, DC: National Council for the Social Studies.

15

MARILYNNE BOYLE-BAISE

The Coalition for Education That Is Multicultural:
A Network of Advocates for Educational Equity

This paper describes and analyzes the creation of a multicultural coalition that was developed as a cooperative effort between the Teacher Education Program at Sangamon State University and Public School District #186, both located in Springfield, Illinois. The mutually beneficial project had as its long-range goals: cooperation, increasing the knowledge of preservice teachers, in-service teachers, and school administrators about multicultural education; promoting the development and implementation of multicultural curriculum in schools and classrooms; and providing placements sites for student teachers with teachers trained in multicultural education.

The definition for multicultural education delineated by Banks and Banks (1989) was used to describe the focus for multicultural projects. Multicultural education is: "an idea, an educational reform movement, and a process whose major goal is to change the structure of educational institutions so that male and female students, exceptional students, and students who are members of diverse racial, ethnic, and cultural groups will have an equal chance to achieve academically in school" (1). Based upon this definition, multicultural education was considered as an approach to curriculum, instruction, and school policies and procedures. This approach advocated and implemented equal educational opportunities for all students, regardless of their race/ethnicity, social class, gender, first-language, or mental or physical ability.

This was a new arena for cooperation between the school district and the university; at the time of this writing, cooperative interactions (e.g., discussions, plans, actions, and reactions) had been going on for almost a year and the project that developed from them, "The Coalition for Education that is Multicultural," was nine-months young. During this time, the coalition developed a successful record: group identity was described, membership was established, a multicultural seminar was taught, resources were identified, a newsletter was developed, informational meetings were held, guest speakers were sponsored, and group existence was strengthened. In the following sections, the record of the coalition is catalogued and considered in terms of several themes: the context for the project; the events and activities of the project; a discussion of the project; and lessons learned about the promotion of multicultural education within the context of school-university cooperation.

THE CONTEXT FOR THE PROJECT

Sangamon State University is a small regional institution with a student population of about 4,500 students. Most students live and work near the university, many are nontraditional (e.g., older, return to the university after working or raising families), and one-third are part-time graduate students. The mission of the university is to provide excellent teaching and promote a public affairs orientation among students; for faculty, teaching is a most important pursuit, and public service work is equated with research. Within the university, the Teacher Education Program has grown rapidly and registers nearly three hundred students, or about 6% of university enrollment.

Springfield Public Schools, District #186 serves approximately 16,200 students. There are thirty-five schools in the district: twenty-nine elementary schools, three middle schools, and three high schools. The district was desegregated during the 1975-76 school year. The racial/ethnic composition of the student population is: 72% European American, 26% African American, 1.3% Asian American, .5% Latino American, and .09% Native American. Of these students: 48% are female, 52% are male, and 10% are in special education programs.

The Teacher Education Program at Sangamon State University (SSU) and Springfield Public Schools, District #186, had a strong positive relationship: the district served as the primary site for field placements for prospective teachers; and the Teacher Education Program provided graduate study for many in-service teachers. The initiation of the project came at a time when several factors influenced stronger ties between the two institutions in the area of multicultural education.

The Teacher Education Program had just completed a five-year review for state recertification. New state guidelines required teacher education programs to include multicultural education in course work; and to provide opportunities for students to acquire and demonstrate abilities to work with children from diverse backgrounds.[1] The program responded to the guidelines by developing five program goals; one of these goals was directed toward the inclusion of multicultural education in all course work.[2] In addition, the program was anxious to provide more field experiences in sites with diverse student populations and with teachers who worked successfully with students from diverse backgrounds. Also, I joined the program with a background in multicultural teacher education, and along with another education professor, Dr. Gary Storm, became interested in promoting multicultural education within the program and the district.

The district had a new superintendent amenable to projects that would increase the quality of education in district schools. He defined quality education as equal and equitable education for all students, and he considered the district only average in providing this type of education. In addition, the district was under pressure from the community to improve education for students of color by, for example, increasing test scores and reducing disproportionate placements in special education classes. The superintendent believed that district educators needed training in multicultural sensitivity, information, and teaching skills. He welcomed proposals for cooperation in the area of multicultural teacher education.

THE EVENTS AND ACTIVITIES OF THE PROJECT

We formed a school-university committee to develop a framework for cooperation. Committee members included: the superintendent (at that time he was assistant superintendent), the assistant superintendent for instruction, the principal of the elementary school that housed the Multicultural Resource Center, and the faculty in the Teacher Education Program. During discussions of this group, the goals cited earlier were agreed upon as general guidelines. Also, there was agreement to support activities within each institution related to these goals.

Initial Interactions between the District and the Program

Based on these meetings, the superintendent invited Dr. Storm and me to attend district-sponsored staff development workshops on diversity in which concepts such as *cultural pluralism* were introduced to district personnel. The superintendent encouraged us to announce plans for an upcoming summer course about multicultural education at the workshops. A short time later, we served as resource people for the follow-up sessions to these workshops.

In addition, the district served as the accounting agent for a grant of funds from the Illinois State Board of Education (ISBE) that helped support the summer school effort. The district also agreed to approve automatically the course for salary steps.

The university approved the creation of the summer course as a new addition to the summer schedule. SSU approved a follow-up multicultural seminar for the fall session as a small part of my regular teaching load (i.e., one hour of credit per semester).

The Summer School Course for Multicultural Education

The summer course was designed as an intensive two-week experience. Twenty-two educators took the course for credit, and others attended, including the Dean of the Teacher Education Program. Key themes for the course were: awareness, empowerment and collegiality. The activities (e.g., readings, discussions, and films) focused on awareness of the following: principles of and approaches to multicultural education, the *monocultural* nature of students' own education, personal experiences related to inequitable discrimination, and the perspectives of people different from oneself. Participants were encouraged to consider their own experiences as part of the curriculum and share information related to their areas of expertise. In addition, the class was encouraged to interact as equal partners in the learning enterprise. This type of learning context was helped by establishing standards for a safe place within the class where all topics were discussed freely and each person was treated with respect. Awareness of issues posed by multicultural education was heightened by sharing personal stories of guest speakers from varied group backgrounds and with varying points of view.

The Formation of the Coalition for Education That Is Multicultural

The last day of the course, we sat around a huge oak table in a conference room and considered future plans. The goals of the district and the program for multicultural education were described. The class wanted to stay in contact and provide support for efforts they made toward multicultural education, and they discussed the possibility of creating a multicultural newsletter to provide information and help communication. I suggested the creation of a coalition or network as an organization to work toward these objectives, and the group heartily approved this idea.

At this same meeting, the group voted to name itself *The Coalition For Education That Is Multicultural*. We chose Grant's definition of education that is multicultural as a guiding definition (1978, cited in Sleeter and Grant 1988). Rather than conceptualizing multicultural education as an addition to regular curriculum, instruction, and school policies, this definition referred to a redesigned educational program and was selected by the group. It is used throughout the rest of this paper for references to the coalition and is considered to be an expansion of Banks and Banks' (1989) definition of multicultural education.

Membership in the Coalition

The only criterion for membership in the coalition was interest in and commitment toward providing an education that is multicultural. However, the coalition was most interested in reaching out to people who, like themselves, were "direct service providers"—teachers, librarians, counselors, and social service staff. Coalition members were leery about the extent to which administrators would work as colleagues with them, even though one class member was an assistant principal.

At the time of this writing, the coalition was nine-months old and membership had grown. However, the coalition did not develop a formal membership system (such as dues and subsequent membership standing). Therefore, the major factor in membership remained participation, with some members being more active than others. On the roster of regular members (e.g., attends most meetings, and/or expresses continual interest) were twenty-eight members, the majority of whom are women. Sixteen of these were European American, eight were African American, one was Latino American, and one considered herself of mixed heritage—European American and Native American. Two members were European American males. Twenty members were elementary level faculty, support staff, or prospective teachers (nineteen were female and one was male). The support staff included: a librarian, two special education teachers, and one counselor. In addition, one member was a middle-school teacher and two were high-school teachers. Of the high-school teachers, one taught government for special education students and the other taught Spanish. One of the men was a high-school administrator. Fourteen schools were represented and three community people were members: an adult educator, a nonprofit agency staff person, and a trainer for a state agency.

Twenty of the members have taken either the summer or follow-up fall seminar for credit. It is clear that the primary source of membership, at that point, was the multicultural seminars. Other members have been students in my courses within the Teacher Education Program, friends of members, or, in one case, a person who heard me speak at a conference.

Soon after the coalition was founded, the superintendent offered the group access to district resources in terms of copying, mailing, and duplicating. He also was willing to give credit toward salary steps for the development of curriculum materials. However, the superintendent also changed the contact person for the coalition project to the newly appointed assistant superintendent who did not share his knowledge of or involvement in the conceptual phases of the project.

Coalition Meetings/Seminars/Activities

A seminar that met once a month throughout the school year also served as the primary meeting time for the coalition. The seminar was planned as a subsequent experience to the summer course; this meant building upon the awareness generated in the summer by providing more information related to multicultural education. A monthly letter was mailed to seminar participants that detailed topics for study, readings, and notice of guest speakers. Also included in the letter were current events of interest to members and requests for information about what they were learning or doing in regard to education that is multicultural.

What happened in these meetings was unlike what one would usually expect in a seminar. Members were hungry for resources and information related to the practical nature of implementing education that is multicultural. They came prepared to share and receive resources, ideas, and information; at least half of the three-hour meeting time was used for this activity. We came to call this activity the round table because we had to monitor turns around the group to permit everyone to participate. This activity was characterized by expressions of support and interest. Almost immediately, we were faced with the problem/opportunity of cataloging and disseminating resources. Except for our round table discussions, other plans for the seminar often were overshadowed by group-building activities. A description of these activities follows. The initial group meeting/seminar was oriented to establishing existence as a group—building an identity. The group created a logo that depicted education as a circle; around the circle were the differences that members wished to celebrate (i.e., race, ethnicity, gender, social class, and ability). The group decided to have the logo adorn sweatshirts, book bags, and signs for doors, walls, or halls.

After several months, it became clear that communication within the coalition was a major challenge since members were scattered in various schools and social agencies. The monthly letter became longer and longer, the program was short on staff to process it, and I found myself doing most of the clerical work involved. When I shared this problem, coalition members decided to create a newsletter to announce events, describe activities in various schools or agencies, and list resources. Developing the newsletter and finding ways to publish and circulate it were among the first of many decisions made. We then addressed ways to help the group continue to function and to inform others about the group's multicultural message. "Keep the group going" and "spread the message" developed into central goals. The publication of the newsletter was made possible by donations from nonprofit agencies staffed with coalition members. The aid from nonprofit agencies made group members aware that concerns about and support for multicultural education extended beyond school walls.

The newsletter was one vehicle for spreading the message, but members found that, when colleagues asked them about the coalition, they were unprepared to give a concise and adequate description of either multicultural education or the coalition. Therefore, we wrote a definition statement for both. However, members reported that handing people a two page statement often was received with a pained expression that said, "oh, more to read." We decided we needed a better marketing tool for our message and developed a trifold brochure that was attractive, succinct, and easy to distribute.

The assistant superintendent agreed to pay for printing the pamphlets and asked that we present principals with the information to formally introduce them to the coalition. Anxious to do this in order to garner support from their school administrators, the coalition gave a presentation for a districtwide meeting of principals in which we introduced the group, its goals, activities, and so forth, and described how the summer course had influenced us to change out ideas and behaviors. The group was asked to give similar presentations for several faculty meetings, and two principals subsequently used their school funds to help sponsor a special coalition event.

The coalition publically demonstrated its existence with a visit and performance by Dr. Burroughs, one of the founders of DuSable African American History Museum. Organizing this event consumed almost all of our seminar and personal time, and coalition members felt it was a coming out of sorts. They worked to "get the word out" through the newsletter, flyers, and personal invitations. Dr. Burroughs entertained several school and teacher audiences successfully. The event extended recognition and gained credibility for the group, and it provided a charge of energy to keep the coalition going.

Members planned workshops for a Multicultural Education Conference held during the summer. Dr. Storm and I made a second request to the ISBE for funds for this conference and it was granted. Coalition members received stipends for presenting workshops at the conference.

What has not been described here is how much time and work it took me and Dr. Storm, my aide-de-camp, to bring the coalition to life and sustain it. We did everything including: processing letters, arranging for sweatshirts, writing most of the articles for the newsletter, coordinating events, developing grant proposals, speaking at district meetings, and training teachers to give workshops. We, too, were involved in keeping the coalition going and spreading the message. These efforts that consumed a considerable amount of time were not part of our regular teaching loads, but they were considered public service. There were few incentives for either of the professors, aside from receiving one hour of teaching credit per semester for the multicultural seminar. Leadership of the coalition called for more hours of our time than should be attributed to service and proved most difficult for me as a person trying to balance expectations for promotion and tenure. On the other hand, SSU recognized the value of such service as part of its public affairs mission.

In addition to limited time, the entire effort was plagued by limited funding. In fact, all of the activities cited above were conducted without a regular budget. Rather, we used district resources, university resources, donations, special funds, and our own money to conduct coalition business. According to reports of others involved in such collaborative ventures, limited funding for these efforts is not unusual (e.g., Goodlad and Sirotnik 1988). Goodlad and Sirotnik suggested that projects should not be considered "special," but that as standard projects should have access to regular budgets. A corollary to limited funding was limited financial rewards for participants in the project. No participants received compensation as an incentive for their participation.

Ongoing Interaction with District Administrators

Pursuing the activities described required continual meetings among Dr. Storm, district administrators, and me. As described earlier, the superintendent had recently been elevated from assistant superintendent and with the change in administration came a new administrative staff. While the new staff was directed to carry out previous commitments by the superintendent, the project was included within the responsibilities of first one assistant superintendent and then another. As a result, some time was spent acquainting each administrator with the project, and in one instance, we changed contact people during plans for an event. This caused confusion within project planning and preparation. On the other hand, the second assistant superintendent wanted to expand school/university cooperation and integrate coalition activities into ongoing school programs.

The Effort of Cooperation

Various factors, forces, and influences shaped this project, such as the effort of cooperation, the vision of education that is multicultural, the coalition as an organization, the nature of coalition participants, and the style of leadership.

Throughout this paper, the term *cooperation* has been used rather than *collaboration*. This is because collaboration seems to refer to a more balanced, or "symbiotic" (Goodlad and Sirotnik 1988) relationship than the coalition project shared with the district. In this regard, Hawley (1990) noted that collaboration is a partnership that cannot function if one party needs the collaboration more than the other. Many of our meetings seemed to center around the messages: "we are here, we are functioning, we are serious, and we need your help." We sensed that while we thought of ourselves as collaborators with the district, it did not consider us as full partners. Rather, we seemed to be held at arms length, acknowledged as a multicultural effort but not integrated into school affairs.

Many related reasons probably caused their uneasy partnership, including inadequate planning, changes in administrative personnel, the need to build a trusting relationship, and general misconceptions and/or apprehension about multicultural education. The coalition came into being within a successful summer course and was in-progress while discussions of the cooperative venture were still preliminary. Therefore, the nature of discussions switched from committee to key people: the superintendent, Dr. Storm, and me. This worked well for accomplishing tasks and garnering commitment quickly, but it did not build an organization that could function independently of the events encountered during the change in administration.

General organization would have been improved by more extensive planning. On the other hand, only after events occurred that built trust in our leadership and provided evidence for the success of the coalition project did administrators express interest in a more pervasive partnership. Only after much work did we learn how much time coalition members had to commit to our efforts, and this resource for expanding the partnership is limited. It seems that preliminary cooperative experience was needed to more adequately determine the shape and focus of further experience. It may be necessary to weave flexibility into any attempts to collaborate while also providing full confidence in and support for the venture from the beginning.

The extent of support for the venture may also have been based on the perceived need for multicultural teacher education among district administrators and teachers. While the superintendent perceived this need as strong, the assistant superintendent had the following thoughts: "I've said all along with this concept, there are too many of our folks who were here twenty years ago and didn't have a good experience with all this that are being resistant to it now . . . we've been there before, we've heard this before, they had a negative experience in some cases, so they're not as open to trying it again" (D.R. 17 January 1992). It seemed that past efforts to introduce multicultural education left negative impressions. This is not unusual but related to a history of inadequate in-service training in this area. (For general responses to original desegregation efforts, see Sleeter 1990.) Nevertheless, this past history may have played a part in the wait-and-see attitude that seemed to characterize the district.

The Vision of Education That Is Multicultural

The concept of education that is multicultural had a special power to hold the group together and direct its main agenda. During a visit with the group during the summer school session, Carl Grant described education that is multicultural education as "a vision for better education for everyone" (19 June 1991). Perceiving education that is multicultural in this egalitarian manner appealed to educators in the coalition; to many it helped name and define ideas, feelings, and images they had maintained for quite some time. From that time on, discussion centered around the notion of "the vision."

The vision of education that is multicultural provided parameters for actions, but it was also a complex concept centered around the interaction of race, class, gender, and ability in curricular, instructional, and policy initiatives. For many, the breadth and scope of this idea proved difficult to comprehend. For example, some members, particularly those of color, were sensitive to racial discrimination. Others, especially special education teachers, were attuned to inequities related to exceptionalities. Many of the members were women, and they could draw on past experiences to think about sexism. But few had a good mental picture of the impact on themselves and others of joint membership in several groups, or of the ways discrimination was built into society and especially into the schools.

Although I do not have any systematic data on this, many discussions I listened to suggested that participants' understanding of the relationships among race, class, gender, and exceptionality concerns seemed to develop over time. I attribute this to several factors. First, the group was defined by an inclusive vision, symbolized by the coalition logo that served as a continual reminder of the relationships among race, class, gender, and exceptionality. Second, provocative readings and films were read, watched, and discussed to increase multicultural awareness. Third, a friendship and trust developed among the group as its members worked together, and they were amenable to listening to the personal stories of others and sharing their own. Fourth, the group was varied enough to provide multiple perspectives; it seemed very important to hear the opinions of people of color, women, and special education teachers (there were no people with exceptionalities). Fifth, I tried to show them that "the personal is political" (Friedan 1976); their stories related to inequities and oppression that existed around them. And, sixth, we learned together over time; this reports details months of study and work rather than the usual one or two days of workshop experiences.

This experience has not, as yet, been documented by concrete data about what happened in classrooms or offices, but the growth in understanding that took place among coalition members provides food-for-thought for staff development toward multicultural education. Research in this area shows that long-term education is needed to increase understanding of the tenets of multicultural education, to provide data about race, gender, class, and ability groups, and to develop attitudes and skills necessary to work with diverse groups. (For a complete review of this literature see Sleeter 1992.) Among the coalition, both long-term and extensive multicultural education have been welcomed.

The Coalition as an External Educational Organization

The coalition existed outside the schools; Lieberman and Miller (1990) noted that teachers may not find support within their immediate environment and may have to seek support outside their own schools. Networks, leagues, or coalitions may serve this purpose. Lieberman and Miller found that several successful coalitions shared common characteristics: common purposes, supportive conduct, voluntary membership, and equal participation of members. Within the coalition, all of these qualities were evident.

The coalition seemed sustained, to me, by projects that involved members in group-building and that taught them about multicultural education. The two goals detailed earlier (e.g., keep the group going, get the message out) relate to common purposes and supportive conduct, and they were in turn related to the need for recognition of the professional efforts by members of the group. In the last few years, the literature on staff development has included discussions of the power of professional growth. There were suggestions that norms for collegiality, expectations for continual learning, and support for collaboration facilitated teacher learning (e.g., Little 1981; Rosenholtz 1989; Holmes Group 1990; Lieberman and Miller 1990, 1991; Melenyzer 1990). These norms were discussed in terms of conditions *inside* schools. This experience provided some evidence that these aspects supported learning *outside* schools. The limitation of the coalition was that it was difficult to take the group force inside school doors; instead, members inside schools were individuals without organized peer support.

The Style of Leadership

This effort took place during a time of change within the culture of teaching. "Collaborative work, characterized by colleagueship, openness, and trust . . . [is replacing] traditions of privacy, practicality, and isolation" (Lieberman and Miller 1991, 105). Leadership is in the process of changing to accommodate this new view of teaching (e.g., Little 1981; Rosenholtz 1989). Relationships between teachers and administrators are described in the following terms: "shared leadership," "teacher empowerment," and the "professionalization of teaching" (e.g., Darling-Hammond 1985; Barth 1988; Lieberman 1988). These terms referred to "more responsibilities, more decision-making power, and more accountability for the results" (Lieberman 1988, 64). Project goals and members' preferences related to the type of leadership that encouraged collaboration and promoted teacher empowerment.

Our experiences as professors were insufficient for this task. The literature on transformative leadership (e.g., Barth 1988; Sergiovanni 1990; Leithwood 1992; Fullan 1992) was helpful in the development of our roles as cheerleaders and facilitators. Ultimately, the coalition was a cooperative venture in which everyone chipped in to build, develop, and sustain the effort. Sergiovanni (1992) described this as "moral leadership" (xiii) in which there is a sense of stewardship among a group for the group. Perhaps this is the secret of promoting multicultural education through an advocacy group; the group took on stewardship for the group and for the concept that defined the group as well.

Lessons Learned About The Promotion Of Multicultural Education Within School-University Cooperation

Certain factors helped achieve the goals of the project, and others were barriers for achieving education that is multicultural within the context of school-university cooperation. For example, it appeared to be the right time and the right place for education that is multicultural. Over the last several years national, state, and local media have paid attention to multicultural education (e.g., refer to cover stories for *Time*, 9 April 1990; *Time*, 8 July 1991; and *Newsweek*, 23 September 1991). Debates over whose culture should be taught in schools are found in scholarly journals and reports (e.g., Ravitch 1990; Bullard 1992). Educational regulations often include some mention of cultural diversity, although this is usually not well-defined (e.g., Illinois State Goals For Education 1985; Illinois Criteria for Teacher Certification programs 1990). This attention made cultural diversity and multicultural education buzzwords in public and educational circles and created a context exists that encouraged attention to the affirmation of human diversity as necessary and positive for schools. These trends helped this project since the district, the program, and the university were anxious to jump on the multicultural bandwagon.

The complexities of the concept of multicultural education were both powerful and elusive. The democratic and egalitarian foundations for the concept, including goals for human freedom, dignity, equality, and pluralism, held strong appeal for teachers and others involved in preparing future citizens. On the other hand, the concept was generally misunderstood, and by some people, disregarded. Misconceptions of the concept usually related to the lack of a common definition for multicultural education. Disregard seemed to stem from past efforts to sensitize teachers to racism—prejudice, stereotypes, and discrimination—that left a residue of ill will. Also, administrators may have some disregard for the importance of multicultural initiatives; only four of thirty-five principals have provided strong support thus far. The extent to which administrators have responded positively to coalition efforts and the relationship of the race, ethnicity, and gender of administrators to that support bears further scrutiny.

The coalition is an organization that supported and facilitated individual change. To a limited extent, individuals were able to promote school change as well: for example, individual members persuaded several administrators to invite the coalition to a few faculty meetings and to fund special events. However, for the most part the coalition existed at an arms length from the district—supported by it, but was not a serious challenge to school structure.

In addition, Dr. Storm and I were tenacious in our efforts to develop and sustain the coalition. District administrators continually made time for us amid busy schedules, and the latest assistant superintendent to come on board was anxious to expand the coalition and school-university relationship. None of us was lukewarm toward the project, and this kept the project percolating.

It was the nature of the coalition to have members scattered throughout many schools and agencies, and this was a barrier to communication. On the other hand, the dispersed nature of the coalition facilitated the perception that the effort was broad based, and it alerted a wide range of people to an organization that might fit their needs. This also made it difficult for the effort to be hindered by any one nonsupportive person.

CONCLUSION

The aim of this work was to foster reflection during the process of a project rather than at the conclusion. This paper served that purpose as it has helped those involved to consider what happened and plan for the future of the project. Several aspects of this project may prove helpful for others trying to promote multicultural education. Developing a coalition worked to connect educators interested in multicultural education across a school district and fostered ownership in the group and thus within the project. Leading, by sharing leadership and encouraging active followership, developed a sense of stewardship for the project. Attending to past history and confusion about multicultural education was necessary throughout the project. Interacting with district administrators took time, patience, and diplomacy to build trust and begin action. Interacting with the same district administrator increased possibilities for positive communication and decisive action. Mentoring coalition members helped deepen and broaden understanding of multicultural education. Learning about multicultural education over time increased understanding of the concept. Promoting multicultural education and the coalition were daily, continual, essential tasks. Enduring the stress, strain, and rush of events were requisites to taking part in the coalition. Enjoying the comraderie, excitement and challenge of charter membership in the coalition was something few of us will soon forget.

Notes

1. Several new state certification criteria mandated attention to human diversity.

Criteria 3—The program develops the candidate's understanding and awareness of the unique nature of distinct cultural and ethnic groups as well as the relationships between these groups.

Criteria 7—The program provides learning experiences enabling the candidate to become aware of, and responsive to, the varied educational needs and distinct cultural backgrounds of students. In addition, opportunities should be available for candidates to acquire and demonstrate abilities to work with students of culturally diverse backgrounds (Illinois State Board Of Education, 1991).

2. The five goals for the Teacher Education Program were:

a. to ensure academic content preparation
b. to ensure preparation in professional skills
c. to develop understanding of the nature of child development and learning
d. to develop sensitivity to and awareness of the needs of individuals from varied backgrounds in school and society
e. to empower teachers as active decision-makers and critical thinkers

To consider where this project should go from here requires reflection of the ways in which facilitators can be strengthened and barriers can be reduced. The time is right to promote multicultural education, and this facilitator for multicultural projects should not be overlooked. However, strong leadership is needed to initiate and sustain such projects. Strong leadership can be shared by members of groups, such as the coalition, if participants feel a sense of stewardship for the group. If these projects take place via school-university cooperation, potential facilitators and barriers should be discussed during planning stages. One important facilitator to consider is the support of administrators and principals. It is necessary to garner the support of administrators and teachers to reform schools from a multicultural perspective.

References

Banks, J. A. and C. M. Banks. 1989. *Multicultural education: Issues and perspectives.* Boston: Allyn and Bacon.

Barsh, R. S. 1988. Principals, teachers, and school leadership. *Phi Delta Kappan* 69(9):639-42.

Bullard, S. 1992. Whose culture: Beyond the rhetoric. *Educational Leadership* 49(4):4-7.

Darling-Hammond, L. 1985. Valuing teachers: The making of a profession. *Teachers College Record* 87(2):204-18.

Friedan, B. 1976. *It changed my life: Writings on the women's movement.* New York: Random House.

Fullan, M. G. 1992. Visions that blind. *Educational Leadership* 49(5):19-20.

Goodlad, J. I. and K. A. Sirotnik. 1988. The future of school-university partnerships. In *School-university partnerships in action: Concepts, cases, and concerns.* Edited by K. A. Sirotnik and J. I. Goodlad, 205-25. New York: Teachers College Press.

Grant, C. A. 1991, June 19. Conversation with the summer seminar class.

Gray, P. 1991, July. Whose America? *Time,* 12-16.

Hawley, W. D. 1990. *The proposals for collaboration between schools and universities to improve American education.* Position Paper, no. 120. TN.

Henry, W. A. 1990, April. Beyond the melting pot. *Time,* 28-31.

Holmes Group, Inc. 1990. *Tomorrow's schools: Principles for the design of professional development schools.* East Lansing, MI: Author.

Illinois State Board of Education. 1985. *State goals for learning and sample learning objectives.* Springfield, IL: Author.

————. 1990. *State criteria for certification for teacher education.* Springfield, IL: Author.

Kantrowitz, B., P. Wingert, P. Rogers, N. Joseph, and S. Lewis. 1991, September. African Dreams. *Newsweek,* 42-48.

Lieberman, A. 1988. Teachers and principals: Turf, tension and new tasks. *Phi Delta Kappan* 69(9):648-53.

Lieberman, A. and L. Miller. 1990. Teacher development in professional practice schools. *Teachers College Record* 92(1):107-22.

————. 1991. Revisiting the social realities of teaching. In *Staff development for education in the '90s: New demands, new realities, new perspectives.* Edited by A. Lieberman and L. Miller, 92-109. New York: Teachers College Press.

Leithwood, K. A. 1992. The move toward transformational leadership. *Educational Leadership* 49(5):8-12.

Little, J. W. 1981. *School success and staff development in urban desegregated schools.* Boulder, CO: Center for Action Research.

Melenyzer, B. J. 1990, November. Empowerment: The discourse, meanings and social actions of teachers. Paper presented at the annual conference of the National Council of States on Inservice Education, Orlando, FL.

Ravitch, D. 1990, October 24. Particularism versus multiculturalism. *The Chronicle of Higher Education,* A44.

Rosenholtz, S. 1989. *Teachers' workplace.* New York: Longman.

Sergiovanni, T. J. 1990. Adding value to leadership gets extraordinary results. *Educational Leadership* 47(8):23-27.

————. 1992. *Moral leadership: Getting to the heart of school improvement.* San Francisco, CA: Jossey-Bass.

Sleeter, C. 1990. Staff development for desegregated schooling. *Phi Delta Kappan* 72(1):33-40.

————. 1992. *Keepers of the American dream: A study of staff development and multicultural education.* London: Falmer Press.

Sleeter, C. and C. A. Grant. 1988. *Making choices: Five approaches to race, class, and gender.* Columbus, OH: Merrill.

INDEX